Divine
Creatures

T0364253

Divine Creatures

Animal Mummies
in Ancient Egypt

◆

Edited by Salima Ikram

The American University in Cairo Press

Cairo New York

The Animal Mummies of the Egyptian Museum thank
Roxie Walker for helping to give them a better home

Exclusive distribution outside Egypt and North America by I.B.Tauris & Co Ltd.,
6 Salem Road, London, W4 2BU

Dar el Kutub No. 13826/14
ISBN 978 977 916 696 9

Dar el Kutub Cataloging-in-Publication Data

Ikram, Salima
    Divine Creatures: Animal Mummies in Ancient Egypt/ Salima Ikram.—Cairo:
The American University in Cairo Press, 2015.
        p.   cm.
        ISBN 978 977 916 696 9
        1. Mummified animals—Egypt
        2. Animal Remains (Archaeology)—Egypt
        1393.30932

1 2 3 4 5   19 18 17 16 15

Designed by Andrea El Akshar
Printed in Egypt

Contents

Illustrations

Figures

Color plates   *following page*

Contributors

Edda Bresciani has been director of the Italian excavations at Medinet Madi, and is professor emeritus of Egyptology at the University of Pisa. She is a member of the Accademia Nazionale dei Lincei, and the author of several books and articles on Egyptian literature, history, and religion.

Aidan Dodson is a senior research fellow in the Department of Archaeology and Anthropology at the University of Bristol and was Simpson Professor of Egyptology at the American University in Cairo for spring 2013. He studied Egyptian Archaeology at Durham, Liverpool, and Cambridge universities, and is the author of some twenty books and over three hundred papers and reviews.

Salima Ikram is professor of Egyptology at the American University in Cairo, and has worked in Egypt since 1986. She has directed the Animal Mummy Project at the Cairo Museum and co-directed the North Kharga Oasis Survey, and currently is director of the North Kharga Oasis Darb Ain Amur Survey. She has excavated and worked all over Egypt, as well as in Sudan and Turkey, and published extensively on diverse topics.

Dieter Kessler is professor emeritus of Egyptology at the University of Munich. He has directed the excavations at Tuna al-Gebel for several years, and has published extensively on animal cults as well as diverse aspects of religion in the later periods of Egyptian history.

Roger Lichtenberg is a physician, radiologist (Institut Arthur Vernes, Paris), and has been a regular collaborator of the Mission Archéologique

Française du Bubasteion (MAFB), as well as being active on several other projects, including wide-ranging work in the Kharga Oasis. He publishes extensively on both human and animal mummies.

Paul T. Nicholson is professor of archaeology at Cardiff University, where he teaches courses on Egyptian archaeology and early technology. He has worked in Egypt since 1983 and has directed excavations at Amarna, Memphis, and Saqqara as well as working at Berenike, Hatnub, Thebes, and elsewhere. His work has involved the investigation of the Sacred Animal Necropolis at Saqqara as well as early crafts and industries, particularly faïence and glass. He has published extensively on these subjects.

Abd el Halim Nur el-Din is professor at Cairo University and has been the director of the Supreme Council of Antiquities. He has worked all over Egypt, and has been involved in the excavations at Tuna al-Gebel. He specializes in the later periods of Egyptian history, as well as continuations between ancient and modern Egypt, and has published on these as well as many other topics.

Donald B. Redford is professor of Egyptology in the Department of Classics and Ancient Mediterranean Studies at Pennsylvania State University. For over forty years, he has excavated widely in Egypt, including Karnak, Mendes, and Tel Kedwa, and has undertaken archaeological and epigraphic surveys in the Eastern Desert and Jordan.

Susan Redford is a senior lecturer in the Department of Classics and Ancient Mediterranean Studies at Pennsylvania State University. She is the director of the Akhenaten Temple Project's Theban Tomb Survey, carrying out field research in several tombs of the Theban necropolis, and is also co-director of the Mendes Expedition.

Alain Zivie is a director of research emeritus at the French National Center of Scientific Research and a visiting scholar at Harvard University. Founder and director of the French Archaeological Mission of the Bubasteion at Saqqara, Egypt, he has also taught and lectured worldwide, and has published several books and many articles, particularly about his archaeological and historical discoveries.

Acknowledgments

I would like to thank the following people, in addition to all the contributing authors, for making this book possible. Christine End for the long hours that she spent working on the bibliography and images, N.Brown and B.I Woodcock, who helped with the revised bibliography, all my students who participated in the experimental work, the Ministry of State for Antiquities and the Supreme Council of Antiquities officials who made all of the research presented here possible, the staff and workers of the Egyptian Museum who opened cases and moved objects, the Egypt Exploration Society for their help with the images, and Roxie Walker, who made the work at the Egyptian Museum possible, and to whom I dedicate this book.

Preface

The civilization of ancient Egypt has long been considered one of the most enduring and admired of the ancient world. The reason for the appeal of the ancient Egyptians is not only that their aesthetic resonates with our modern tastes, but also that their very 'otherness' is intriguing. One of the most obvious manifestations of this difference is the Egyptian practice of mummifying their dead. While one can come to terms with the mummification of humans as an effort to provide a 'house' for the soul, the mummification of animals is less easy to understand and accept. The oddity of this habit was also remarked upon by the ancient Greeks, who found it one of the more peculiar aspects of Egyptian culture. Nonetheless, it seems that ultimately some of the Greeks and later the Romans came to accept and even adopt this practice, leaving us with a legacy of millions of animal mummies.

These animal mummies were so closely identified with ancient Egypt by travelers and tourists, that the cleric Father Géramb quipped in 1833 that "No one would believe that one had been to Egypt unless they returned with a mummy under one arm and a crocodile under the other." This is borne out by the collections of museums throughout the world: even very small, provincial museums in Europe and the United States have an animal mummy or two tucked away as a part—or in some cases, as the whole—of their Egyptian collection.

This book is an initial attempt to begin to understand the Egyptian phenomenon of mummifying animals, including the different types of mummies, the religious reasons that led to their creation, the practicalities of mummification, and some of the major cult centers which have proved to have been the sources of many of the animal mummies found throughout the world. The different authors whose essays are included in this volume have worked on museum collections of mummies or at sites where these mummies are found. The work is arranged from the general to the specific, and thus starts with an introduction to the range of animal mummies found in Egypt, together with a discussion of the different reasons behind the phenomenon. It continues with a survey of the methods of mummification, together with the evidence of experimental work, and continues with more animal and site-specific essays. These range from a study of ram cults from the Delta to Aswan, the different bull cults and their association with kingship, the crocodile cult of the Fayum and Kom Ombo, the multiple animal necropoleis found at Saqqara and Tuna al-Gebel, and the results of the Animal Mummy Project in Cairo's Egyptian Museum. These essays cover a wide range of topics, sites, and species; however, they are by no means the dernier mot on animal mummies as work remains to be done on the economics of the enterprise, the practicalities of where the primary raw materials—the animals—were raised and kept, the people for whom these mummies served as a manifestation of their personal piety, as well as further research into other religious aspects of this phenomenon. It is hoped that this volume serves as a basis for future work and a catalyst for other investigators and types of investigations.

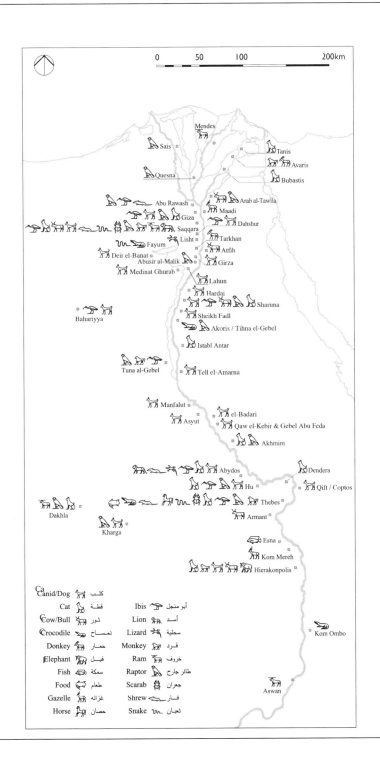

Map of selected
animal cemeteries.
Drawn by
Nicholas Warner.

Selected List of
Animal Cemeteries

Abu Rawash (Shrews, Raptors, Crocodiles)
Abukir/Canopus (Raptors)
Abusir al-Malik (Ibis, Cats, Ovicaprids, Crocodiles)
Abusir/Taposiris magna (Ibis, Raptors, Fish)
Abydos (Ibis, Raptors, Dogs, Shrews)
Akhmim/al-Hawawish (Ibises, Raptors, Canids, Cats, Snakes, Shrews)
Alexandria (Birds, Cattle?)
Arab al-Tawila (Raptors, Cattle)
Armant (Cattle, Ibises, Raptors, Cats)
Asyut (Canids, Hyenas, Ibises, Raptors, Cats)
Atfih (Cattle)
Avaris (Donkeys, Monkeys)
Badari (Cats, Dogs)
Bahariya (Ibis)
Bahnasa (Ibises, Raptors)
Batn al-Herit (Ibises, Crocodles)
Beni Hasan/Stabl Antar/Speos Artemidos (Cats, Dogs)
Dakhla (Raptors, Ovicaprids, Cats)
Deir el-Bersheh (Dogs)
Dendera (Ibises, Raptors, Cats)
Dimeh (Crocodiles)
Edfu (Raptors, Ibises)
Elephantine (Ram, Ibises, Raptors)
Esna (Fish, Crocodile)
Gebel abu Feda (Cats, Canids)
Gebelein (Crocodile, Ibises)

Gerzeh (Dogs, Sheep)
al-Gharaq (Ibises, Raptors, Crocodiles)
Ghoran (Ibises, Raptors, Cattle, Crocodiles, Cats, Dogs)
al-Hagarsa (Crocodiles)
Hardai/Cynopolis (Dogs)
Hawara (Crocodiles, Raptors)
Heliopolis (Cattle, Ibises, Scarabs)
Herakleopolis (Shrews, Raptors)
al-Hiba (Crocodiles)
Hierakonpolis (Elephants, Cattle, Baboons, Cats, Dogs)
Hu (Ibises, Raptors, Cats, Dogs)
Kharga (Canids, Raptors)
al-Khawalid (Cattle, Sheep)
Kom abu Billu (Cattle)
Kom al-Adami (Cattle)
Kom Ausim/Letopolis (Shrews, Crocodiles)
Kom Mereh (Gazelles),
Kom Ombo (Crocodile, Snakes, Raptors, Ibises)
Koptos (Dogs, Cats, Gazelle)
Krokodilopolis (Crocodiles)
Lahun/al-Lahun (Crocodiles, Dogs, Snakes)
Lisht (Lizards, Sheep, Snakes, Dogs)
al-Maabda (Crocodiles)
Maadi (Gazelle)
Manfalut/es-Samun/al-Maabda (Crocodiles, Cattle, Ibises, Snakes,
    Fish, Canids, Cats)
Medinet al-Fayum (Ibises, Crocodiles)
Medinet Gurab (Cattle, Fish, Dogs, Sheep)
Medinet Madi (Ibises, Crocodiles)
Medinet al-Nahas (Crocodiles)
Meidum (Dogs)
Meir/al-Qusae (Cattle, Crocodiles)
Qasr al-Banat (Ibises)
Qaw (Ibises, Cats, Dogs, Crocodiles)
Qus (Ibises, Raptors, Fish)
Roda /Tell al-Amarna/ Wadi Deir al-Bersheh (Ibises, Raptors)
Sa al-Hagar/Sais (Fish, Snakes)

Saqqara (Canids, Crocodiles, Snakes, Cattle, Dogs, Ibises, Raptors, Monkeys, Shrews, Cats, a lion)

Sharuna (Ibises, Raptors, Cats, Dogs, Cattle)

al-Shutb/al-Borsa (Sheep, Ibises, Raptors)

Tanis/San al-Hagar (Cats)

Tarkhan (Ovicaprids)

Tehna al-Gebel (Rams, Crocodiles, Ibises)

Tell Abu Yasin (Ibises, Raptors, Cattle)

Tell Baqliya (Ibises)

Tell Basta/Bubastis (Cats, Shrews, Mongooses)

Tell al-Fara'in/Buto (Raptors, Shrews, Mongooses, Snakes)

Tell al-Kom al-Hisn (Cattle)

Tell al-Rub'a/ Mendes (Rams)

Tell Muqudam (Lions alleged, but none found)

Tell Nebira/Naukratis (Sheep)

Thebes (Ibises, Raptors, Crocodile, Shrew, Monkeys, Cats, Dogs, Gazelles, Snakes, Fish, Scarab Beetles)

Thinis/Nag al-Mesheikh (Fish)

Tuna al-Gebel (Ibises, Raptors, Monkeys, Shrews, and a few examples of many more species)

Umm al-Burigat/Tebtynis (Crocodiles, Raptors, Cats, Ovicaprids)

Zawiyet Barmasha (Ibises, Falcon)

Zawiyet al-Maitin (Raptors)

Zawiyet al-Aryan/Giza (Ibises, Raptors, Shrews, Cats)

Brief Chronology
of Egypt

Period	Dynasties	Dates BC
Predynastic Period		5000–3050
Early Dynastic Period	1–2	3050–2663
Old Kingdom	3–6	2663–2195
First Intermediate Period	7–mid-11	2195–2066
Middle Kingdom	mid-11–13	2066–1650
Second Intermediate Period	14–17	1650–1549
New Kingdom	18–20	1549–1064
Third Intermediate Period	21–25	1064–525
Late Period	26–31	525–332
Ptolemaic Period		332–30
Roman Period		30–AD 395

1

Divine Creatures
Animal Mummies

Salima Ikram

For most people mummies are synonymous with Egypt. However, it is less well known that the ancient Egyptians mummified animals as well as humans. For the ancient Egyptians, the act of mummification ensured that the body of a creature would be preserved forever, and thus conferred the potential for eternal life upon it. Throughout history, however, animal mummies, like their human counterparts, had little value as artifacts. Indeed, they were used as ballast for ships, as fertilizer (Maspero 1912: 272), as fuel, and as medicine in powdered form (Ikram and Dodson 1998: 72). Despite these vicissitudes, many animal mummies have survived, and are now valued as sources of information on the culture and environment of ancient Egypt. Broadly speaking, animal mummies can be divided into four different types: beloved pets, buried with their owners; victual mummies, consisting of funerary food offerings for humans; sacred animals, worshiped during their lifetime and mummified with pomp upon their death; votive mummies, dedicated as offerings at the shrines of specific gods to whom these animals were sacred. Although most animal mummies fit into these categories, especially if they are from a known context, not all of them clearly conform to these divisions. Thus, some mummies that come from human cemeteries (for example, the Valley of the Kings) might not be pet mummies, but might have some cultic function or be dedicated to the god of that locality.

Pets

Pet mummies are certainly the most endearing of animal mummy types. From the Old Kingdom (2649–2150 B.C.) onward, Egyptians are pictured in their tombs with their pets. The magical or religious power of these images ensured the continued joint existence of both owner

Fig. 1.1 The wooden sarcophagus of Khu and his dog, Meniu-pw (JE 36445), from Asyut. Photograph by Salima Ikram.

and pet in the Afterlife. Occasionally, pets had their names carved above their image(s), providing further insurance for an eternal life, or even full texts, such as was done for the royal guard dog Abuwtiguw, buried in Giza c. 2180 B.C. (Reisner 1936; 1938). Pets are often found buried with, or else in close proximity to their owners. Some of what are presumed to be the earliest pet burials come from an archaic grave at Tarkhan, Grave 2052, and consist of donkey and duck burials, with the animals placed within their own coffins (Petrie 1914). In cases where they predeceased their owners, they were interred within the tomb; if they died at a much later time they might have been buried in the tomb's forecourt. It is possible that some animals died shortly after their owner, and thus would be able to have been buried with the owner, as the mummification of small animals did not take as long as that of humans (see Ikram on mummification, this volume). This would be especially true of dogs as they frequently pine and die after the death of their master or mistress. The mummified baboon and horse found outside Senenmut's tomb (Theban Tomb 71) could have died after the burial chamber had already been sealed (Lansing and Hayes 1935–1936: 7–11; Ikram and Iskander 2002: 46). This might also have been the case with the recently excavated monkey mummy that was buried outside Theban Tombs 11 and 12.[1] The dog of King Psusennes I was found within the burial chamber of his tomb (NRT III) at Tanis (Monet 1951). The only clear examples of pets that were deliberately killed appear to date from the royal tombs of Dynasty I at Abydos. There, rulers of the First Dynasty had lions and donkeys buried around their tombs. Four of their dogs, complete with funerary stelae of their own, were also buried there (Dreyer et al. 1993: 59). Although there is no clear evidence that these animals were killed, the similar burials of the kings' human dependents show that they at least had been deliberately put to death.

At the site of Hierakonpolis the burials of animals that might have been pets or part of an exotic menagerie, indicative of a leader's wealth and status, have also been found (Friedman 2003: 9–10, 2012; Van Neer and Linseele 2003: 11–12; Warman 2000: 8; Merceron 2003: 13–14).[2] Like the examples from Abydos, these animals do not appear to have been killed, although work is still being carried out on the remains to ascertain this. Diverse creatures, including elephants, cattle, baboons, a hippopotamus, and a wildcat were found buried in tombs in a cemetery (HK6) at the site (van Neer and Linseele 2002: 7). One of the elephants seems to be the proud owner of the earliest elaborate superstructure to its grave, dating to the Naqada II Period (Friedman 2003: 9–10). These animals showed evidence of basic (and very early) attempts at mummification, with textile wrappings and some blackening of the skin that might have been the result of oils or resins applied to the animals' bodies.

Fig. 1.2 This dog, a cousin to the Saluki, was found in tomb 50 in the Valley of the Kings, and might have been a royal pet (CG 29836). Photograph by Anna-Marie Kellen.

On the whole, pets were allowed to live out their natural lives, and when they died they were carefully mummified and placed in coffins or sarcophagi of their own (e.g., Isitemkheb's gazelle, CG 29835 [Ikram 2000a: 58–61; Ikram and Iskander 2002: 25–26]). Some pet-lovers went so far as to include their pets in their own coffins—perhaps they had slept together during life, and wished to continue the practice through-out eternity. A man called Hapymin was buried with his pet dog curled up at his feet, very much like the medieval tomb carvings of Europe that feature knights and ladies with their respective hounds.[3]

It is sometimes difficult to ascertain if an animal mummy is a pet mummy or has a separate religious significance. The dog and monkey mummies found in the Valley of the Kings (KV50 and KV51) are among these enigmatic mummy types (Ikram and Iskander 2002: 26–28). They appear to have been pets, as the baboons were divested of their canine teeth to avoid the risk of injuring anyone seriously while alive, and were very healthy and well looked after, unlike the baboon mummies found in sacred contexts (see Kessler, this volume). Furthermore, mummified dogs are rarely, if ever, found as religious offerings in the Theban area, and the type of mummification carried out on all these animals would suggest that they were pets rather than votive mummies. It is unclear, however, to whom the animals belonged. Based on proximity of tombs their owners might have been Amenhotep II (c. 1427–1401 B.C., buried nearby in KV35), or Horemheb (1319–1307 B.C., buried in KV57).

Food or Victual Mummies

The second category of animal mummy—food offerings—consist of mummified foods ready for human consumption, which were placed in tombs so the tomb-owner could feast for eternity. In many instances these mummies were placed in individual wooden coffinets carved to the shape of a joint of meat or a poultry carcass, or in rectangular boxes. In some instances, they were held in baskets or other containers. The species thus prepared included cattle, ducks, geese, pigeons, as well as ovicaprids. Beef, generally coming from juvenile animals that were less than two-and-a-half years of age, was the highest-status food offering (Ikram 1995a: Appendix II). Thus far no fish or pork victual mummies have been found, although both types of animals were consumed; per-haps their lower status excluded them from the offerings. They certainly form no part of offering lists found in funerary contexts. It is possible that some wild antelopes were included in this mummy type, as they also appear in offering lists. They are, however, difficult to identify and separate from young cattle and ovicaprids unless the bones are exposed— radiographs are not always precise enough for this type of identification.

All kinds of cuts of meat were mummified, ranging from ribs, steaks, and entire legs. The latter are usually cut off above the hoof (i.e., at the carpals or tarsals), although examples of hoofs are not unknown.[4] The poultry was prepared to be ready to roast: plucked and with the head, wing-tips, and feet removed. The internal organs (liver, gizzards, etc.) are removed, wrapped separately, and then replaced in the body cavity should they be needed for gravy. Most victual mummies come from the cemeteries of the New Kingdom (1550–1070 B.C.) in Thebes, although the origins of this practice extend back to the Old Kingdom. Internal organs, such as the liver and lungs, were also offered, as can be attested in the funerary assemblage of Isitemkheb D (Ikram and Iskander 2002: 30). There seems to have been no strict rule concerning how many victual mummies should be included in a tomb: Tutankhamun had over forty such cases of food mummies buried with him to sustain him in the Afterlife. These victual mummies are very useful not only in explaining beliefs in the reification of offerings, but also practical questions concerning butchery, food preparation, and the types of creatures that were considered high status (and thus preferred) foods for eternity.

Sacred Animals

Sacred or cult animals are generally identified as special animals that were chosen on account of a set of specific and unusual markings to represent the physical presence of a god, and worshiped as a living incarnation of that god throughout their lifetime.[5] The god's 'divine essence' was thought to have entered into the animal transforming it into a divinity. During its lifetime, this animal was worshiped and treated as if it were a god, and upon its death buried with great ceremony, just as the pharaoh was buried. The spirit of the god would then find its way into another similarly marked animal, which would then be worshiped until its death. This can be compared to the Tibetan beliefs concerning the Dalai Lama (Ray 2002: 19) or the current Nepalese practice of the Living Goddess. Thus the Apis bull at Memphis was revered as Ptah and Osiris, the Buchis bull at Armant was the embodiment of Montu and Re,

the crocodile in the Fayum and at Kom Ombo was an incarnation of
Sobek, and the ram at Elephantine was the personification of Khnum.
These animals were kept in special stalls or enclosures, such as the area
of the Apis in Memphis, or the cage made of rectangular limestone slabs,
attached to the southwestern corner of the temple of Osiris-Baboon,
that was found at Tuna al-Gebel (Kessler and Nur el-Din: 1999). For the
sacred ibis at Saqqara, the temple courtyard at the Sacred Animal
Necropolis was planted with trees or bushes to make it a more pleasant
place for the god (Martin 1981: 12), as well as to invoke the primeval
landscape. These divine creatures were served by their own hierarchy of
priests (Ray 1976: 140–145), and the temples were supported by their
own endowments, such as fields (both near the temple as well as some
that were scattered throughout Egypt), as well as by royal grants (Ray
1976: 136, 144; Kessler and Nur el-Din, this volume; Reymond 1972:
254–255, 257), and donations given by pilgrims or other believers.

When the animals died, the entire area would be plunged into
mourning. For Apis bulls the mourning period lasted seventy days
while the animal was mummified, after which its funeral would be celebrated. Priests of the animal, and even the people of the area, wore
mourning garments, did not cut or wash their hair, and mourned loudly
and publicly for the loss of their god. For the first four days of the
mourning period they fasted, and ate only bread and vegetables for the
remainder (Vercoutter 1962: 41–43, and 125; Vos 1993). Once
mummified, the sacred animal would be taken to the special cemeteries
that had been established for them, placed in coffins and sarcophagi,
some of which had canopies over them (Emery 1971: 3–13), and had
the final rites administered. After the burial and the establishment of
the new god, life would continue as usual.

The basis of animal cults is not totally clear. Certainly, animals were
regarded as special beings, belonging to this world as well as to other
realms. As such, they may have had access to the gods who were also
denizens of another sphere.

From the earliest times standards bearing totemic animals were used
to symbolize and represent specific geographic areas of Egypt or groups
of people ('clans'). These animal standards can be seen on the Narmer
palette as well as earlier slate palettes, and are common throughout later
Egyptian history as emblems of specific localities. These local animal

gods sometimes merged with other divinities, and joined together to form the pantheon of the unified Egyptian state, in some cases becoming a combination of zoomorphic and anthropomorphic entities.

Perhaps this link between animals and gods was also extended to the early rulers of Egypt. The intimate association between royalty and animals is obvious in the Protodynastic–Early Dynastic Periods, where the names of early rulers are those of animals—catfish, scorpion, serpent, etc.—which perhaps serves to underline the divine nature of both. The king was also being gifted with the particular strengths of his name-animal. In some ways, the burial patterns for cult animals reflected that of royalty from earlier periods of pharaonic history: the central tomb-complex was dedicated to the god-animal, while cemeteries surrounding it were dedicated to its (primarily female) family members.

Animal cults have existed in Egypt from the Predynastic Period onward, gaining in popularity in the New Kingdom, and most especially in the Late Period and thereafter.[6] Certain animal cults, such as that of the Apis Bull of Memphis, are securely attested from the First Dynasty onward (Simpson 1957), and enjoyed a renaissance in the Eighteenth Dynasty under the reign of Amenhotep III, as is demonstrated by the construction of the Serapeum galleries and the cat sarcophagus dedicated by Crown-Prince Djhutmose.[7] Others came into being, or at least became popular, from the Twenty-sixth Dynasty onward. The roots of the popularity of these cults lay in their accessibility to the public and the upsurge of personal piety and personal gods that occurred during the New Kingdom (Davies and Smith 1997: 122–123). The nature of the later cults seems to have differed slightly from that of the earlier, more established ones in their general accessibility and the identification of most of the creatures with aspects of Osiris, as well as the king, although this is still a matter of some conjecture (Kessler website: 11; Kessler 1989: Chapter 3).

The reason for the proliferation of animal cults that started in the Late Period and continued into the Greco–Roman Period is unclear. Perhaps these cults started as a form of religious archaizing that paralleled the artistic archaizing of the period. At this point in Egyptian history the Egyptians were no longer the proud rulers of their country; it had been attacked, invaded, occupied, and ruled by a variety of peoples, including Libyans, Nubians, and Assyrians. By emphasizing things uniquely

Egyptian and distinct from the religious customs of the various invaders, the Egyptians perhaps were asserting the strength of their own culture and religious traditions in the face of these interlopers. Many Classical writers commented scathingly on the oddity of the Egyptian's obsession with animals and their manifestation as divine beings. However, ultimately this did not stop either Romans or Greeks (or indeed other nationalities) from participating in aspects of the cult (Clarysse 1988: 7–10). The range of popularity of these cults increased markedly in the Ptolemaic Period and persisted, to some extent, into the Roman era until A.D. 379 when the Edict of Theodosius closed down pagan temples. The Christian Emperor Honorius (A.D. 395–423) had the Serapeum razed to the ground. Thus, animal cults became not just a manifestation of Egyptian religion, but also a means of separating and defining 'Egyptian' as opposed to foreign, and was a reaction against the alien peoples who ruled and inhabited Egypt. These cults were extremely popular, perhaps as they offered guarantees of salvation for those who served them or those who put themselves under their protection (Smith 1992: 219).

Animal cults had other components in addition to the worship of the god. Prime among these were oracles, dream interpretation, and incubation (see Kessler and Nur el-Din, and Redford and Redford, this volume). The oracular power of divine animals was perhaps the most significant of these components (Kurth 1986), as the names of many animals would suggest: e.g., 'The Face of the Ibis Speaks.' Texts found at such temple sites also indicate the importance of the oracular nature of the cult. The Buchis bull, known as 'The Bull Who is in Hermonthis, Lord of Medamud, Who is in Tod,' was renowned for his oracle (Mond and Myers 1934: 47). The Ram of Mendes also seems to have played an important role as an oracular divinity from the Twenty-fifth Dynasty onward (Kakosy 1981b: 141), and appears in many priestly autobiographies. Texts also tell us that the particular movement of a sacred scarab beetle would be interpreted by an oracle priest (Jasnow 1997). Oracles became increasingly important in Egyptian religion from the Late Period onward, perhaps as they permitted people a more intimate relationship with the gods than had been previously available. Even Alexander the Great went to Siwa to consult the Oracle of Amun (perhaps in the form of a ram). As oracular animals, questions would be addressed to the animal manifestation of the god, and the response, whether audible or gestural, would be interpreted by priests, and the results passed on to the petitioner. Perhaps some sort of book existed, like the dream books, which had rules for interpreting the animal's response. In some instances the oracles seem to have been interpreted (or if one is cynical, to have been made) by a group of priests who met in a council chamber, such as the one described by Kessler and Nur el-Din (this volume).

Incubation and dream interpretation also drew people to animal cults as it permitted them to have intimate contact with a god. The dreams were interpreted by priests, and in some cases, perhaps the priests themselves had dreams that answered the prayers or queries of the pilgrims. The priest Hor, whose archive was found at Saqqara (Ray 1976), was frequently visited by Thoth in his dreams, while the priest Sematuitefnakht writes in his autobiography that the god Khnum came to him in a dream and gave him advice that saved him (Kakosy 1981b: 141). Incubation, together with the prescriptive advice contained in interpreted dreams, was also supposed to have been very effective in curing people of their ailments. The Buchis bull was supposed to be particularly effective in curing eye diseases (Mond and Myers 1934: I, 48), while many other animal cult centers were famed for their ability to encourage fertility.[8] Even after their death specific animals continued to be worshipped by name; a certain sacred baboon had not only stelae, but also offering tables dedicated to it after its death; clearly it must have been a particularly effective god (Ritner 1993: 267). The sacred animal cults clearly had vast appeal to the population of Egypt, as the gods were not only visible, but also effective.

Votive Mummies

The votive mummy is generally identified as an offering consisting of a specific mummified animal that was dedicated to its corresponding divinity so that the donor's prayers would be addressed to the god throughout eternity. Votive mummies acted much in the same way as the candles purchased and burned in churches, except they were longer-lasting. Thus, cats were offered to the goddess Bastet, the goddess of pleasure who was manifested as a cat, while ibises and baboons, totemic animals of Thoth, the god of learning and wisdom, were given to him, and dogs and other canids were offered to Anubis, god of mummification and travel who was shown as a canid.[9] They differed from the sacred animals in that they were not unique, and lacked the special markings that identified them as the god; instead, they acted as the pilgrims' emissaries to the gods, and were purchased and offered by pilgrims at shrines dedicated to the relevant gods (Martin 1981: 9). These mummified creatures were prepared in special embalming houses (*wabets*). After their purchase, they would then be presented to the god by the priests and kept in storage. Once a year, during a special festival, the mummified animals would be taken in procession, and buried en masse in extensive catacombs that would then be sealed with mud-brick walls until the next celebration (Ray 1976: 140). These extensive catacombs were known as Houses of Rest (Ray 1976: 140), and have been found at many sites such as Tuna al-Gebel, Armant, and Saqqara. These vast animal cemeteries, that have yielded millions of mummies, were a particular feature of the first millennium B.C., and proliferated particularly during the Ptolemaic Period.

It should be noted that some scholars, particularly Dieter Kessler (1989 and this volume), have provided an alternative interpretation of these animal mummies. He has suggested that they were not necessarily votive offerings per se; rather, that any animal that lived within the temple enclosures, or on temple land and died on it, was consecrated to the god, and essentially sacred as it had lived in a hallowed place, and thus was to be mummified and kept in these catacombs dedicated to the god. Thus, other animals that were not manifestations of the god, such as flamingos, nightjars, and other creatures that are found mummified in the Tuna catacombs, probably just died in the sacred confines of temple-owned land and were mummified as creatures associated with the god's sacred domain. According to this school of thought, many of the mummies of animals that were associated with the god (i.e., ibises), were not the god's particular avatar, but rather ibises that lived on the god's land within the temple confines, and were revered due to their resemblance to the god, rather than worshipped as a god. However, a significant number of animal mummies that have been identified as belonging to the category of 'votive,' contain animals that have deliberately been killed. This ritual sacrifice would argue against the idea that anything living and dying on the god's land was elevated to a sacred or revered being that was mummified and interred in the hypogea. Until more textual evidence concerning this mummy type is discovered and studied, the identification of these mummies as votive offerings must remain debated.

As with conventional votive offerings, there seems to have been different 'grades' or qualities of animal mummy, depending on how much a pilgrim wished to spend, or how important the request was. Presumably the more lavishly wrapped mummies with cartonnage masks were more expensive, while more simply presented creatures were cheaper. Coffins and sarcophagi of stone or wood, or cartonnage casings were also provided. Some took the shape of the animal they housed, while others were rectangular boxes. In the early Ptolemaic Period elaborate cast bronze coffins were made. The examples used for falcons often have wooden flaps set into the ventral surface so that the mummy could be inserted once the coffin had been chosen, and then secured by sealing the flap using leather or thread tied through a hole.

Fig. 1.3 Votive statues of cats made of bronze. Photograph by Salima Ikram.

In addition to mummies, more conventional votive offerings in the forms of images of the god and inscribed stelae were presented to the animal form of the deities, and also interred in the galleries. Perhaps these had a different value, both monetary and spiritual, than the mummies, or were given under different circumstances. These ex-votos were made of different materials, including faïence, wood, and metal, with the latter being the most common. The stelae were all made of limestone and either inscribed or painted. Some of the larger images of animals that were made of bronze (or even wood) were hollow and contained an animal mummy. The donors of such pieces were clearly taking no chances in currying favor with the gods.

The majority of animal mummies found in museums today belong to the category of votive mummy. This is hardly surprising if they represent the offerings of pilgrims. It is estimated that ten thousand birds were buried annually in the Sacred Animal Necropolis, based on an estimated total finding of four million ibises (Ray 1976: 138). Cats buried at Bubastis and Stabel Antar were so numerous that they were used as ballast for ships going back to Europe, where they were used as fertilizer. A single shipment of cat remains sent to England from Egypt in the nineteenth century weighed approximately nineteen tons, and contained about 180,000 cat mummies (Malek 1993: 129). Animal mummies, like human mummies, were also used as fuel when there was a shortage of wood, and ibises were used as fertilizer by villagers as recently as the late nineteenth century. To achieve such a large volume of production, undoubtedly many of these animals must have been specially reared in or around the temples.

Evidence for the breeding of these animals has been found at several sites. Recent discoveries at Medinet Madi (see Bresciani, this volume) have revealed egg hatcheries and a small crocodile-rearing pen attached to the temple. At the Sacred Animal Necropolis at Saqqara a find of several ibis eggs in a courtyard has led to its identification as the ibis hatchery (Davies and Smith 1997), while texts from the Archive of Hor, a priest of that necropolis also indicate the existence of a building or complex of buildings where ibis eggs were incubated and the young birds reared (Ray 1976: 138). In other areas which had ibis temples there is also evidence for special breeding areas (Vandorpe 1992: 115, Traunecker 1987: 147–158). Texts also discuss supplying the ibises with the clover and bread that they ate (Ray 1976: 138; see Kessler and Nur el-Din, this volume). Dogs, too, seem to be bred for sacrifices (Ikram et al. 2013). Some of the baboons that seem to have been bred and kept in captivity were not always well-looked after; some show signs of rickets, periotitis, and deformed heads (Moodie 1931: 56). Quite possibly the sacred animals, as well as the votive animals, were also bred in captivity, as has been suggested for some of the baboons (Goudsmit and Brandon-Jones: 2000: 116). Others, though, were imported from Africa proper, contributing to an active trade in live animals.

The upkeep of animals that were bred for dedication to the god was not without its problems. Priests attached to the temples were in charge of feeding them, keeping them clean, acting as veterinarians when they were hurt, and mummifying them when they had to be given as offerings. However, the priestly caretakers of the animals were not always above reproach. The Archive of Hor tells us that the food of the ibises was stolen and the birds were hungry, some even dying of hunger and neglect (Ray 1976: 37, 123), although this might have been a slight exaggeration for dramatic effect. Ultimately, six priests were arrested and punished, and the cult of the ibis continued to be administered without, we hope, any additional problems for the birds (Ray 1976: 73–76).

As time progressed, the diversity of animals found in these cemeteries increased dramatically. Perhaps with the passing of time the original beliefs behind these cults had evolved and changed, leading to a larger scale celebration of the gods through their manifestations in the animal world. This syncretism and diversification of animals associated with gods, and indeed the gods themselves, is attested from spells and prayers of this period (Ritner 1986: 103, n. 28). In the Roman Period a composite deity, Har-thoth, was made up of Horus, who symbolized the sun and the day, and Thoth, who symbolized the moon and the night. Together, the two birds invoked a host of other deities that were part of the great creation of Egypt and the world (Ray 1976: 137). Occasionally curious combinations of animals have also been found wrapped together in single bundles: rams and crocodiles (Kessler 1989: 56), falcons and shrews (Nicholson, this volume; Ikram, in press). Some are due to obvious theological reasons (shrews and falcons are the respective manifestations of the nocturnal and diurnal aspect of the sun god), while other combinations remain obscure. It appears that animals became sacred, or increased in their importance during this period, in order to emphasize an additional aspect or role of the god. Thus, all sorts of animals were mummified during the Greco–Roman Period: cattle, baboons, rams, lions, cats, dogs, hyenas, fish, bats, owls, gazelles, goats, crocodiles, shrews, scarab beetles, ichneumons, ibises, falcons, snakes, lizards, and more. Even crocodile eggs and dung balls were wrapped up and presented as offerings.

Unlike pets and sacred animals, votive mummies were not, for the most part, allowed the luxury of a natural death. Many of the animal mummies that have been identified as votive offerings show that they were killed deliberately. This rather argues against the idea that all animals in sacred area that looked like the god were sacred. Many of the cat mummies found at the Bubasteion (Zivie and Lichtenberg, this volume), as well as examples in museum collections (Armitage and

Clutton-Brock 1981; Ikram and Iskander 2002) show that they were killed by having their necks broken, while others had their skulls crushed with a blunt instrument. A particular pattern also seems to emerge in the age at death of the British Museum's collection of cat mummies: they died either between the age of two to four months, or between nine to twelve months (Armitage and Clutton-Brock 1981). The ones in the Egyptian Museum had a less clear age of death curve, although several were between two and four months when they died, while the ones in the Louvre were between ten and fifteen months old when they met their end (Charron 1990: 209–213). The natural life-span of a cat can be as long as twelve years, which might have been the age achieved by some of the sacred animals. Other animals, such as ibises and raptors might also have been summarily dispatched by being dipped into vats of melted resin or pitch (Nicholson, this volume), while canid mummies show signs of strangulation (Lortet and Gaillard 1909: 257–260, 283–286, 294), and crocodiles might have had their nostrils slit (Bresciani, personal communication).[10] At Lahun, two tombs of crocodiles were found, in which one crocodile was sliced up (de Gorostarzu 1901: 182–184)!

When examined either by radiographs or by unwrapping, some of these votive mummy bundles are either empty or filled with bits of fur or feathers or even fragments of different animals, sometimes even different species. These have been identified as ancient fakes, made by the priestly embalmers to dupe the pilgrims. Interestingly, the more elaborate the wrapping (especially in the Roman Period), the more likely it is to contain a fake. On a more charitable note, mummies might have been made when few animals were available. The priests may have used the idea that a part might symbolize the whole, and with the correct spells and incantations the fragments of an animal would become complete offerings for the gods. This might hold true for raptor mummies, which number a high percentage of fakes, as these birds are difficult to breed in captivity. Kessler has posited (1989 and this volume) that the jars or bundles filled with fragments of animals suggest that the animals were held so sacred that even parts of them that were found in the wild (or pieces left in the detritus of mummification) had to be properly mummified. This might indeed have been true for some periods, but certainly not all as some of the texts from the Archive of Hor prove. The texts mention abuses perpetrated by the embalming priests who were accused of putting empty jars into the catacombs or putting in bundles of ibises that contained only a few bones. The priests in question were tried and punished and the rule of 'one god in one vessel' instituted (Ray 1976: 142–143). Certainly many examples of votive mummies, whether they are meant to belong to ibises, lizards, or cats have been found to be fakes. It is hoped that the gods accepted the honest prayers of the pilgrims, despite the trickery of the priests.

Notes

1 The excavation was carried out by the Djehuty Mission to TT11/12 under the direction of Jose Galan. I am grateful to J. Galan for the information and for the invitation to work on the animal and human mummies from this area.

2 It has also been posited by the excavators that these might have been kept for temple sacrifices, although this is still one of several hypotheses concerning these animals. In addition to the publications referred to above, up-to-date information on these burials is available at www.archaeology.org. Also, see Nekhen News, www.hierakonpolis-online.org

3 Both the man and his dog are in the University Museum, Philadelphia, and numbered E16220a and E16219, respectively. They were excavated by W.M.F. Petrie at Abydos, and date to the Thirtieth Dynasty, although the early Ptolemaic Period has also been suggested as a date (Petrie 1902: 39–40).

4 The leg of a calf (CG 29853) from the victual mummies belonging to Isitemkheb D is also unusual in its preparation as some fur, just above the hoof remains in place. It was more usual to skin the creature and to prepare it for consumption prior to mummification. The unique offering of a mummified head of a calf, also from this assemblage (CG 29841), also retains its fur (Ikram and Iskander 2002: 29–33).

5 It should be noted, however, that Kessler (1989: 253–290) believes that all the sacred animal cults, especially those of the later periods of Egyptian history, were linked to the divine apotheosis of the king, rather than to the manifestation of different divinities. This might be the case, but until more evidence is forthcoming it must remain a hypothesis.

6 For a detailed examination of the evidence of Predynastic animal burials and their links to later dynastic practices see Flores (2003).

7 At Abydos Petrie discovered a tomb with a pyramidal superstructure and chapel containing seventeen cat skeletons with offering pots of milk (Malek 1993: 52). It is unclear whether these were pets or sacred animals.

8 In some cases, temples with animal cults were also dedicated, in whole or in part, to Imhotep. The cult of Imhotep, the architect for Djoser, who was hailed as a wise-man and doctor, as well as an architect, was particularly popular in the Late and Graeco–Roman Periods, when he became a focus of personal piety. Imhotep's relationship to animal cults was partially due to the belief that his mother, Khereduankh, was supposed to have been fathered by the Ram of Mendes (Wildung 1977: 52–53).

9 Some animals that signified certain divinities do not have exact parallels in nature as they are made up of composites of a type, and are thus 'super-canids' or 'super-hawks' (Houlihan and Goodman 1986: 48), manifesting the best and most prominent characteristics of all such animals. With the advent of Christianity, Anubis seems to have been translated into Saint Christopher, the now decanonized patron saint of travel.

10 It is interesting to note that Lortet and Gaillard record cuts in the muzzles of certain crocodiles perhaps to stop them from biting people after their capture (1909: 295–299).

2

Manufacturing Divinity
The Technology of Mummification

Salima Ikram

A lthough a great deal of research has been carried out on the mummification of humans, less attention has been paid to their animal counterparts, both in antiquity and the present.[1] As many, if not more, variations in mummification technology were practiced on animals compared to humans. The study of these methods has involved considering the mummies themselves, together with embalmers' workshops and embalming detritus, ancient texts, whether written by the ancient Egyptians themselves (Sauneron 1952, Möller 1913), such as the Apis Embalming Ritual (Vos 1993), or by visitors to Egypt, (e.g., Herodotus of Halicarnassus, the fifth century B.C. historian), the results of recent scholarship, and experimental archaeology.[2]

Work carried out on the animal mummies in the Egyptian Museum, as well as in other collections, shows that, like humans, animals were mummified in a variety of ways throughout Egyptian history. Several different methods were employed during the same chronological period, perhaps dependent on the atelier used (Ikram and Dodson 1998: 109). Some types of mummification are more particular to specific groups of creatures, such as dipping in resin for birds (see Nicholson, this volume, and below), while other methods are used for a broader range of species. There is no evidence to indicate whether the ancient Egyptians practiced different ways of mummification on animals prior to using them on humans, or vice versa. In this case, it was possibly the humans who served as the 'guinea-pigs,' as in the earlier periods of Egyptian history human mummies far outnumbered the animals.

The foundation of our knowledge concerning techniques of mummification comes from classical authors, with Herodotus's descriptions (II: 86) being the most comprehensive. This, supplemented by information gathered by studying the mummies themselves, as well as ancient Egyptian texts, suggests that at least three basic methods (Ikram and Dodson 1998: 103–136), with some variations, bringing the total number of methods to five, were possible. Some of these additional methods may have been used exclusively for animal mummification. In an effort to correlate our knowledge of animal mummification derived from textual evidence with the physical remains, experimental mummification has been carried out on rabbits, ducks, and fish (see p. 29).³ These experiments, together with observations culled from examining the mummies and sites associated with mummification (the Apis Embalming house at Memphis [Jones 1982, 1983, 1985, 1987, 1988; Dimick 1959] and the embalming room at Tuna al-Gebel [Gabra 1971: 171]), help to elucidate the technology used to make many of the animal mummies that have been found throughout Egypt.

Fig. 2.1 Raw natron as available currently in Cairo. Photograph by Engell Brothers Media.

Mummification basically involves the desiccation of the body using common salt or natron that draws out the bodily fluids leaving the dry husk. Natron, a naturally occurring substance in Egypt, is not only a desiccant but has additional deodorizing and anti-bacterial properties. It should be noted that due to the earlier translations of Herodotus the desiccation process was misunderstood, and scholars thought that the bodies were put into a bath of *liquid* natron. Actually, the term 'bath' has caused confusion; in reality it meant that the bodies were submerged in a tub of *dry* natron. This was clarified by the experimental work of Lucas on pigeons, and Garner on mice (1979), although S. Buckley renewed the debate in 2011 on television ("Mummifying Alan"), but thus far no published evidence is available.

Evisceration and Desiccation

The highest quality method, practiced during the Middle, and especially the New Kingdoms, involves the removal of the brain (in humans through the nostrils, generally the left nostril—this would only be relevant for larger mammals whose cranial material would contribute to putrefaction [Leek 1969]), followed by the extraction of the viscera (lungs, stomach, intestines, and liver) through a cut in the left side of the body, or from a ventral incision. Then the body was cleaned and deodorized by washing it with water and sometimes palm wine, before desiccating it using natron (a mixture of sodium bicarbonate, sodium carbonate, sodium sulphate, and sodium chloride). In humans this process was supposed to take forty days; in animals it could probably take more or less, depending on the size of the creature. Texts indicate that the Apis bull might have taken as many as fifty-two or more days (Vos 1993: 34). Experimental work has shown that to make good quality mummies, the natron had to be changed regularly. The experiments have also shown that bags filled with natron are the most effective method for drying the interior of the body (see p. 35), while loose natron was used to dry the exterior. Once the body was dry, it was anointed inside and out with sacred oils (such as castor, lettuce, and balanites), and in some instances resins, and then wrapped in linen bandages. The so-called embalming room found at Tuna al-Gebel could have been used for these activities as it contains an inclining stone bed that is covered with black substances, a deep jar containing embalming materials (natron, salt, resins), and the whole area is covered with oily and resinous deposits (Gabra 1971: 171–172). However, its size (3 x 2 m) argues against large-scale usage. The excavators posit that it was used for the Opening-of-the-Mouth ceremony (Kessler and Nur el-Din, this volume). Certainly this area could not have been used for desiccation as the space is too small, and as experimental work has shown, sunlight is necessary for the success of the operation (see p. 31).

The viscera were similarly prepared separately. Variations on this method include a briefer drying time, and the application of huge amounts of oils, resins, and even bitumen to compensate for the resulting poorer quality of desiccation. This shorter method is particularly common from the later Third Intermediate Period onward, becoming the norm in the Greco-Roman era.

Fig. 2.2 A calcite table in Memphis that was probably used in the mummification and funerary rites of the Apis Bull. Photograph by Salima Ikram.

The best quality of traditional mummification (see Rabbit 4, p. 34) can be seen in mummies coming from the Eighteenth (CG 29836–8, monkeys and dog) and Twenty-first Dynasties (CG 29835, a gazelle), as well as in a monkey mummy found by the Spanish mission working at the tomb of Djehuty, in Thebes, in the area of TT11 and TT12. None of these examples however, with the exception of the gazelle, seem to have had the cranial cavity totally voided. These mummies were all eviscerated (from incisions in different areas), and well desiccated. The changing of the natron and its reuse is evident from the curious items that are found wrapped up in the bandages and with the mummies: feathers appear on and around mammals, and dried insects or reptiles can be found together with the 'main' mummy. As the experimental work showed, these extraneous elements were not necessarily placed inside the 'main' mummy for any symbolic reason; probably, they had fallen into the natron or resin, when the mummy was being prepared for bandaging, and had not been removed.

The monkeys all seem to have been eviscerated from their sides, lower abdomen, or anal area. However, the turpentine method (see below) was not used, as the animals from the Egyptian Museum collections preserve their windpipes and other fragments of internal organs, as do human bodies that have been eviscerated from the side. The monkey from TT11/12 is missing its bottom half, so it is difficult to judge how he was eviscerated. The gazelle (CG 29835) and the dog (CG 29836) were eviscerated by a cut in the abdomen. A pair of sacred crocodiles, also in the Cairo Museum collection (CG 29628, CG 29630), might have been prepared similarly, and the cut lavishly covered with resin, as with others from Kom Ombo. The amount of solid resin in the crocodiles' bodies nearly doubled the animals' weights and virtually obliterated the incision.

The body cavities of the gazelle (CG 29835) and the monkey from the tomb of Djehuty were well filled with packing material. The gazelle was given the plump shape that it would have enjoyed in life with a filling of sandy soil and bandages; the monkey's torso was filled out with rolls of loosely woven linen bandages that had been rolled tightly and filled the cavity so completely that the monkey's skin was stretched taut over them. This re-stuffing using soil is typical of good-quality human mummification found in the Twenty-first Dynasty; certainly the gazelle dates to that period. Although the monkey might also date to the same time, ceramic evidence suggests that it dates to the Eighteenth Dynasty, as this is the other time period where linen-stuffed, high-quality mummies were commonly produced.

Desiccation and Anointment

The second method of mummification involves the washing out of the intestines, and then drying the body, using natron, before anointing and wrapping it. A variation on this method, not described by the Classical authors, but observed in actual mummies, requires pouring vast amounts of black substance (resin, oil, pitch, bitumen—without proper scientific analysis it is difficult to determine the exact nature of this black material) over the body and especially in the area of the torso after some desiccation, and often without benefit of evisceration. These substances inhibit bacterial growth.

This type of mummification, and variations on the theme, seems to have been most commonly used on the mass poroduced votive mummies. These shortcuts might have developed due to economic reasons, the need to produce a large quantity of mummies quickly, or a loss of knowledge as to how to carry out the better qualities of mummification.

All types of creatures were prepared in this manner. The majority of votive mummies seem to have been desiccated with natron, but the natron was rarely changed, if at all, and evisceration was also less common. This resulted in the general disintegration of the corpses, which is clearly demonstrated in x-rays of mummies of this period that show the collapse of the skeleton's articulation and the presence of a black powdery substance: the disintegrated flesh. Mummies prepared thus also smell differently from the ones prepared using less in the way of oils and resin. The hot resins/pitch/bitumen applied on the body have often burned through the wrappings, or pooled in the area closest to the ground; this enables one to see how the creatures were placed. Some of the bird and cat mummies (CG 29645, CG 29657) in the Egyptian Museum collection show that they were thrust into the ground, like standing skittles, while they dried. The sand and gravel on the ground has adhered to the damp bandages to the level of insertion. In the Egyptian Museum several cat mummies seem to have been prepared thus, while other similar examples come from the Bubasteion at Saqqara (see Zivie and Lichtenberg, this volume).

The application of hot resins and oils to badly dried bodies resulted in the burning of the flesh and its subsequent speedy disintegration. In fact, in the case of very young or small animals with delicate bones and little flesh, the combination of improper drying (and often the retention of the viscera) and the extreme heat of the applied materials has resulted in a sort of combustion, leaving only a black powdery deposit as the trace of the body (CG 29712, CG 29785). Perhaps this is one reason why the quality and complexity of the external bandaging improved in direct proportion to the decline in the

Fig. 2.3 A chamber beside the entrance to the Tuna al-Gebel galleries that was probably used for heating resins and oils that were used to anoint mummies. Photograph by Salima Ikram.

quality of mummification. The best and most elaborate bandaging comes from the Greco-Roman Period, and the bodies of these mummies are invariably the worst prepared.

Smaller animals or animals with minimal viscera were also similarly prepared, especially in the Late Period and thereafter. Shrews, snakes, and sometimes groups of young crocodiles were desiccated in natron, and then heavily coated in resins and wrapped together, sometimes of twenty or more!

Enemas

The third method of mummification uses no incision for evisceration. Rather, oil of cedar or pine (equivalent to turpentine)[4] was injected into the anus (like an enema), the orifice plugged, and the liquid left to melt the viscera. The body was desiccated using natron. After a number of days the body was taken out of the natron and the anal plug removed, releasing the body's contents, which had been liquefied (see p. 37). The body then underwent the standard anointing and wrapping procedure. This method, mentioned by Herodotus, has been disputed, particularly with regard to the Middle Kingdom royal and non-royal women found at Deir al-Bahari who were thought to have been prepared in this manner. Although it is difficult to determine if this was indeed the mummification method used for these women, a clear example, probably dating to the Roman Period, has been examined by the author: a certain unnumbered Lady X, in the Egyptian Museum.

Examples of animal mummies made using some sort of cedar/juniper oil are few, although this material is referred to in the Apis Embalming Ritual (Vos 1993: 201, 256). Contrary to its name, the incomplete papyrus does not provide guidelines for mummification, but rather for the final wrapping and accompanying prayers that were to be used when preparing the Apis bull for its eternal rest. The best known examples of mummification using the enema technique are the Buchis Bulls and the Mother of Buchis (CG 29859) mummies found at Armant (Mond and Myers 1934: I, 62–64). At this site the actual enemas that had been used in the process were found by the excavators, bearing a remarkable resemblance to the ones that were used by modern-day veterinarians (Mond and Myers 1934: I, 100–102). Unfortunately the mummies themselves were destroyed by ground

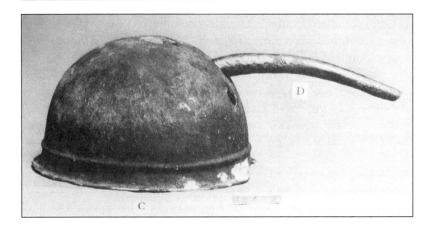

Fig. 2.4 An enema found during the course of the Bucheum excavations.
Courtesy of the Egypt Exploration Society.

water, and thus it is difficult to evaluate the method and the quality
of their mummification. The excavators of the Buchem suggested that
a combination of evisceration and the enema was used to achieve
mummification (Mond and Myers 1934: I, 100–102). An emetic evisceration method was experimented with quite successfully (see Rabbit 5,
p. 37); in fact, thus far this was the best preserved of all the rabbit mummies produced during the course of the experimental archaeology.
After the enema-evisceration, it is believed that the animals were further
desiccated and then wrapped after the application of oils and resins.
The use of bitumen in the preparation of a bovid mummy in the
Munich Museum has also been identified (Boessneck 1987: 86).

Once voided of viscera and desiccated, the Buchis Bulls were placed
on wooden boards in the position of a sphinx, achieved by cutting the
tendons of the hind legs. A few animals had the hind legs extended.
The tail was passed under the right hind leg, and the head was held
upright by a wooden chin rest. The mummy was clamped onto a
wooden board (c. 2.5–3 cm thick) using bronze or iron clamps
through which linen bandages were passed to secure the animal
(Mond and Myers 1934: I, 58). Huge amounts of linen were used;
some investigators have calculated that at least two-hundred meters of
linen were used in the wrappings of these animals (Moodie 1931: 58).

The same pose and wrapping is outlined in the Apis Embalming Papyrus (Vos 1993). These bovid mummies tended to be very elaborately wrapped, with cartonnage coverings, inlaid eyes, crowns, and gilding (Mond and Myers 1934, Boessneck 1987, Rose and Dietze 1978).

Defleshing

A fourth method used on some animal mummies involved defleshing. The examples are all Greco–Roman mummies, and this fact might be related to their being *ex votos* offering. Examination of some animal mummies suggest that the bodies were defleshed, anointed with oils and resins, and then wrapped (e.g., CG 29676, CG 29758, Brussels E.1870, BM 6772, BM 6774). The manner in which they might have been defleshed, and the reasons for this are unclear. Some young bovid mummies (CG 29676, Brussels E.1870) show that the bones are piled into the mummy bandage and then wrapped. The epiphyses of some of the bones, visible through the wrappings in CG 29676, are covered with resin or pitch suggesting that the bare bones were collected, smeared with resins and oils, and then bandaged to make them resemble complete bovid mummies. Were these animals cooked and eaten before burial of their bones took place, as has been suggested with the Apis bulls (see Dodson, this volume), or were these animals buried, allowed to rot, and then exhumed and wrapped? Other animals that seem to have been similarly prepared are dogs (CG 29758) and ovicaprids (CG 29675). Radiographs show that the dog mummy (CG 29758) consists of a mass of disarticulated dog bones (apparently from one dog) that are wrapped together and placed inside a wooden statue of Anubis. It is unlikely that the flesh of the dog would have been consumed, so perhaps the idea of extracting bones from burials and preparing these as mummies is more feasible. Whether this was related to the mass burials of animals associated with festival days of the particular divinity is unknown (see Chapter 1). Some bird mummies also consist merely of bones. Sami Gabra, the first major excavator at Tuna al-Gebel, wrote that some of the ibises were injected with terebinth resin, causing the body to dissolve, leaving only the bones. The bones were wrapped in linen, and groups of these mummies were placed in pottery vessels that were sealed and later placed in Gallery C (1971: 111).

Fig. 2.5
A proposed
restoration of
the Buchis
Bull. Courtesy
of the Egypt
Exploration
Society.

Immersion

A fifth, and final, variation on mummification involved the total immersion of live birds in vats of melted resin/pitch/bitumen, and was also used as a speedy and economical way of mummification. (Moodie 1931: 58, Nicholson, this volume). The idea is that the embalmer held the creature by its feet and plunged it into the vat of boiling liquid. This would have simultaneously killed the animal and 'frozen' it. Except for the desiccation, this follows on the principle of the second type of mummification described above. No such experimental work has been carried out, so it is difficult to assess its viability. It is also possible that the birds were killed by strangulation (some of the ibises might have been thus dispatched), and then immersed in or painted with these substances prior to bandaging. This would explain the poor quality of preservation of many of the avian mummies.

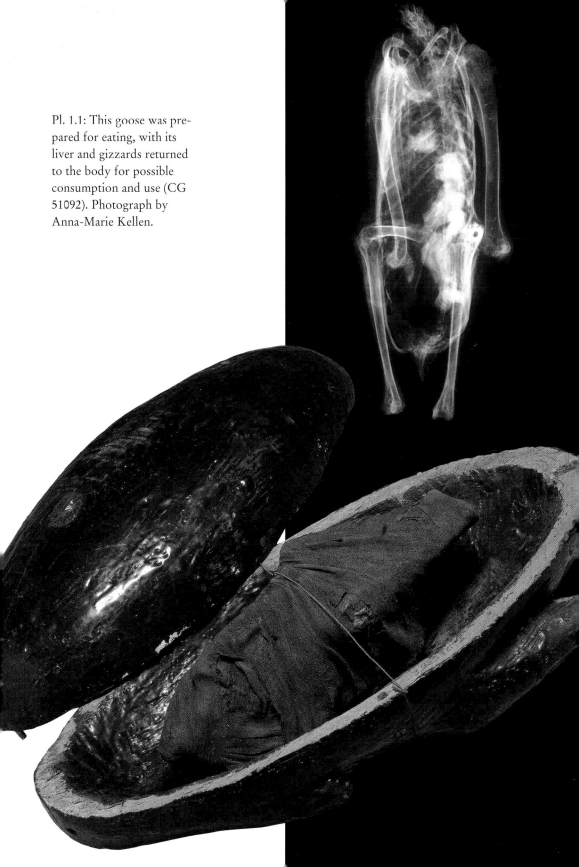

Pl. 1.1: This goose was pre-pared for eating, with its liver and gizzards returned to the body for possible consumption and use (CG 51092). Photograph by Anna-Marie Kellen.

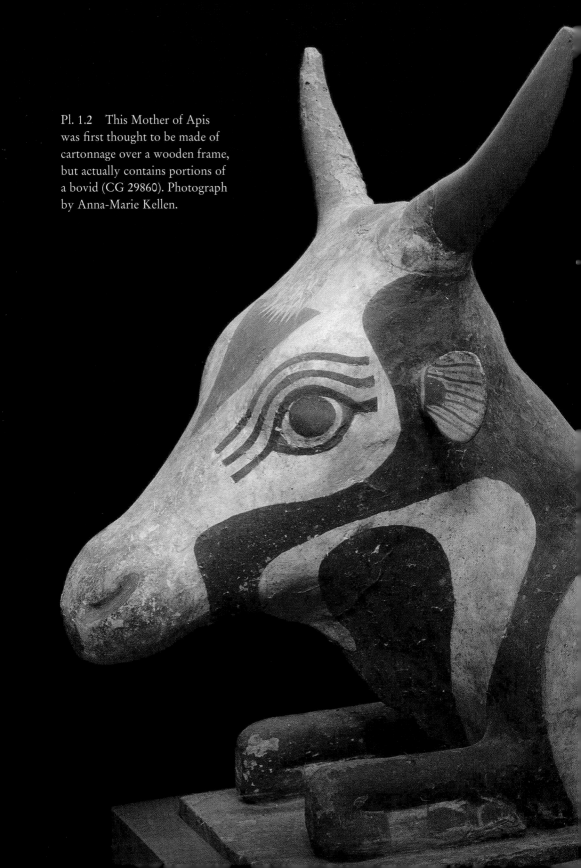

Pl. 1.2 This Mother of Apis was first thought to be made of cartonnage over a wooden frame, but actually contains portions of a bovid (CG 29860). Photograph by Anna-Marie Kellen.

Pl. 1.3   Part of a stela showing the Apis bull being revered. Photograph by Salima Ikram.

Pl. 1.4   A limestone sarcophagus of a cat, dedicated by Prince Djhutmose
of the Eighteenth Dynasty (CG 5003). Photograph by Salima Ikram.

Encasement

A variant on the theme of preservation that is unusual and not well understood seems to be unique to the baboons found at Saqqara (Nicholson, this volume). The baboons were mummified, presumably in a conventional way, using natron, resins, and oils. They were then placed in a squatting position that was common for these animals (see below), and were put inside rectangular wooden shrines that were filled with gypsum plaster so that the mummies were completely encased.

Victual Mummies

The production of food mummies raises some additional questions. These mummies consist of joints of meat or entire pieces of poultry that are ready for consumption. The meat was jointed and skinned prior to preservation, while the poultry mummies were plucked, eviscerated, and had their wing-tips and feet removed, just as one would prepare them for eating, with the gizzards and liver wrapped, and reintroduced into the body cavity (Goodman 1987: 67–77; Ikram 1995a: Appendix II; Ikram, this volume [Pl. 1.1]), as is the case with prepared fowl found in modern supermarkets.

The mummies were prepared by being desiccated in natron, possibly of a quality that had a higher salt content than the more refined type that would have been used for higher status human burials, as has been demonstrated through the use of Scanning Electron Microscopy.[5] Some of these mummies show evidence of oils and resins being used on them, while many more show evidence of this in their coffinets.[6] Some researchers had suggested that the application of hot oil or resin gave the desiccated pieces of flesh the appearance of burning or being cooked. This could indeed be the case. Until now it has not been possible to determine if these pieces of meat were cooked, salted, and thus preserved, or if they were only salted, covered with resin, and then wrapped. With victual mummies, as with the other examples discussed, the final step was the wrapping. Frequently the linen bandages are knotted into position, rather than sealed with resin.

Last Rites

Naturally, minor variations occurred within these different mummification methods depending on economic criteria, the particular style of each embalming house (perhaps based on its geographic location), and what fashion might have been particularly popular during a certain

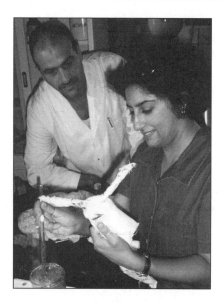

Fig. 2.6 Experimental work, sealing bandages using resin on a catfish mummy. Photograph by Engell Brothers Media.

era. The type of mummy itself also plays a part in determining these variations; the favorite pets of wealthy individuals would have enjoyed a better quality of mummification than mass-produced votive mummies.

The final preparation of the mummies varied a bit depending on how they had been desiccated. Generally, after the animals had been dried using natron, they were removed from the substance, dusted off, and then anointed with oils. As experimental work has shown (see p. 29ff.), this served a dual purpose: certain oils were linked to the revivification rituals that facilitated the animals' eternal existence, and the oils restored some of the suppleness to the limbs that they had enjoyed in life, permitting the embalmers to arrange the body in an appropriate position. Thus the oils were both practical and metaphorical means/symbols of reanimation for the hereafter. Once the oils, unguents, and resins had been applied to the body, amulets were placed on it, and it was wrapped with linen bandages while appropriate prayers were read (Ikram and Dodson 1998: 153–165; Vos 1993). This traditionally took thirty days, although with animals of different sizes it was bound to vary. Once bandaged, masks were frequently placed over the heads of the creatures. Several cartonnage, and even ceramic, masks were made for cats, dogs, hawks, and even rams (CG 29655, CG 29685, CG 29863, CG 29862, CG 29767, and CG 29804–06; Evans 2001). Occasionally an animal was entirely encased in a cartonnage covering, just as was done for humans in the Ptolemaic period (CG 29816 *bis*).

Wrapping

Mummy wrappings varied considerably: until the Roman Period they remained relatively simple, consisting of linen bandages spirally wound around the creature (presumably this was a bit different for bulls and cows, as their size made bandaging difficult). For victual mummies the bandages were generally knotted into place, while other animal mummies had a more elaborate system for sealing that involved copious amounts of resin. Some animals have layers of different wrappings in addition to their linen bandaging. There are several instances when the body was first wrapped in a papyrus or reed mat, perhaps to provide extra protection and bulk to the desiccated creature, and then covered with the conventional linen wrappings (CG 29661, CG 29728). Wrapping votive offerings and even sacred creatures was not always a task that commanded the embalmer's complete attention: there are examples where the exterior of a wrapped mummy fails to match the interior: a small crocodile (CG 29713) is wrapped so that it seems to have a very definite head and tail. X-rays show that in actual fact, the animal's head is where the tail should be. Occasionally the reverse occurs and the embalmer lets his imagination and technical skill takeover. Some wrapped animals are almost sculptures: a kid or a lamb (CG 29668) forms the basis of a much larger mummy that is basically a seated goat made almost entirely of linen. One cat in the Cairo Museum (CG 29660) has bandages that are cunningly painted to give the impression of a brindled cat. The outermost wrappings of mummies dating from the Roman Period are often quite elaborate. Some have bi-colored coffering in square or lozenge patterns, while others are wrapped in a herringbone or a basket pattern. Some of the plain packages of Greco-Roman mummies were often enhanced with appliqué images of divinities or animals, or even the features of the animals themselves (eyes, nose, mouth, etc.).

Orientation

The positions of animals within their wrappings are also diverse, and are somewhat dependent on the method of mummification: if the animal has been reduced to a pile of bones, it will be wrapped differently from an articulated and complete animal. Some poses do become standard: monkeys are wrapped in a squatting position, cats tend to be placed as if they were sitting down, with their tails pulled up between the legs, lying over the abdomen. Cats are also wrapped as if they were standing up (see Zivie and Lichtenberg, this volume), as are a few dogs, although this is rarer. Dogs are buried in a variety of positions, while bovids tend to be put into a sphinx-like position that is achieved by cutting the tendons in their hind legs. Some snakes are coiled and wrapped, while other larger ones were often mummified straight, creating a long stick-like object. Sometimes resin is put into the mouths of poisonous snakes, perhaps as an attempt to render them harmless, or is maybe an artifact of mummification, or possibly a part of some ritual (CG 29728; some vipers in the National Museum of Antiquities in Leiden [Falke 1997: 57]) Birds take diverse positions. Ibises tend to be positioned as if they were sitting down, with their heads either twisted down onto the belly, or twisted and pushed onto the back. Falcons were often mummified as if they were standing. Interestingly, many falcons were wrapped as if they were standing humans. This caused some confusion amongst early excavators, as they identified the larger examples as infant humans!

A combination of the study of animal mummies, texts, mummification sites, and experimental archaeology shows that a variety of methods of mummification were possible at any given time to create the animal mummies that are found in Egypt. Further study on this subject might clarify questions regarding enemas and submersions. At present we are still working toward a better understanding of animal mummification techniques used in ancient Egypt, and the information derived from this will shed light not only on the process of animal mummification, but also that of humans.

Experimental Mummification

Experimental archaeology can shed light on many different aspects of an ancient culture, especially where technology is concerned. In order to understand better Egyptian mummification, both animal and human, a series of experimental mummifications were carried out in Egypt on rabbits, ducks, and fish. The rabbits and one duck were prepared in 1999, a second duck in 2000, and the fish in 2002.

The rabbits were purchased from the butcher, and thus were meant for the pot (the other creatures came from a poulterer and fishmonger, respectively). The animals that were successfully mummified could, like their ancient Egyptian counterparts, enjoy an eternal existence in the Fields of Iarru. A total of five rabbits were used for experimentation, with different methods used on each. The brain was left intact in all these animals as it is not of sufficient dimensions to affect significantly the desiccation process, and almost all the similarly sized ancient examples that have been studied retain their brains. The rabbits and the fish are all, at the time of writing, in fine form. One of the rabbits has also donated its tail for DNA testing in order to monitor the disintegration of DNA in mummified tissue.

Materials Used[7]

An effort was made to replicate ancient Egyptian technology and materials. Thus, natron, resins, beeswax, incense, oils, and linen bandages were all purchased in Cairo in herbalists' shops. The natron was first ground as it would have been in ancient Egypt: by hand, using rocks or pounders to smash up the large pieces. As several kilograms were used (over 70) and time was limited, the bulk of the natron was ground professionally using industrial-scale coffee and grain grinders. The solid resins (and incense) were also purchased; most originated in Ethiopia or the Sudan (more probably traded through the Sudan, rather than originating there), although some came from Syria. Palm wine was unavailable, so local gin was used for disinfection, and pure professionally produced turpentine was used. It is hoped that at some point pine juniper or cedar oil/essence will be produced experimentally and then utilized for this purpose. The oils used were lettuce and castor oils, both of which were produced in antiquity as well as today. Other oils, such as almond oil, were no doubt available by the Late Period or the Ptolemaic, and could have been used for mummification, but we chose to use the more common, easily available, and cheaper (although not particularly fragrant) types.

Rabbit 1 (Flopsy)

The first rabbit, weighing 850 g., was killed by strangulation. This method was in keeping with what was done in ancient Egypt as it was used on the mummified cats (Ikram, Zivie and Lichtenberg, this volume; Armitage and Clutton-Brock 1980). There was some bleeding. As some smaller animal mummies do not show clear evidence of evisceration, this animal was left with its viscera intact to see how it would react. It was then placed on a layer of natron on its side, and then covered with more natron. About 20 g. of frankincense was sprinkled over the natron in the hopes that the odor would be controlled. It was then left in a chamber with humidity and temperature controls set to replicate conditions found in the desert. On the second day we were informed that the rabbit had exploded, smelled unpleasant, and had been disposed of. Presumably the gases and fluids reacted internally, causing the rabbit to bloat and then release these rather dramatically. In nature this process would continue, and ultimately, in the desert, the animal would desiccate due to the sun and the sand. Certainly, this is what occurs with corpses

Fig. 2.7   The rabbit that was eviscerated and exsanguinated being removed from the natron. Photograph by Basil Foda.

that are disposed of in the desert and have been observed by this author.

Rabbit 2 (Mopsy)

The second rabbit also weighed 850 g., and was also strangled. Then three holes were made in the body to permit gases to escape in order to see if this would prevent damage to the animal prior to its desiccation. It was then placed on natron, covered with natron, and placed on the roof of the laboratory, in direct sunlight. This would have been closer to the ancient Egyptian conditions in an embalmer's workshop, particularly for the initial desiccation of the corpse where sunlight would not only provide heat, but also cleansing ultraviolet rays (Ikram 1995b: 87). The rabbit was checked after two days. It was malodorous, and had started to swell. Another hole was made in the torso, and the rabbit flipped over after the natron had been stirred so that drier natron was next to the body. On the fifth day the rabbit was rechecked. It was even more bloated and smelly. Another puncture was made, and the natron moved around. On the seventh day the rabbit was examined again. Dermestid beetles were swarming around the animal. The head had exploded completely leaving the skull intact within a brownish colored gooey substance (the disintegrated flesh), with the pelt completely separated from the skeleton. The stomach had also exploded and the flesh had almost completely disintegrated. Presumably, if the animal were left after a repetition of the usual treatment it would eventually turn into a natural mummy. However, due to health and sanitary considerations this corpse was also interred and the experiment terminated.

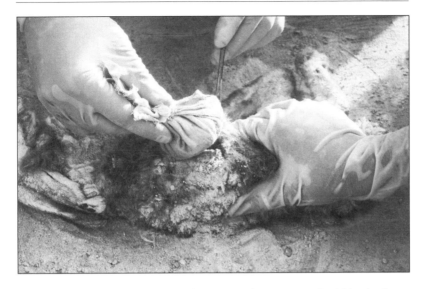

Fig. 2.8 Fresh natron bags being thrust into the eviscerated rabbit's body cavity. Photograph by Basil Foda.

Rabbit 3 (Thumper)

The rabbit weighed 950 g. It was killed (and bled) by the severing of its carotid artery, and was then eviscerated ventrally. After the removal of the internal organs it was reweighed, with its weight being 506 g. The interior cavity was then washed with local gin (Bold's Dry) due to the unavailability of palm wine. The body cavity was then rinsed, and dried using linen. The rabbit was still a bit damp. A container was filled to the height of 10 cm with natron, then two wooden blocks were placed on it, and the rabbit balanced on these before being covered with more natron, with more of that substance being used to fill its interior cavity. This arrangement, which allowed the height of the animal's body to vary, parallels the wooden embalming beds that have been found in Thebes and elsewhere (Ikram and Dodson 1998: 107). The viscera was also treated in the same manner, and the heart was left inside, as was the custom with human mummies. The rabbit was then placed on the roof of the biology building in the sunlight.

The rabbit was examined after two days and the natron changed. The natron near the body was crusty and slightly damp. The rabbit was also turned over so that both sides of the body would have access to the sun's rays through the natron. The natron was once again moved around and added to on the third day. The rabbit was left alone until the sixth day when dermestid beetles were found in the natron. The natron was changed, with the old natron being spread out in a container in the sun to dry so that it could be reused. On the seventh day the animal was flipped over and the natron stirred about a little, but not changed. Dermestid beetles were still visible, but their number was limited. On the ninth day some of the natron was changed as it was damp; this was repeated on the following day. No insects were found in the natron. On day 13 the wet natron was stirred. The rabbit was fairly dry, smelly, and relatively insect-free. The following day the natron was changed and allowed to dry. Some of the animal's fur was falling off and had mingled with the natron. On the sixteenth day the rabbit was examined again. It appeared to be entirely dry, with its fur beginning to fall off, and some small insects still making their home in and around the body. The animal's position was readjusted and it was returned to the natron. On the twentieth day the rabbit was removed from the natron as it was very dry. Some of the hind leg bones (tibia) were sticking out through the skin. Although only twenty days had passed, the animal was dry and ready for bandaging. Perhaps its size and the regular changing of the natron sped up the desiccation process.

The natron was cleaned off the very stiff creature by gently scraping and brushing it with linen, sticks, and reeds. It was not rewashed as this would have rehydrated the animal and been counterproductive to successful mummification. Castor oil was then poured directly into the abdominal cavity and a piece of linen and fingers were used to massage it into the skin to increase pliability so that it could be arranged in a proper position for wrapping. As this was the first mummy, we were unsure of the amount of oil that was viable to use. Both human and animal mummies found in museums and on excavations seemed to have deteriorated due to the oils poured over them. Two small linen balls were inserted into the body cavity and a band of linen was tied around the rabbit's waist to keep the interior packing intact. A seal, made by softening beeswax and modeling it into shape, as can be seen on human mummies, was placed over the evisceration cut of the abdominal cavity. As the rabbit's leg was broken, it was mended with linen. Melted beeswax was used to keep the linen in place and to strengthen it. A scarab was placed in the chest cavity. The extremities (legs and ears) were wrapped first, followed by the head and torso, with other amulets included amongst the body wrappings. Care had to be taken, as the animal was very brittle. Resin was melted and applied on the bandages as a seal. The resin had to be kept hot and melting as it cooled and hardened very quickly once it was off the fire. The liver was separately wrapped and kept with the rabbit.

Rabbit 4 (Fluffy)

This large rabbit weighed 1.5 kg. It was killed by strangulation and eviscerated through a small incision (2.5–3 cm) made in the left side of its abdomen. The animal was massaged and pressed to encourage the exit of any easily removed bodily liquids, and then washed with Bold's Gin, as palm wine was unavailable. The gin was introduced through the incision and then the body was rocked to and fro. The gin was then poured out of the body, which was then not washed with water, but cursorily dried with a linen swab, and filled with natron. As with Rabbit 3, the animal was buried in natron, as was its liver, and placed in the open air on the roof of a building.

On the second day the rabbit was checked, and all the wet and crusty natron on the outside was exchanged for fresh. The natron inside the rabbit had become extremely viscous and malodorous. As much natron as possible was dug out from the inside of the rabbit through the embalming incision using wooden sticks. This was an extremely time-consuming and unpleasant process. After clearing the cavity to the best of our abilities, it was restuffed with natron that had been tied into linen squares, forming bags. Such bags are frequently found as part of embalmers' caches. The experiment clarifies why such bags were used: they are easy to put in and take out of the body cavity, do not smell as much as loose natron, and can be recycled with ease. On the third day the rabbit was removed from the natron and all the soggy natron replaced with fresh; the interior packet was not changed. No insect activity was noted. On the sixth day the animal was again examined, all the natron changed, including the inner bag. Prior to replacing the bag of natron, the abdominal cavity was once again scraped with the wooden tools. The body was very squishy, and gave the impression of containing trapped air. When the animal was pressed, air escaped, in addition to a greenish yellow puss that emerged through various cavity holes within the abdominal wall. Part of the rabbit's nose and ear seemed to be blackened and decaying, so extra natron was placed over those areas.

The following day showed that the rabbit was bloated and puffy, with a quantity of wet natron surrounding it. The animal was once again pressed and massaged, and various liquids and gases (all odiferous) escaped. Then its internal bag was again changed, together with the external natron. The natron that was extraordinarily saturated was discarded, and the remainder spread out to dry in the sun for later reuse. On the ninth day the rabbit's natron, both internal and external was changed. The stench had decreased noticeably. The following day the surrounding natron was again changed and the creature flipped over, although the internal sack was left in place. The fur was molting and the animal was still moist. No insects were detected, perhaps due to the massive amount of natron covering the body. The procedure was repeated on the thirteenth day, and the internal natron removed. Accidentally, the internal cavity was refilled with loose natron. An unidentified insect was found crawling inside the abdominal cavity.

When the rabbit was examined on the fourteenth day, its hind legs were very spongy. As the desiccation process had progressed, the loose natron that had been inadvertently poured into the body cavity was relatively easy to remove. The animal was placed with the incision side down and rubbed and thumped gently. Most of the natron came out quite quickly, with the residue being extracted with a small piece of wood. It was replaced by a natron bag, before the animal was returned to the natron after being flipped. The skeleton could be felt quite distinctly through the skin with the drying of the flesh. On the sixteenth day the animal was checked again. The surrounding natron was not noticeably wet in most areas save for between the legs. A point was made of filling this space with fresh dry natron after the animal had been flipped.

On the twentieth day the animal was checked again. Rabbit 3 had been removed on this day as it had been completely dry. Rabbit 4 was not. This was probably due to its size and the fact that it had not been exsanguinated and less thoroughly eviscerated. The internal packet of natron was wet and the hind legs were also still moist. Accordingly, the natron bag was changed and fresh natron introduced around the hind legs. Some of the fur in the area of the forequarters was pulling away from the skin. The rabbit was not checked for another five days, when it was removed from the natron. It was insect-free, not particularly smelly, and the body was fairly stiff, including the hind legs. The natron was stirred about and the animal flipped. On the twenty-seventh day it was removed from the natron; the internal bag was slightly moist, but the rest of the animal was totally dry, and ready for wrapping.

As with Rabbit 3 the natron was removed, then the body anointed with castor and lettuce oils. In this instance more oil was used; this permitted the manipulation of the joints so that they were convenient for wrapping, and also more in keeping with the animal's natural position. The internal area was partially filled with hot, melted resin and used to coat the entire internal space. Then, four small linen bags filled with natron were inserted into the cavity, together with some dry chunks of resin, such as have been seen in x-rays of animal mummies,[8] and found in the body cavities of human mummies. A heart scarab was placed in the chest, and the abdominal cavity sealed with wax. Then the animal was wrapped carefully as its bones were quite brittle. Clearly, some of the broken bones and disarticulated skeletons found in x-rays of animal mummies are the result of careless handling by the embalmers. The legs were first wrapped, followed by the ears and tail, and then the torso with the bandages being kept in place with melted resin, and amulets placed throughout. In keeping with ancient Egyptian practices, some of the bandages were inscribed with spells from funerary books, incense was burnt, and spells recited during this process.

Rabbit 5 (Peter Cottontail)

This rabbit weighed 800 g.; it was killed by strangulation. Instead of evisceration through an incision, an enema of 168 ml of rectified turpentine was poured into the anus via a glass tube in order to dissolve the viscera, and the anal aperture plugged with linen.

The body was massaged so that the turpentine could spread throughout the interior cavity of the rabbit. Then it was placed in natron, as was done with the other rabbits. The following day the rabbit was checked; it smelled pleasant, was insect free, and the natron was not overly wet, so it was left unchanged. When the animal was examined on the third day, the natron was damp due to the seepage of the turpentine through the animal's pores. It was re-placed in fresh natron. On the seventh day, when the creature was examined, it was very puffy; the fur was detaching itself from the skin. The skin itself became grayish-black, and turpentine was seeping through the pores. The linen plug was removed from the anal cavity and it was massaged, head downward, so that it could start to drain. The liquid had eaten away a part of the area of the left hind leg, and this provided an additional drainage passage. The liquid that came out of the rabbit was greenish-black, but smelt only of turpentine. The animal was not completely emptied as many of the internal organs remained partially intact. The natron was not changed. On the ninth day the natron was changed as it was very wet, due, in part to the fact that the hole in the hind leg had allowed the melted viscera, together with the turpentine, to drain out of the body. A large quantity of material was massaged out of the rabbit; most of it was liquid, but some recognizable chunks of viscera also emerged. The heart, although intact, had become disengaged and started to move out of the body cavity, but was pushed back into it. The semi-liquid emissions had an unpleasant odor.

The animal was next checked on the twelfth day when the natron had to be changed as it was very wet. It only smelt of turpentine; no more visceral emissions were noted. The animal's fur continued to fall off as the follicles had been drastically weakened by the turpentine. There was no insect activity. On the fourteenth day the natron was again changed as it was wet with turpentine. The fur was very loose near the stomach area, though in other areas it was attached more securely. The head was well desiccated, the ears flexible, and the fur fluffy. The rabbit was next checked on the twenty-first day, the natron changed, and the animal returned to it. Due to practical considerations, the rabbit was not checked again until the thirty-fifth day, when it was removed for wrapping. The natron was almost completely dry at this time, with only one or two small damp patches that smelled of turpentine.

The rabbit was freed of the natron; it was quite flat due to the squeezing out of the viscera. Otherwise, it was the best preserved and most pleasant-smelling of all the rabbits prepared. The quality of the fur was also better as it was softer and fluffier. Castor and lettuce oil were poured into the body cavity from the anal passage and the hole in the leg, while more was poured over the animal itself and massaged in. The hind legs, in particular, became far more flexible with the addition of the oils. Melted resin was applied to the inner ears, and the anal cavity and the rupture in the skin of the hind leg were sealed with resin. The extremities were wrapped first, with bandages inscribed with spells from the Book of the Dead. As usual, these were sealed with melted resin. The body was given more shape with linen pads; amulets were included in the wrappings. Additional bandages were added to the neck area to provide support. This is often found in the wrappings of animal mummies as their fragile necks are often in need of support as they are wrapped in their own images, as opposed to the more abstract rendition of human mummies whose necks are not defined separately in the bandaging.

Catfish *Clarias sp.* and Nile Perch *Lates niloticus*

As examples of mummified *Clarius* sp. (catfish) and *Lates niloticus* (Nile perch) have been found, experiments were also carried out on these types of fish. Examinations of mummified specimens, carried out by Lortet and Gaillard (1905) reveal longitudinal cuts made on one side of the fish, or completely gutted through a cut made in the belly. The two fish currently in the Cairo Museum collection (CG 29588 and 29592) show that they were gutted from the belly, rather than the side, as described by Lortet and Hugonunenq (1902); this would have been especially important for the enormous Nile perch that measures 1.45 m. These would have been dried in plain natron, and then wrapped: the method used for both the fish mummies.

The fish were gutted, washed, then dried with linen, before being submerged in natron. As with the rabbits, the natron was changed, but only after the third, seventh, and twelfth days as the fish exuded less liquid. The *Lates niloticus* (named Mongo Fish) was quicker to dry as it is a less greasy and lighter fish, while the catfish (named Augustus 'Catfish' Hunter, a.k.a. Gussie) took longer. The *Lates* was removed from the natron after fifteen days, and the *Clarias* after seventeen days. They were then massaged with generous amounts of lettuce oil, and then

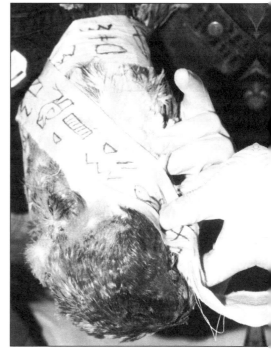

Fig. 2.9 Bandages, inscribed with funerary spells, being wrapped around a desiccated rabbit.
Photograph by Basil Foda.

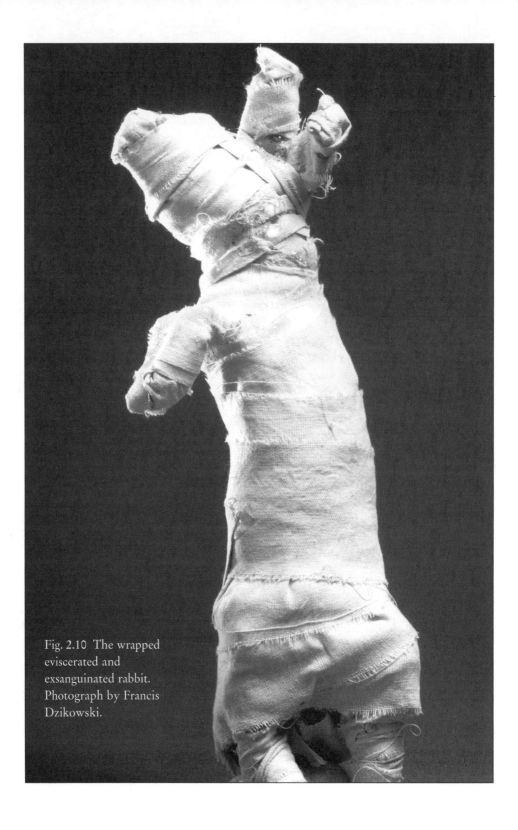

Fig. 2.10 The wrapped
eviscerated and
exsanguinated rabbit.
Photograph by Francis
Dzikowski.

Fig. 2.11 The completed eviscerated rabbit. Photograph by Francis Dzikowski.

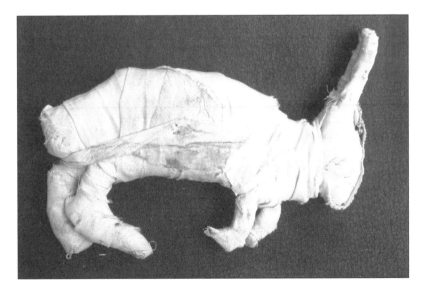

Fig. 2.12 The rabbit prepared using an enema. Photograph by Salima Ikram.

wrapped with linen bandages kept in place with melted resin. The catfish was difficult to wrap as, in keeping with the ancient examples, its whiskers had to be individually wrapped. It should be noted that one of the catfish mummies produced in this way was left out in the sun after being wrapped, and proved to be extremely attractive and tempting (still) to a local raptor who flew away with it.

Poultry

Experiments on ducks were carried out with two students, William Clifford and Matthew Wetherbee (2004). A brief summary is provided here. Work was carried out on two ducks of a similar weight. Both, acquired from the poulterer, were killed by having their necks' wrung. They were then eviscerated. The first duck was submerged in dry natron, which was then changed after every five days, being finally removed on the thirty-fifth day. The second duck was left in the natron, checked only once, and removed on the thirty-fifth day. The duck that had its natron changed was mummified successfully, while the second bird remained damp and partially decayed. They were both wrapped in linen using resin to secure the ends.

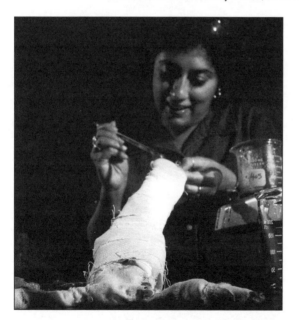

Fig. 2.13 The completed fish. Photograph by Engell Brothers Media.

The State of the Experimental Mummies in 2014

After five years, Rabbits 3, 4, and 5 are still in good condition, showing no external signs of deterioration. They exude an odor that is similar to that of ancient Egyptian mummies, but far less intense. The fish are also stable. The ducks had to be disposed of as they became unbearably malodorous. In future years the rabbits will be re-radiographed to monitor the state of their respective skeletons, and if necessary, or scientifically useful, unwrapped (or perhaps scanned using new imaging machinery), in order to gauge the success of the experimental mummification. The DNA samples that were taken will also provide useful information concerning the rate of deterioration of DNA in mummified tissue, as well as the difficulties involved in its extraction from animals thus prepared.

Notes

1 A notable exception to this is the work of the Manchester Museum Mummy Project, especially the work of R. Garner. Although this work concentrated on human mummification, they carried out experiments in mummification on laboratory rats and mice. See Garner in David, ed. 1979: 19–24.

2 Experimental mummification on a human body has been carried out by Bob Brier and Ron Wade (1996, 1999).

3 The experiments on rabbits were carried out as part of the Animal Mummy Project and a class on "Death in Ancient Egypt" taught at the American University in Cairo in 1999, and then again in 2000 and 2002. I am extremely grateful to Andrew Main and to Zein al-Abeddin Ahmed, and the Biology Department at the American University in Cairo in general for their assistance and support in these experiments. The students who participated particularly in this class and in the experiments were: P. Bell, W. Clifford, J. Eyster, B. Foda, S. Fukagawa, B. Jewell, N. Lazarides, H. Sayed, T. Thompson, M. Wetherbee, and F. Yates. Additionally, further work on ducks was carried out by the author, M. Wetherbee, and W. Clifford (Clifford and Wetherbee 2004). The work on the fish was executed by the author and another group of students: K. Bandy, J. Berman, M. El Dorry, M. Hanna, and A. Shearer.

4 This would probably have been an impure oil of turpentine or pyroligneous acid made of wood tar and turpentine. Such a mixture has been described by Pliny (XV: 7, XVI: 21). The identification of possible examples of this are discussed in Serpico 2000: 267.

5 Some scholars (Lortet and Gaillard 1907: 307) have suggested that these mummies were made by immersion in resinous natron, but research carried out by the author does not support this view (Ikram 1995b: 283–289).

6 Or: (Clark et al. 2013; Ikram 2013)

7 For a brief overview of mummification materials, see Ikram and Dodson 1998: 106.

8 These have been noted by several people when studying museum collections, and by the author during her examination of the animal mummies in the Egyptian Museum, see chapter 9, this volume.

3

The Sacred Animal Necropolis at North Saqqara
The Cults and Their Catacombs

Paul T. Nicholson

Introduction

North Saqqara is, for many reasons, a special place.[1] It was special to the ancient Egyptians as the necropolis in which some of the most important figures in Egyptian history were buried, ranging from officials and Kings of the Early Dynastic and Old Kingdom to high officials of the Amarna Period and beyond.

The Sacred Animal Necropolis at Saqqara is also special. Parts of it were known to scholars through the writings of classical authors such as Strabo, whose *Geography* enabled Anthony Harris (1790–1869) to suggest the location of the Serapeum which was then discovered by Auguste Mariette (1821–1881) in 1851–1852 (Mariette 1857; Taylor 2001: 249; Dodson, this volume). Other parts of it were also known to early European travelers, even before the time of Napoleon (below). The discovery of the Serapeum must be regarded as one of the great discoveries of Egyptian archaeology and did much to boost popular interest in the country and its antiquities.

North Saqqara is, however, important for another reason. It is the location of the first pyramid, that of King Djoser of the Third Dynasty (2649–2575 B.C.), but still more importantly, from the viewpoint of this essay, it is the location of the burial place of the pyramid's architect, Imhotep. Although his tomb remains undiscovered, the search for it is intimately bound up with the discovery and study of parts of the Sacred Animal Necropolis.

Imhotep

Imhotep held the titles "Chancellor of the king of Lower Egypt, the first after the king of Upper Egypt, administrator of the great palace, hereditary lord Greatest of Seers, Imhotep, the builder, the sculptor, the maker of stone vases"—usually translated simply as 'Vizier' and 'Architect' of Djoser (see Wildung 1977). In life he enjoyed considerable privilege, to the extent that his name appears on the base of a statue of Djoser (Cairo JE 49889) (Gunn 1926c). His name was still associated with the construction of the Step Pyramid at Saqqara many centuries after this death, so much so that Manetho, writing in the third century B.C., credited him—under the Greek form of his name (Imouthes)—with the invention of building in stone. It is surely the impact of the monument he had constructed for his master, which led to the association of his name with learning and wisdom. He is said to have been the author of several wisdom texts or "instructions," but none have come down to us. Indeed, John Ray (1978b: 150) refers to him as the "first universal genius known to man" but notes that "most of the sources about him are closer in time to us than they are to Imhotep."

He was deified due to his wisdom, probably during the Late Period (712–332 B.C.), a rare honor for a commoner. He was associated with writing, medicine, and wisdom, giving him a connection to the gods Ptah, and especially Thoth, the former being a creator god, and the latter being hailed for his wisdom. The Greeks identified him with their god of medicine, Asklepios, and through the connection between him and Thoth—the Greek Hermes—he is loosely connected with the Hermetic literature which survived into the modern world.

Saqqara became the focus of the cult of Imhotep, and probably focused around his supposed burial place.

Fig. 3.1 Base of statue of Djoser (JE 49889) with the titles of Imhotep, Cairo Museum.

The Sacred Geography of North Saqqara

The 'sacred geography' of North Saqqara relates to its role as the necropolis of the ancient capital of Memphis, and of the relationship of that place to the Apis bull (Dodson, this volume). The best overall description of this geography has been provided by Ray (1978a, b).

The Apis was regarded as the living herald of Ptah (his ba) and was chosen by the priesthood from among the cattle of Egypt on account of its unique markings, in a process "reminiscent of the cult of the Dalai Lama" (Ray 2002: 19).

Once selected, the Apis was brought to Memphis where it lived a life of great luxury within the precincts of the temple of Ptah. Its arrival at Memphis was marked by a coronation of royal splendor, but "nothing in the Apis's life quite became him like the leaving of it; amid national mourning, often displayed hysterically, the bull was embalmed, encoffined and escorted out to the western desert, finally to lie in a massive granite sarcophagus in . . . the Serapeum" (Ray 1978b: 151) (see also Smith 1974; Taylor 2001: 247–254; Dodson, this volume).

Although the Apis is known to have been venerated from at least as early as the First Dynasty (2920–2770 B.C.), little is known about his cult prior to the construction of the first Serapeum at Saqqara around 1300 B.C. (Ray 1978b: 151). It is to later developments, however, that we owe the creation of Ray's "mummified zoo" (1978: 151). While the living Apis was the *ba* of Ptah, on his death he became identified with Osiris to become Osiris-Apis, or Osorapis. Since the dead were justified and living in truth it was logical that the Apis should be capable of giving oracles in death as he had in life. As a result, North Saqqara became a community of the living as well as of the dead, with facilities to cater for pilgrims—interpreters of dreams and oracles, makers of statuettes, embalmers of animals, astrologers, hostelers, and the like.

Not only was Apis venerated, but after a time his mother also came to be regarded as divine. This elevation of the cow, identified with Isis, probably dates to the sixth century B.C. (Ray 1978b: 152). She too required a burial place, and as a result a further hypogeum was constructed at Saqqara (although the earliest burial place was in the temple of "Hathor lady of the sycomore" at Memphis). Thus a balance was established between Osiris and his wife-mother Isis.

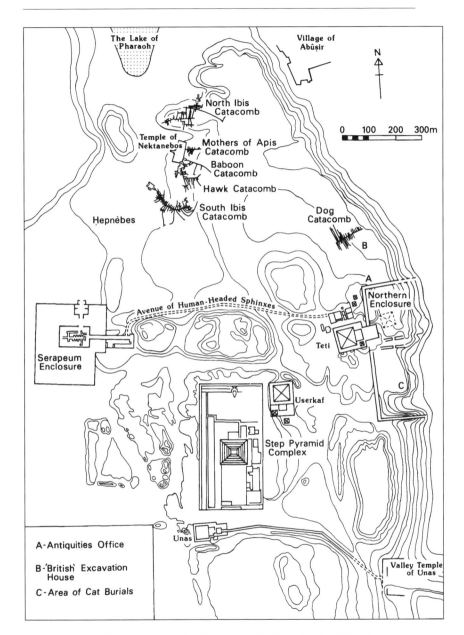

Fig. 3.2 Map of the Sacred Animal Necropolis. Drawing by J. Hodges.

Subsequently, probably at some time before the reign of Nectanebo II (360–343 B.C.), the father of Isis was introduced to North Saqqara. In the local mythology this was Thoth, the ibis-headed god of learning and a lunar deity (Ray 1978b: 152) who could also be represented by the baboon. Burial places for both the ibis and baboon were also constructed at North Saqqara.

In the same way that the Osiris bull had to be counterbalanced by the Isis cow, so the lunar ibis was balanced by the introduction of the solar hawk, representing 'Horus, the avenger of his father,' whose father was in fact Osiris, already present in the form of the deceased Apis.

The story is not complete however. We must consider why the ibis and baboon burial places in particular were located where they were, and not immediately next to the Serapeum. One reason might be the association of Imhotep with Thoth. It is very likely that the great sage found rest near the Step Pyramid, the tomb of his king. The area chosen for the catacombs of the ibis and the baboon is beneath the area of Third Dynasty tombs where Imhotep may well have been buried. Indeed, it is likely that those responsible for establishing the catacombs believed that they knew where his tomb lay, and so chose the area very deliberately.

The location of the catacomb of the Mothers of Apis may well have been sited nearby so that the cow was near to Thoth, her father. The fact that temples were already in existence at the sites of the ibis, baboon, and falcon catacombs would also have made the location of the Mothers of Apis catacomb beside them a logical one, forming a focal point for the cults.

These however, are not the totality of the cults at Saqqara. On the opposite, east, side of the escarpment from these creatures we have the catacomb of the dogs identified with Anubis, and a little to their south are the burials of cats associated with Bastet (Zivie and Lichtenberg, this volume). The cats do not seem to have had a specially built catacomb, but rather were deposited in tombs used for human burials of earlier times, including that of Aper-el, Vizier of Akhenaten (1353–1335 B.C.).

To the northwest of the escarpment into which the catacombs were cut was "the lake of pharaoh" known from demotic papri discovered at the site (Ray 1978b: 153) and probably to be identified with the later lake of Abusir. It is likely that this was the breeding place for the ibises whose earthly remains eventually found burial in the nearby escarpment.

The Functioning of the Cults

Saqqara during the Late Period, when the animal cults were at their height, was very different to the site that we see today. This was not the sort of quiet, deserted, space where burials might be made in many societies of our own time, rather it was a thriving community.

The busy life of Saqqara toward the end of the Late Period, and particularly in the Thirtieth Dynasty, reflects an increased desire to appease the gods following invasions by the Assyrians (671 and 669 B.C.) and Persians (Twenty-seventh Dynasty, 525–404 B.C.) earlier in the period. This must have been seen as a measure of the gods' lack of satisfaction with the Egyptians, and this could be put right by a return to traditional values: An early example of more recent 'back to basics' campaigning. The building of shrines and temples, the embalming and burial of sacred animals all hearkened back to earlier, less troubled times, and by building more and burying more than before surely things could only get better. The animal cults became a religious expression of nationalistic feeling.

The new temples had their priesthoods, and those who served in other capacities as mourners or as recluses. From Ptolemaic times we know of a category of recluse known as *katachoi* who were permanent residents at some of the temples at the site (Ray 2002: 131–132). In addition there would have been masons to maintain the shrines and vendors of votive items such as the ubiquitous bronze figurines, known in such profusion from the site.

The reason for all of these individuals being at Saqqara was, of course, the sacred animals, and these we can divide into three broad groups. The Apis, as we have already seen, was unique, as was its mother. The as-yet-undiscovered catacomb for its calves would presumably have housed all such offspring it produced.[2] Next in line we have creatures such as the baboon of Thoth. There might be several of these animals, or their substitutes in the form of monkeys, housed in the Temple of Ptah under his Meringa Tree at any one time. Consequently, they might be more numerous than the Apis, but are to be numbered in their hundreds rather than thousands. Finally, we have those animals such as the ibis, falcons, cats, and presumably dogs, which found burial in the thousands, and even hundreds of thousands. Over time the whole species of ibis came to be regarded as sacred and all were, theoretically, worthy of burial.

Needless to say, such a great number of sacred corpses called for a number of specialist embalmers, and in the case of the birds, potters would also have been employed to make the jars and their lids, which were to house the embalmed bird. Our knowledge of the embalming is largely drawn from the examination of specimens, but it is clear that there were different standards. The most simple seems to have involved simply dipping the corpse into bitumen or resin; better examples have simple bandaging while the most 'expensive' might have elaborate bandaging and added appliqué work depicting the god or an emblem relating to him.

Pilgrims would come to Saqqara and pay for the burial of one of these representatives of Horus, Thoth, or Bastet. They might do this purely out of piety or in fulfillment of a vow, or in the hope of some favor from the god concerned. Alternatively (or additionally) they might, for similar reasons, choose to leave a votive figurine at one of the temples. So numerous did votive donations become that from time to time they filled the sanctuaries to overflowing and had to be removed. As sacred objects they could not legitimately be recycled, and so were buried within the sacred precincts, sometimes within the catacombs themselves (Green 1987).

Such pious giving did not go on silently. The popularity of the sanctuaries was because they served an important function in popular religion by providing oracles. A petitioner could approach the priest at the sanctuary and that person would convey the question or request to the deity. In due course an answer would be returned, either via a priest serving as the voice of the divine, or via the priest himself, or even by the perceived fulfillment of a request. Some cults seem to have been particularly venerated by certain sections of society; thus at Saqqara the cult of an otherwise unknown deity known as Thutmose, who took the form of a young ibis, seems to have been particularly popular among women (Ray 2001: 347). As a result the surface structures at Saqqara would have been as significant as the subterranean labyrinths, on which this chapter largely concentrates.

The Discovery of the Sacred Animal Necropolis

Just as we might regard Imhotep as fundamental to the location of certain catacombs of North Saqqara, so he is certainly fundamental to the rediscovery of those catacombs. However, it is only in relatively recent times that they became lost.

Fig. 3.3 Elaborately wrapped Ibis mummies. Courtesy of the Egypt
Exploration Society.

We have many surviving accounts from European travelers of the so-called 'bird pits' or 'tomb of the birds' at Saqqara. Indeed these were a greater attraction than the Step Pyramid. Amongst the earliest travelers to record a visit to the bird catacombs was Vansleb (1678) who gives a graphic description of the condition of the monument he visited:

> The first Well that we saw was that of Birds Embalmed. When we had caused the Sand that stops the Wells Mouth to be removed, through which we were to go down, and from thence to enter the Cave; we caused our selves to be let down one after another, by tying a double Rope about our middles. As soon as we were at the bottom, and that every one had lighted his Taper, and several Matches that we had brought, we went into the Cave creeping upon our Bellies. The Cave is an Alley in the Rock about the height of a Man, and about the breadth of a Perch; and of an extraordinary length. We found there many other Alleys on both hands, cut in the Rock, where were many large stores, full of Earthen Pots, covered over with Coverings of the same substance. In these Pots were Embalmed Birds of all kinds, every Bird in its own Pot. And as I thought at the remembrance of a Custom so ancient, and superstitious, was worthy of our notice, I brought about half a dozen with me; some I have sent to the King's Library. We found also some Hens Egs [sic], empty, but entire without any ill smell or crack (Vansleb 1678: 89–90).

The location of the "Tombeau de Momies d'Oiseaux" was marked on Tome V Plate I of the Napoleonic *Description de l'Égypte* (1826) while volume 10 of the text, *Explication des Planches,* describes Plate 4 figure 2, which shows a part of the catacomb itself and describes its location.

Belzoni too visited Saqqara and mentions it in his account (Siliotti 2001: 92); he was aware of the bird pits but did not actually enter them, being content instead to examine a mummy jar which he initially took to be a forgery on account of its good condition.

There is however, a difficulty in using these early accounts. As Martin states: "In the published accounts of the early visitors to the subterranean galleries at Saqqara, brief for the most part, it is not usually possible to differentiate between the two catacombs called by us the North and South Ibis Galleries. Nor are the plans published in some of these early publications illuminating in this respect" (Martin 1981: 3–4). By the last quarter of the nineteenth century the bird pits had ceased to be a tourist attraction, perhaps because the nature of tourists themselves had changed, and the difficulty of access of the catacombs was considered unsuitable for this new breed of 'traveler.' Whatever the cause the location of the bird burials was lost; only the Serapeum remained.

In 1964 Professor W.B. Emery (1903–1971) turned his attention to North Saqqara. He was not concerned with the sacred animals per se, rather he aimed to locate the tomb of Imhotep. His accounts of his discoveries, published as a series of preliminary reports in the *Journal of Egyptian Archaeology* from 1965 until his untimely death in 1971, make fascinating reading and reveal the reasoning behind his search for the tomb in the North Saqqara escarpment.

In the late 1950s Emery had noted Third Dynasty remains juxtaposed with the remains of ibis mummies in lidded pottery jars in an area some 700 meters from the Step Pyramid enclosure and saw the possibility that here "we might discover the Asklepieion and the tomb of Imhotep" (Emery 1965: 3). The 1964–1965 season of work in this same area, conducted on behalf of the Egypt Exploration Society, revealed a large tomb [3508] of the Third Dynasty with the remains of sacrificed bulls around it, and above them fragments of Ptolemaic–Roman offering pots and the remains of ibis mummies (Emery 1965: 4). Excavation of the main burial shaft at the south end of the superstructure yielded the skeleton of another bull, laid on clean sand and below that "hundreds of ibis mummies in their lidded pots" (Emery 1965: 4). Some of the elaborately wrapped ibis mummies had appliqués clearly indicating their connection with Thoth and Imhotep (see fig. 3.3). Work on two other tombs, 3509 and 3510, was begun and on December 10, 1964 and while working in the latter of these "at a depth of 10 m we broke into a vast labyrinth of rock-cut passages" (Emery 1965: 6). The shaft of 3508 was later found to be part of this same complex, which ultimately became known as the South Ibis Catacomb. The Sacred Animal Necropolis had been rediscovered.

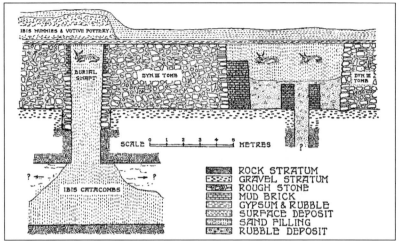

Fig. 3.4 Section of Mastaba 3058 showing the gallery. Courtesy of the Egypt Exploration Society.

Work in later seasons moved slightly to the northeast, close to the foot of the escarpment of the plateau, and the location of what proved to be the temple terrace on which the shrines to the various cults had stood. Clearance of rubble from behind one of these shrines, designated C, led to the discovery in the 1968–1969 season of the entrance to the Baboon Catacomb (Emery 1970: 7). When entered it was discovered that the upper level of this hypogeum contained, among other finds, anatomical *donaria* such as were well known from the temple of Aesculapius in Rome, further reinforcing the connection between Imhotep, Asklepios/Aesculapius, and animals representative of Thoth. Later in the season a large mastaba, numbered 3518, overlying the baboon catacomb was investigated (Emery 1970: 10). Its main entrance area contained *donaria* of the kind found in the catacomb, suggesting that this mastaba may have had a role in the Asklepios cult. However, the fill of the southern shaft of 3518 was believed to be original and if this view is correct it could not have provided a link between the Upper Baboon catacomb and the mastaba (Emery 1971: 4).

By the end of January 1969 the Baboon Catacomb had been cleared and a break in the wall between two widely separated niches for the burial of baboons was investigated. This proved to lead to a further catacomb filled with mummified birds (Emery 1970: 9). Initially these were thought to be ibises, and the catacomb probably part of the one found in 1964. In fact, it later became apparent that this catacomb was actually independent

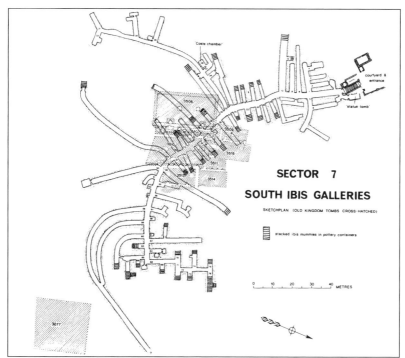

Fig. 3.5
Plan of the South
Ibis Catacomb.
Courtesy of the
Egypt Exploration
Society.

of the first and contained not ibis mummies, but those of birds of prey, mostly falcons/hawks (Emery 1971: 5). This was however, the source of temple furniture relating to the cult of the ibis Thutmose (Ray 2001: 347).

The main object of the 1969–1970 season was to discover the burial place of the Mothers of the Apis, which Emery believed to be in the vicinity of the temple terrace, based on finds of cow remains from the area. With this in mind most of the workmen were moved to the area known as Sector 3. On February 9, 1970 in the extreme northeast corner of Sector 3 near the dividing wall between it and Sector 2, a small rock-cut room was found, and in it a pit which when cleared revealed an opening in its west wall. This opening proved to be a plunderers' entrance into the Mothers of Apis Catacomb (Emery 1971: 10). It was found to comprise a broad, flat-roofed main gallery with vaulted side chambers where the actual burials were made. The four chambers nearest the original entrance, located from inside, were cleared during the season.

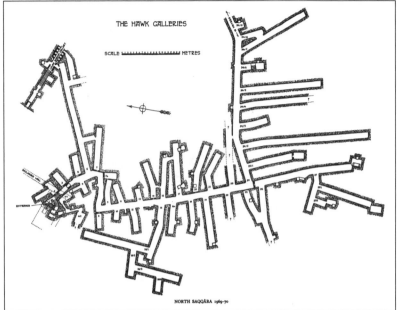

THE HAWK GALLERIES

SCALE |||||||||||||||||||||| METRES

NORTH SAQQÂRA 1969-70

Fig. 3.6 Plan of the Falcon Catacomb. Courtesy of the Egypt Exploration Society.

The 1970–1971 season of work was marked by Emery's tragic death while working at Saqqara.[3] In the days immediately before this event a second ibis catacomb, known as the North Ibis Catacomb, was discovered in a spur of the escarpment immediately overlooking the former lake of Abusir. This new catacomb received only minimal attention as a result of the events that season and was not completely planned and investigated until renewed work by the writer in the 1990s (Nicholson 1996). During the new work it was realized that part of the catacomb is that illustrated in a sketch in one of the notebooks of Karl Richard Lepsius[4] (1810–1884) during the work of the great Prussian Expedition of 1842–1845 (Nicholson et al. 1999).

In subsequent years Emery's work was completed by Professor Geoffrey Martin (1973, 1974) and by Professor Harry Smith (1976) along with David Jeffreys (Smith and Jeffreys 1977), although no further catacombs were located at this time.

There are, however, two further catacombs which should be mentioned, and which are not part of the work undertaken by Emery. They are the Catacomb of the Dogs and the "Catacomb" of the Cats. At the

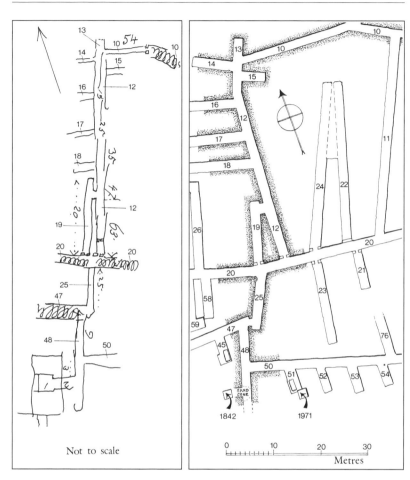

Not to scale

0   10   20   30
Metres

Fig. 3.7 Part of the North Ibis Catacomb as sketched by Lepsius (left, measurements in ells) and remapped by the recent EES expedition. Courtesy of the Egypt Exploration Society.

time of writing I have been unable to locate records dealing with the discovery and clearance of the Dog Catacomb, but it does feature on the map published by de Morgan (1897) and was presumably investigated at some time shortly before this. The second "catacomb" is that of the cats sacred to Bastet, located on the eastern side of the escarpment. These have been known since the late eighteenth century, but were lost again until the recent work of the French expedition. Since this work is treated elsewhere in this volume (Zivie and Lichtenberg, this volume) they will not be further dealt with here.

The Catacombs

Before examining the individual catacombs prepared for the sacred animals at North Saqqara some general comments should be made concerning them. First, it must be borne in mind that the catacombs themselves are but a part of a much wider complex, and that in the immediate vicinity of each stood a temple or shrine where pilgrims could go to make their devotions, to present offerings and to receive oracles. Furthermore, these catacombs and their temples were but a part of an overall sacred landscape. The pilgrim visiting Saqqara would have seen, and understood, a much different landscape to the one we see today (see Smith 1974; Ray 2002).

Cutting a Catacomb

The excavation of rock for the construction of a catacomb was clearly a major task, and in the case of the bird catacombs seems to have been approached in a fairly uniform way. The strata chosen for the galleries is one of soft calcareous stone known as *tafl* which is up to ten meters thick, and both under- and overlain by hard limestone (see Martin 1981: 7). Deliberate use seems to have been made of earlier features such as tombs of the Early Dynastic and Old Kingdoms. Thus we find that the steps from the entrance courtyard of the South Ibis Catacomb enter close to the so-called "Statue Tomb" of the Late Old Kingdom (Martin 1981: 115). Although never thoroughly documented because of the poor condition of the rock, this tomb was presumably used as part of the ancient complex and not simply incorporated by accident. Emery (1965: 6) states that he believed the tomb to have been restored and painted in the Late Period, reinforcing their deliberate use in the Catacomb. When discovered the statues were visible, but beneath them was two meters of debris which was later cleared to floor level revealing two deep pits, which were not further examined (Emery 1966: 5). Emery does not say whether the debris removed comprised ibis pots or not, but if so this may have been a room reserved for the most important burials, or alternatively have been a cult room which was filled only during the last phase of the use of the catacomb.

A similar pattern is found in the Falcon Catacomb, where the entrance area makes use of the burial chambers of several Old Kingdom tombs. The North Ibis Catacomb is more difficult to comment upon.

X11KV90

Pl. 1.6 X-rays show that
the hawk mummy contains
only either a twig or a bone
fragment, giving the idea that a
part symbolizes the whole
(CG 29881). Photograph by
Anna-Marie Kellen.

Pl. 1.5 This hawk is wrapped
in a herringbone pattern typical
of the Roman Period (CG 29881).
Photograph by Anna-Marie Kellen.

Pl. 2.1   A crocodile completely encased in a cartonnage covering that is equivalent to a Ptolemaic Period carapace coffin used for humans (CG 29816 *bis*). Photograph by Anna-Marie Kellen.

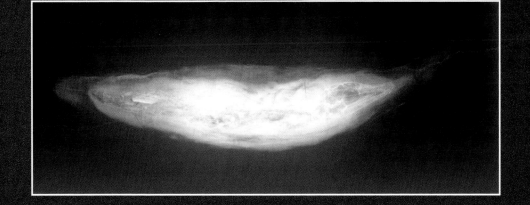

Pl. 2.2 This crocodile looks as if it is wrapped carefully, but x-rays show that the head and tail are reversed (CG 29713). Photograph by Anna-Marie Kellen.

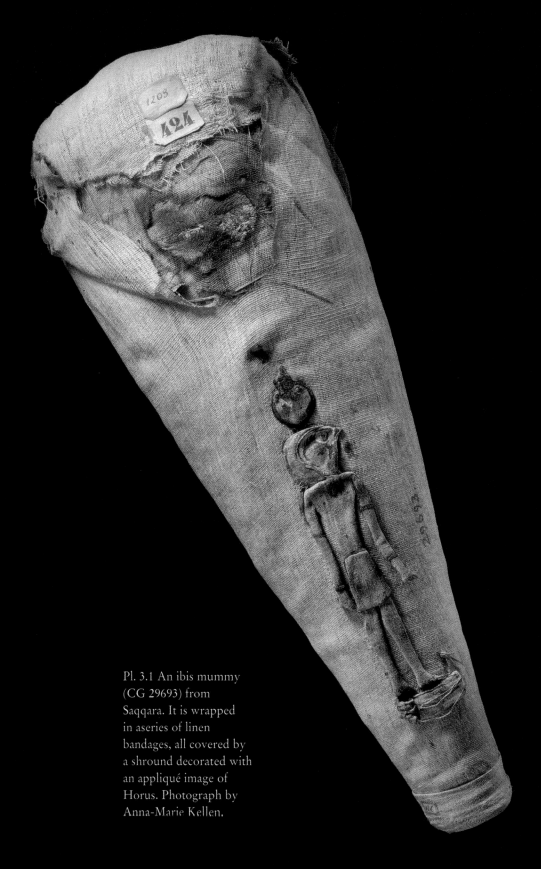

Pl. 3.1 An ibis mummy (CG 29693) from Saqqara. It is wrapped in aseries of linen bandages, all covered by a shround decorated with an appliqué image of Horus. Photograph by Anna-Marie Kellen.

Fig. 3.8 The main
entrance to the
South Ibis area and
the courtyard in
front of it. Courtesy
of the Egypt
Exploration Society.

Fig. 3.9 Statue Chamber, South Ibis Catacomb. Courtesy of the Egypt
Exploration Society.

Immediately east of the entrance stairway is a short gallery running north–south, exactly analogous in its positioning to the "Statue Tomb" in the South Ibis Catacomb. However, this gallery is now outside the accessible area of the Catacomb and buried beneath many meters of sand; as a result it cannot be said with certainty to be an Old Kingdom tomb. If it is then there seems to have been a preference on the part of the builders of the catacombs for making the entrance near to an older tomb, which perhaps served some special function in the cult.

What is clear in all the bird catacombs is that Early Dynastic–Old Kingdom tomb chambers and shafts were utilized at other points. It is surely not merely a matter of coincidence that the shafts of so many mastaba tombs intercept the galleries of the South Ibis Catacomb—for example, shafts from 3508, 3509, 3510 all intercept parts of the central area of the catacomb (see Martin 1981: Plate 2A) and there are numerous others not shown on Martin's plan. The same situation is found in the North Ibis Catacomb where galleries 34, 38, 48, 49, and 51 (to give but a few) all either incorporate an older tomb as a short side gallery or have an older burial shaft leading to them. In the Falcon Catacomb we find older shafts descending into many of the galleries—for example, 13, 16, 17, 20, 25, and 27.

Not all the shafts that intercept the galleries were reopened (either accidentally or deliberately) by the tunnelers. There are many examples where, with the benefit of modern lighting, it is possible to see the compacted fill of a shaft suspended above a gallery where the tunnelers have planed through it, no doubt incorporating the burial chamber into the tunnel as they went. This begs the question of why so many shafts were included. I am not convinced by the argument that they were simply included as an accident of tunneling, that the workers cut through them simply 'because they were there.' It seems to me that at least some of the shafts must have been intentionally used to provide light and air for those working below ground (c.f. Martin 1981: 8). They might also have provided a convenient means by which spoil could be removed from parts of the catacombs, which were distant from the entrance. It is possible that on occasions tunneling was begun from several different points. If a shaft had been discovered accidentally it would be possible to mark it on the surface and then align the top of another shaft with it and so tunnel toward it. Emery (1965: 6) states that the tunnelers blocked the shafts as they tunneled, and this may well be so in many cases. However, the fact that mummy pots seem sometimes to have occupied the lower part of some of the shafts suggests that not all were blocked immediately—they may have stood open during tunneling and been sealed later.

At times, whether or not the shafts were used to aid navigation, there seem to have been problems in finding direction. The Falcon Catacomb is particularly disorienting, and when walking along the main axial corridor of the catacomb visitors frequently believe that they are heading east, when they are actually going south, toward the South Ibis Catacomb. It is possible that the tunnelers experienced some similar confusion when they reoriented the axial aisle outside gallery 7A and headed west, before eventually turning south.

As one might expect of such extensive structures, the catacombs seem to have been constructed in sections. A length of axial aisle was cut, and opening from it on either side were cut side galleries in which the mummy pots themselves would be stacked. Occasionally a decision was made to create a secondary, or new, axial aisle or even to convert what may have begun as a side gallery into an axial. The result is that in all of the bird catacombs the overall layout is somewhat erratic. Individual stretches of the catacomb are neatly laid out while others seem to be almost unplanned.

It would appear that at the end of the period of use of a catacomb the axial aisle would begin to be filled. Vessels were stacked, but not quite up to ceiling level, so that access to the rear parts of the catacomb could still have been gained if necessary. Why this might have been necessary is uncertain, since the side galleries were generally sealed once filled and no further access would be necessary for any practical purpose. Occasionally it might be necessary to cut a second, completely new, catacomb for the same sacred animal, such as was the case for the ibises.

Subterranean Architecture of the Bird Catacombs

The catacombs cut for the interment of the ibis and falcons are not mere tunnels; rather they have a variety of elaborations, which make for distinctions between the side galleries and between different parts of the catacomb. At the time of writing only work on the South Ibis Catacomb has been published (Martin 1981) and the work is largely concerned with the surface structures. No attempt was made to phase the individual side galleries or sections of the catacomb itself. The Falcon Catacomb is about to be published (Smith and Davies, forthcoming) and will give a full description of the catacomb and the phasing of the individual galleries. The writer examined the North Ibis Catacomb, but work on phasing is not yet complete. The following therefore represents a summary of the key features of the bird catacombs in general.

Axial Aisles

Axial aisles, or galleries, form the arterial routeways through the bird catacombs. From these open the numerous side galleries in which the mummy pots were placed. These axial aisles seem to have been deemed to have a particular importance, probably because they were the routes taken by the burial parties and can therefore be seen as extensions of the sacred way. Their importance is marked by their architecture. The most immediately notable feature, particularly in the Falcon Catacomb, is the presence of a series of niches cut into the walls of the aisle. These niches are simply cut from the soft rock of the catacombs and are designed to take miniature limestone sarcophagi in which were placed certain of the mummified falcons. These bird mummies might be placed in the sarcophagi simply in pottery jars or in wooden coffins without a jar. The lids were usually sealed with gypsum mortar. These birds presumably represent offerings made by particularly wealthy individuals and/or the burial of birds of special importance.

Niches seem to be less common in the North Ibis Catacomb. However, the condition of that monument—still choked with debris—makes this uncertain. Further niches may well be obscured by the remains of broken vessels, roof collapse, and other debris. No limestone sarcophagi have been recovered from this monument, although lids from two are known, both of them from the area near the monumental entrance to the structure. In that same entrance aisle we see evidence of a different kind of niche, rock-cut like those in the falcon catacomb but this time lined with pink plaster and preserving the shape of a mummy-pot. The vessel had been cemented into position and then sealed in with a limestone slab or slabs, the impression of which remained in the plaster. The practice of sealing niches with such slabs seems to have been relatively common in this catacomb, and one excellently preserved blocking slab is known, standing in front of its robbed niche, from one of the other axial aisles within the monument. The face of this blocking had been carefully smoothed as if to receive an inscription, but either this was never added or has not survived. In this instance there was no trace of a pot having been cemented into the niche, suggesting that the ibis must have been placed in the niche simply as a mummy in a wooden coffin or in a stone sarcophagus. The South Ibis Catacomb seems to be devoid of niches although the writer was not able to examine the whole catacomb during the work in the 1990s, and it is clear that the axial aisles often contain a considerable depth of stacked mummy pots, which may have buried such niches as existed.

It is clear from both the North and South Ibis Catacombs that the axial aisles were themselves used for burials. However, the chronology of these is less certain. It might provisionally be suggested that these burials represent the last phase in the use of the Catacomb, and provided a substitute for the cutting of new side galleries. The fact that the burials are not stacked floor-to-ceiling but leave at least some gap suggests that it was felt that access even to the more distant parts of the catacomb might be deemed necessary at some time.

Doorways

Within the Falcon Catacomb, on the main axial aisle, are two elaborate doorways. These are constructed of dressed limestone blocks. The second one is surmounted by a cavetto cornice in limestone and clearly showing the bolt hole by which the wooden doors it must once have supported were sealed.

The first of these doorways is located between galleries 3 and 5, and may have served to shut off the main part of the catacomb when it was not in use. It may be that those galleries located outside this door originally had a somewhat different purpose to those beyond it. Perhaps they served as the place where the mummies in their pots were cached prior to the mass burial, which took place once a year. At this time these galleries would be emptied and the vessels removed to their intended resting place. Only at the end of the life of the catacomb would these galleries then be sealed and used as actual burial places.

The second doorway is of considerable interest. It blocks the axial aisle between galleries 25 and 26, and immediately north of it, on its

Fig. 3.10 A limestone doorway with cavetto cornice. This divides one section of the Falcon Catacombs from another, and is situated on the main axial aisle. Courtesy of the Egypt Exploration Society.

east side, the axial gallery 24 opens up. Behind the doorway there are only four galleries. Interestingly, the axial itself does not seem to have been used for the stacking of mummy pots, suggesting that even at the end of its life the catacomb was not considered so full as to merit the partial filling of these routes.

Gallery Blockings

The Falcon Catacomb also has a series of stone doorway-type block-ings to the side galleries, but before describing these and their relation-ship to the other catacombs something must be said about the purpose of the blockings.

According to the archive of the scribe Hor of Sebennytos (second century B.C.) the burial of the sacred birds took place only once each year (Ray 1976: 140). Prior to this they were cached in a 'rest house,' which may, perhaps, have been the purpose of the gallery or galleries closest to the entrance of some of the catacombs. They were then taken into the catacomb and stacked in the appropriate side gallery or, toward the end of the life of a catacomb, along the axial aisle itself. In either case the placing of the vessels was carefully done. The pots were laid on clean sand and each layer of vessels was separated by a further covering of sand. Because the vessels tapered markedly they were stacked in rows, alternating between top and tail so that the surface of each layer was roughly horizontal.

We do not know how many burials were made at any one time, but it is likely that on many occasions it was not sufficient to completely fill a side gallery. At these instances it may be that the face of the stack, from floor to ceiling, was sealed with a layer of mud plaster. This would have the effect of stabilizing the stack and preventing sand from trickling out from between the ends of the vessels. It may equally be that this practice of sealing with mud plaster does not represent the end of one depositional event but was carried out in order to stabilize the stack as it was constructed. Whatever the case, the stack of mummy pots would eventually reach the junction of the gallery with the axial aisle. At this point it would be sealed off.

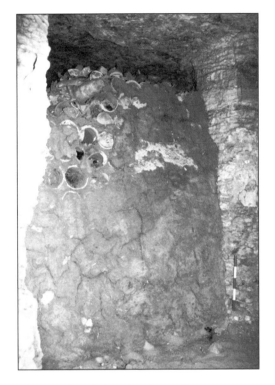

Fig. 3.11 A sealed gallery in the Falcon Catacomb (no. 6/2). Some galleries have a plastered mud-brick blocking, while others, like this, are simply sealed by mud-plaster. Photograph by P.T. Nicholson, reproduced courtesy of the Egypt Exploration Society.

Several types of blocking are known. That closest to the stone doorways discussed above comprises a wall and threshold of dressed stone with a carefully constructed doorway. These occur at several places in the Falcon Catacomb, for example at the end of gallery 14, and are sometimes the ground on which demotic graffiti or drawings are to be found. It is not always clear how the doorway itself was blocked in these stone examples from the Falcon Catacomb, however, there are parallels from the North Ibis Catacomb.

Fig. 3.12 In the North Ibis Catacomb blockings between various parts of the monument take different forms. Behind the figure the axial aisle has been blocked completely by filling in a doorway-type blocking, while in front of the figure another doorway remains open. The reddening of the brickwork comes from the burning of this part of the monument at some time in the past, probably during the time it was opened to the earliest tourists. Courtesy of the Egypt Exploration Society.

The rock of the North Ibis Catacomb is of particularly poor quality, and the tunnelers were aware of this. As a result they seem to have used doorway-type blockings as a means of supporting the ceiling in parts of the catacomb. This implies that these blockings, at least in this catacomb, were put in place before the burials were made—hence the need for a doorway. Not only do we have several examples of these, but also find numerous instances where the brickwork is extended to form a lining to the tunnel, helping to support the poor quality rock. A particularly elaborate area of such brickwork and doorway-type blockings is to be found on axial aisle 20 where it is met by gallery 31, itself possibly a secondary axial gallery. Here, across 20 itself, we have a doorway-type blocking which has actually been sealed using neatly inserted mud-bricks; immediately to its north is the open doorway of gallery 31, and running north from it brick tunnel lining. Extending east from the blocking of 31 is a length of tunnel lining with a carefully fashioned bull-nose differentiating two areas of brickwork. Still further along we find the aisle narrowed by a pair of buttresses, not projecting far into the routeway, and so not qualifying as a 'doorway' but nonetheless helping to support the ceiling. Many of the features of the brickwork in this area show especially well as a result of a conflagration, perhaps the result of early visitors using flaming torches, which has fired the brickwork to a bright orange color.

The doorway-type blocking across gallery 20 is significant. Since it has been infilled with brickwork it suggests that areas of the catacomb were sometimes sealed off permanently and considered to be full. Unfortunately the area of the catacomb to the west of the blocking has been extensively robbed and it is not possible to say whether the axial aisle itself was filled, or partially so, with stacked vessels.

The doorway-type blockings are, however, the exception. The norm was a blocking made of mud brick, which extended right across the end of the gallery, where it met the aisle, and was then often plastered over. Work in the North Ibis Catacomb has suggested how this was put in place. The brickwork is normally about a half-meter thick, comprising two rows of stretcher bricks laid side by side. This was built up until it reached to about two courses from the ceiling. At this point the blocking was completed with a single thickness of brick laid—obviously—from the axial aisle. The gallery was thus sealed. It is possible that part of the brickwork was put in place before the final burials in a gallery were made. This might make the construction process easier, and might also provide some support to the rock, however, we cannot be certain of this. The exterior face of the blocking was often plastered over.

Occasionally, as in gallery 6/2 of the Falcons, the end of the vessel stack came so close to the axial aisle that it was not possible to construct a brick blocking without it protruding into the aisle. In this instance the face of the stack was simply plastered over, as in the case of the more temporary stack faces discussed above. Information on the blockings of the South Ibis Catacomb is limited, but the practice of sealing the gallery end with plaster in this way is also known there. This catacomb shows many variations on the others and it is unfortunate that it has not been possible to document it more fully.

In the North Ibis Catacomb however, we find that blockings are sometimes made especially thick and protrude into axial aisles, apparently to serve as large buttresses to support the ceiling. This is notable at the junction of gallery 33 with 31 and across axial aisle 36 (another instance where a part of the catacomb appears to have been deliberately and finally sealed).

There are several variations on these blockings known from the North Ibis Catacomb. A whole series of galleries opening from axial aisle 10 appear to have been crudely blocked using a mixture of mud bricks and

Fig. 3.13 North Ibis Catacomb Gallery 61 has an impressive raised molding across its blocking. Now badly damaged, this may have represented a large door-bolt. Courtesy of the Egypt Exploration Society.

lumps of limestone. Unfortunately, aisle 10 is so choked with debris that the ceiling is now less than a meter from the debris covered floor, and often much less, so that only the upper courses of these blockings can be seen.

The opposite end of the spectrum is offered by the blocking of gallery 61. Here the brickwork extends across the opening in the usual way, but at approximately half the height of the gallery the brickwork has been built outwards as a horizontal band, before resuming its normal width further up. The whole face of the blocking has then been plastered, giving the effect of an enormous door-bolt spanning the width of the gallery. It is also clear from this, now very damaged, blocking that it had already been completed and plastered before a supporting tunnel-lining was built to its south in order to support (unsuccessfully as it turned out) a particularly dangerous area of the ceiling.

Although now very difficult to access, it is likely that the North Ibis Catacomb may have been the most spectacular of the bird catacombs in terms of its subterranean architecture. What remains is only a hint of its former grandeur, it does however, tie in to what we know of aspects of the architecture of the other bird catacombs.

The Baboon Catacomb

The baboon catacomb is entered through a small doorway surmounted by a cavetto cornice. On entering it is immediately apparent that it shares few similarities with the bird catacombs. Most striking is that it is on two levels, a lower gallery having apparently been cut beneath the original one at a later stage in the history of the monument. The cutting of this gallery was evidently intended to replace the upper one, since its construction made access to the upper gallery almost impossible without the use of some kind of removable walkway.

The Upper Gallery, like the lower one, runs approximately due east, but unlike the bird catacombs there are no side galleries, only axials. The burials themselves are made in individual niches, one for each animal. The niches are rock cut, but after all had been filled a second set was built in masonry on the north side of the gallery. These niches would have held the mummified remains of the animal within a rectangular wooden box or shrine. At the eastern end of the upper gallery the masons found that they had broken into the shaft of mastaba 3518, and so cut two further galleries running roughly north–south. Each of these also encountered Old Kingdom tomb shafts and so was abandoned (Smith 1974: 41).

The Lower Gallery, reached by a stairway, runs roughly west–east beneath the Upper Gallery, but extends to approximately twice the length of the former, avoiding the shaft of 3518 a little to its north.

The baboons were mummified in a squatting position and were placed inside rectangular wooden shrines. Into these gypsum plaster was then poured such that the mummy was entirely encased in a block. The shrine would then be placed within its designated niche. This is a different method of mummification to that used at Tuna al-Gebel, where the squatting mummy is placed into its shrine without a plaster jacket.

The niches in both galleries were originally sealed with limestone slabs, inscribed with short biographies of the animal, giving its name, place of birth, and date of death along with prayers. Only one niche was found intact during Emery's excavations, the rest having been vandalized by the Christians who had settled on the Temple Terrace in later times.

The Mothers of Apis Catacomb

The resting place of the Mothers of Apis is now a poor reflection of its former grandeur. In form it is closely similar to the Serapeum itself, and since that monument has already been discussed (Dodson, this volume) it will be described only briefly here.

The catacomb, at first referred to as "the Iseum" (Emery 1971) comprises some eighteen individual vaults of a size sufficient to take the burial of a Mother of Apis cow. There is also a smaller vault (1a) more consistent with the size of a human burial. The vaults consist of an arched vault, with their floor level below that of the rest of the gallery. The vaults were originally lined with fine white limestone blocks, but this has almost entirely been robbed away. At the sides of the vaults, at the level of the gallery floor, there are recesses where a man could stand while the sarcophagus was lowered. It is likely that the vault itself would have been filled with sand to the level of the walkway, the sarcophagus would have been swung through ninety degrees and maneuvered into the vault whereupon the sand would have been removed from beneath it via the niches.

Once the sarcophagus was in place, the burial placed within it, and the lid moved into position the vault would be closed. This was done using a wall of the same white Tura limestone as had been used for lining the vault. This provided a suitable surface on which the 'Divine Fathers' of the Temple of Ptah at Memphis could write their commemorative inscriptions (Smith 1974: 37). Between the blockings there were areas of rock wall, and in niches cut into these the masons left their own stelae recording their work at the site (Smith 1974: 37). The latest inscription from the catacomb refers to Year 11 of Cleopatra VII "when the Queen was in Syria" namely 41 B.C., the time when she had gone to meet Anthony after Philippi. The earliest recorded inscription is of the Twenty-ninth Dynasty usurper Psamuthis (393 B.C.). Inscriptions found at the south end of the temple terrace refer to burials made under Amasis in 533 B.C., Smith notes (1974: 39) that there were originally no more than twenty vaults in the catacomb plus three in the cliff face, and that these are insufficient to cover the burials of Mothers of Apis spanning some four centuries, and that the burial place of the cows in the Persian Period (Twenty-seventh Dynasty) may remain undiscovered.

The Dog Catacomb

Work on this important monument is ongoing, though at the time of writing, I have been unable to ascertain to whom its discovery should be attributed; it first appears on de Morgan's 1897 map of the area. Unlike the other catacombs discussed in this chapter it is located on the east side of the Saqqara plateau, somewhat farther north than the cat burials and in the area of the archaic tombs. The catacomb has been surveyed and some of the remains studied (Nicholson et al. 2015; Ikram et al. 2013), and a final publication is in preparation. The details given here are of a preliminary nature. This catacomb takes the form of an axial aisle with galleries opening off it, with piles of dog mummies between 0.75–1.4 m deep. Parts of the dog burials are disturbed, and in some instances have been removed entirely, perhaps as sabbakh. However, some better preserved specimens survive. The animals do not normally appear to have been placed in any kind of container, though scraps of linen suggest that they were originally bandaged.

Several galleries contain niches. Some contain a single animal, others more. It has tentatively been suggested tht these were considered worth of higher status burial.

Notes

1 The author is grateful to the Egypt Exploration Society for its support of the work at North Saqqara, and to all those who have taken part in the project over several seasons and whose work has contributed to this article. Particular thanks are due to Professor H.S. Smith and Mr. K.J. Frazer for making their knowledge of the Emery seasons freely available to us. We are especially grateful to Dr. Zahi Hawass and our colleagues in the SCA who have permitted our work and assisted us in it.
2 It is possible that these are located further to the north in the area between the Serapeum, the Sacred Animal Necropolis, and the Lake of Abusir, as numerous cattle bones and their fragments cover this area (ed.).
3 An obituary can be found in *The Times*, March 13, 1971.
4 Lepsius 1849–1859, Text: 141.

4

Bull Cults

Aidan Dodson

A number of bull cults were current in ancient Egypt. The detailed ideas behind their inceptions are nowhere set out, but it seems very likely that there are connections with the broad concept of the bull as a manifestation of physical and sexual power. This kind of link certainly lay behind the adoption of the tag of 'Strong Bull' as part of the Horus names of the pharaohs of the Eighteenth through Twenty-second Dynasties. The best attested bull cults are those of the Apis at Memphis (sacred to Ptah), Buchis at Armant and al-Tod (Montu), and Mnevis at Heliopolis (Re). Others existed elsewhere, including Cynopolis (Bata), Athribis (Kemwer), and in Nome UE11 (Hesbu) (Otto 1938/1964).

Apis (𓄿𓊪𓃒, *Ḥp*)

The Apis was in essence an incarnation of the Memphite creator-god, Ptah, although as time went on his affiliations became more complex, particularly with reference to the Hellenistic deity, Serapis (cf. Otto 1938/1964: 23–34). Evidence for the existence of the Apis goes back to the very earliest times. An inscription on a bowl formerly in the Michaelides Collection, naming the Horus Aha alongside Apis, appears to bear out a statement by the Roman writer Aelian that the cult was founded by Menes (Simpson 1957). The Palermo Stone mentions the Apis twice in sections probably referring to the reigns of two First Dynasty kings, Horus Den and Anedjib, confounding Manetho's statement that the cult was begun in the reign of the second king of the Second Dynasty. He is also mentioned two, and possibly four, times in the Pyramid Texts.[1]

As depicted in the Eighteenth Dynasty tomb D, the Apis is black and white, with a black head, back, and rump, a white blaze on its forehead, and similarly colored sides, undersides, and legs. A rectangle of red is also shown on the bull's flanks. This does not wholly correspond with Herodotus' statement (III: 28) that the Apis was "black, with a white diamond on its forehead [and] the image of an eagle on its back, and a beetle on its tongue." It is possible, however, that the features of the bull may have

Fig. 4.1 Painting from the wall of Tomb D showing the Apis and the Four Sons of Horus; reign of Horemoheb. From Mariette 1857, pl. 3.

changed in the intervening millennium: unfortunately, inspection of bronzes closer to Herodotus' time is inconclusive. Another aspect of the Apis is its horns, which are frequently shown as straight, angled outwards at forty-five degrees and, in the Eighteenth Dynasty at least, shown gray. This may suggest silver sheaths. On the other hand, such horns are by no means universal at any period, although the better quality monuments seem to have the straight horns.[2]

Concerning the identification of the Apis, Diodorus Siculus (I: 84) states that

> whenever one has died and has been buried in splendor, the priests who are charged with this duty seek out a young bull which has on its body markings similar to those of its predecessor. When it has been found the people cease their mourning and the priests who have care of it first take the young bull to Nilopolis [near al-Wasta], where it is kept for forty days, and then, putting it on a state barge fitted with a gilded stall, conduct it as a god to the sanctuary of Hephaestus at Memphis.

The bull appears in various contexts, and seems to have been associated with the *heb-sed* festival, but little is known of its cult, other than the arrangements made for its interment from the latter part of the Eighteenth Dynasty onward. Prior to this, nothing is known of the disposal of its body. It has been suggested that the Old Kingdom burial-place of the bulls might be represented by the extensive galleries that lie under the western part of the Step Pyramid enclosure, but no substantive evidence has been forthcoming (Ibrahim and Rohl 1988: 23, seconding an old idea of Mariette's). Alternatively, it is possible that the remains may have been simply deposited within the precincts of the Ptah temple itself, perhaps after being partly consumed in a ceremonial feast. A number of later Apis tombs (A, C, E, and F) held large crude pottery jars, containing ashes and burnt bones, while the bovine remains were found to have been fragmentary (see below). A connection has been posited between this occurrence and the so-called 'Cannibal Hymn' of the Pyramid Texts (§273–274), which speaks of the king devouring the gods to take on their powers (Lichtheim 1973: 36–38): perhaps the death of the divine bull was followed by a feast at which Pharaoh devoured the erstwhile incarnation of Ptah on Earth (Mond and Myers 1934: I, 5–7), and might have had some connection with the Cannibal Hymn.

Whatever arrangements had previously existed, they underwent dramatic revision in the reign of Amenhotep III, with the construction of the first of a long series of burial places, known collectively as the Serapeum. Some areas seem to have been entered early in the eighteenth century, by Paul Lucas, and others. A number of canopic jars were removed around this time, some from apparently intact chambers.[3] Then, in 1848, Anthony Charles Harris (1790–1869) suggested that sphinxes at Saqqara represented an avenue leading to the Serapeum, the temple and tomb of the Apis bulls, long known from the classical writers (Málek 1983). The major work carried out here, however, was by Auguste Mariette from November 1850 onwards (Mariette 1857 and 1882).[4]

No further substantive work was carried out until 1985–1986, when Mohammed Ibrahim Aly reopened a long-closed section of complex and discovered a considerable amount of new material (cf. Ibrahim Aly 1993, 1996; Ibrahim Aly, Nageb, Devauchelle and Herbin 1986; Ibrahim and Rohl 1988). However, work was not continued, and many areas remain in need of further work, albeit hampered by the poor state of the local rock, exacerbated by recent earth tremors affecting the Cairo area.

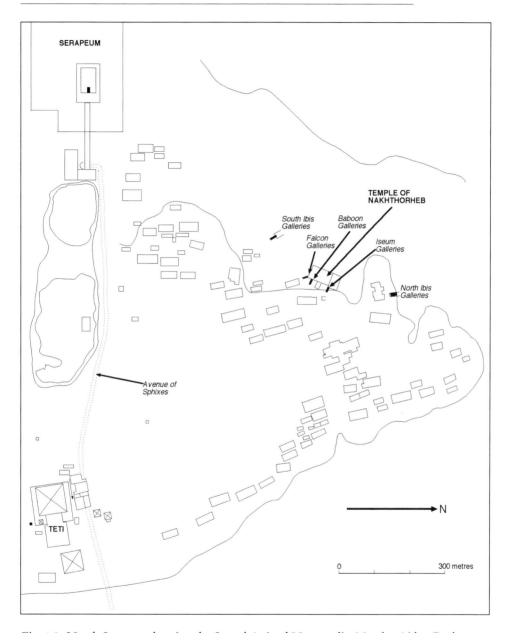

Fig. 4.2 North Saqqara, showing the Sacred Animal Necropolis. Map by Aidan Dodson.

The Isolated Tombs

The earliest known Apis burial (A)[5] was carried out under the authority of Crown Prince Djhutmose (Dodson 1990: 87–90). It forms the prototype for subsequent interments down to the middle of Ramesses II's reign, and comprised two elements. On the surface was a cavetto-corniced platform, approached by a flight of steps; upon this stood a naos-roofed chapel, supported at the corners by columns, with walls ornamented with reliefs.[6] A sloping passage led below the chapel to a rectangular chamber, which appears to have been largely robbed. The principal objects recovered were four canopic jars (Dodson 1999: 59–61), a set of magic bricks found in niches in each wall of the chamber (Louvre N 842: Monnet 1951), and a number of stone and pottery vessels, some inscribed with the prince's name (Louvre N 482, 484, 455, and AF 153).

Two similar tombs, B and C, belonged to Apis 18.2/II and 18.3/III,[7]

Fig. 4.3
The eastern extremity of the Greater Vaults of the Serapeum. The sarcophagus lid belongs to Apis 31.1/XLVI. Photograph by Aidan Dodson.

and date to late in the reign of Amenhotep III or early in that of Amenhotep IV (Akhenaten),[8] and Tutankhamun, respectively. Canopic jars survived in both sepulchers (N 394 5A–D: N 394 2A–D; Dodson 1999: 61–62), while from tomb C Mariette recovered pieces of the bull's wooden coffin and three glass pendants, which provided the king's name (Louvre N 2271 A–C: Mariette 1857: pl. 2).

Tomb D/E lay north of the previous three sepulchers, and is dated to Horemheb's reign by a block bearing his name found in the debris of the chapel (Mariette 1857: 8; 1882: 126). While earlier burial chambers had been plain, Chamber D (Apis 18.4/IV) had its walls smoothed with plaster and painted. The west wall (Fig. 4.1) showed the bull together with the Four Sons of Horus, the latter being repeated on the side walls, followed on one wall by Anubis-khentysehnetjer and Isis, and by Anubis-imywet and Nephthys (Mariette 1857: pl. 3). Chamber D had been extensively robbed, only a single canopic lid surviving (Louvre N 394 3: Dodson 1999: 63). However the northern wall was false, revealing a small, irregularly-hewn chamber (E), probably originally the cinerary chamber of the tomb. This held the intact burial of Apis 18.5/V, which lay in a paneled, vaulted lid wooden sarcophagus, which had been placed in a lidless, stone-built, outer sarcophagus. The 'mummy' comprised a bull's head, devoid of flesh and skin, resting upon a black mass, wrapped in fine linen, and composed of broken bovine bones and pieces of gold leaf embedded in resin; this is suggestive of the bull having been at least partly consumed prior to burial.

The canopic jars (Louvre N 394 4A–D, AF.1731) stood at the four corners of the sarcophagus, and may have been damaged by rock-falls, which certainly caused damage in tomb G (Dodson 1999: 63). Excavation under the floor revealed a dozen large crude pottery jars, containing ashes and burnt bones. Fourteen such jars were also present in the next tomb to be constructed, that for Apis VI (F), which may be dated to Seti I's time on the basis of a relief-fragment in the debris of the chapel (Mariette 1857: 12; 1882: 137). It had been robbed out, with the exception of its cinerary chamber, which was intact. Only the four largely undamaged canopic lids (Louvre N 400, AF.1730; Dodson 1999: 63–64) apparently remained from the burial itself.

The next burials to take place were overseen by Khaemwaset, fourth son of Ramesses II. The first burial for which he was responsible took place in his father's Year 16. A tomb (G) was cut just north of Seti I's tomb F, of simple design, lacking the side-rooms seen in the previous two sepulchres, but proving to hold a pair of intact burials (Mariette 1857: 12–15; 1882: 61–65, 137–142). Its chamber had been decorated; although rather faded, on the south wall Khaemwaset and Ramesses II could be seen offering to an anthropomorphic Apis. A sumptuous touch was the covering of the lower parts of the chamber walls with gold leaf. A niche high up in the center of the south wall contained two painted quartzite shabtis of Khaemwaset, each over 30 cm high (Louvre N 445 A–B: Mariette 1857: pl. 8); there is some doubt as to what occupied the niche(s) elsewhere in the tomb, due to a contradiction between the plate and the descriptions in Mariette 1882: 138–139. A pair of pottery jackals upon pylon-form bases occupied niches in another wall. The bases contained four faïence shabtis in the name of the Vizier, Paser. Niches of the north wall contained amulets and some flakes of gold leaf.

A large rectangular wooden sarcophagus lay in the center of the chamber, varnished with black resin, with the lower part covered in gold foil (Apis 19.2/VII); four large alabaster canopic jars lay with it (N 396 A–D; Dodson 1999: 64). To the right lay another sarcophagus of the same dimensions, accompanied by a life-size gilded wooden figure of Osiris, but without any canopics. Cuttings in the floor contained 247 shabtis in hard-stone, calcite, and faïence, some dedicated by a whole range of dignitaries, others simple bull-headed examples in faïence (Aubert and Aubert 1974: 85–90; Mariette 1857: pl. 7).

The right-hand sarcophagus, of Apis 19.3/IX,[9] had been damaged by the fall of a part of the ceiling, which had broken the lid and knocked away one of the sides. Two further rectangular coffins lay nested within, without decoration, the innermost containing a huge anthropoid coffin-lid, with a gilded face. This lid lay directly on the floor of the rectangular coffin, a cavity in this, 120 cm long, 60 cm wide, and 17 cm deep, being filled with a black mass. This contained a haphazard collection of small fragments of bovine bone, as had been the case with Apis 18.5/V, but with the difference that in this case there was no sign of the skull. With the bone fragments were fifteen bull-headed shabtis, items of jewelry and several votive shabtis and amulets. The contents of the Apis 19.3/VII sarcophagus were similar, with the same combination of rectangular coffins and inscribed anthropoid lid as its fellow.

A room (H), cut in the south side of the entrance incline, had been almost completely robbed-out, but seems to have been the canopic chamber of Apis IX, preserving a single jar (Louvre AF 10997; Dodson 1999: 64–65). The entranceway to the tomb revealed thirteen stelae, two were inscribed in Year 30 of Ramesses II, and record the death of an Apis in that year, as well as one which died in Year 16—clearly Apis

19.3/IX and 19.2/VII respectively. One also notes another bovine death in Year 25, which Mariette allocated to his putative Apis VIII. In actuality, the bull in question was the Mnevis of Heliopolis (see below).

The Lesser Vaults

For the next Apis that died, a catacomb was inaugurated in which successive animals could be interred. These are now known as the Lesser Vaults. They were entered via a cutting about 15 meters northwest of tomb G/H. This led west, before turning south, and finally east,[10] to enter a long, roughly rectangular, hall, its roof supported by five square pillars. A temple lay above ground in which the cult of the dead bulls could be celebrated, equipped with a dedicatory inscription by Khaemwaset.

When opened by Mariette, the Lesser Vaults were in total disorder, probably the result of both robbery in antiquity, and the apparent penetration of the complex in the eighteenth century. As a result, the nature and exact location of some burials is rather unclear, exacerbated by a number of serious inconsistencies within Mariette's accounts and plans,[11] as well as between his results and those of the 1985–1986 excavations. In particular, of the five burials in the vaults attributed to Ramesses II's reign,[12] Mariette's notes talk of one twin and three single interments, yet his manuscript plan shows two twins and a single. To this one must add the fact that chamber J, the alleged location of the latter single burial, seems actually to be a Late Period work (Ibrahim and Rohl 1988: 14; Ibrahim Aly 1996: 5).

Logically, the earliest burial chamber would seem to have been I, lying as it does in pride of place at the southern end of the pillared hall. Mariette later attributed two bulls to it, Apis X and XI (19.4 and 19.5). Since J now appears ruled out as the tomb of Apis 19.6/XII, it would make sense to place him in room 1, left unattributed by Mariette. This would put the earliest Lesser Vaulted Apis in tombs at either end of the central, columned part of the new complex.

However, for subsequent burials, chambers were cut off a new passage, running northward from the hall. The first chamber to be used in this new section seems to have been K, in which two burials were made. At an unknown date, a considerable part of the roof of the gallery directly beyond chamber K collapsed; most of rooms L and 3 were lost, and a vast pit had opened up in the ground above. The edge

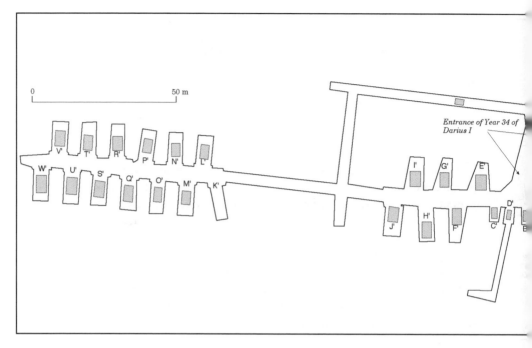

Fig. 4.4 Plan of
the Serapeum
vaults. Plan by
Aidan Dodson,
after Mariette.

of the collapse buried what seems to have been one of chamber K's occupants.[13] Designated Apis 20.2/XIV, it comprised a wooden sarcophagus, largely embedded in the ground, with its upper part largely crushed. Inside, there was a mass of fragrant resin, containing a quantity of disordered bone, made into the shape of a human mummy, its face covered by a somewhat crude gold mask.[14] A text on the wall gave a 'Year 55,' presumably referring to either Apis 19.7/XIV or the other interment attributed to the chamber, Apis 19.8/XIII, probably the later of the two, buried after Khaemwaset's death and his succession as crown prince by Merenptah.[15]

Mariette does not assign canopic jars to any of the bulls buried in the Lesser Vaults, nor their successors, the Greater Vaults. However, to the later Ramesses II Apis, 19.4–19.8 (X, XI, XII, XIV, and XIII), must be assigned a group of vases found in the eighteenth century, which appear to derive from four sets,[16] plus one 'odd' jar found by Mariette (Louvre N 5438; Dodson 1999: 67). The latter probably belonged to Apis 19.8/XIII, with the other sets probably falling to his predecessors.

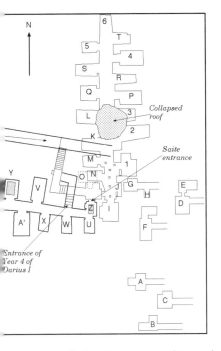

After Apis 19.8/XIII, the next firmly identified bull, Apis 20.2/XV, died in Year 26 of Ramesses III. Even if the former bull died in the very last years of Ramesses II's long reign, which would seem not unlikely, on the basis of known bull life spans, this would leave a gap of around fifty years without a burial. Accordingly, at least one or two additional bulls must be added to the list.

A bull life span of around fifteen to twenty years would take us to the end of the reign of Seti II and, interestingly enough, a faïence vase of the begining of the reign of his successor, Siptah, found its way into the burial of the Twentieth Dynasty Apis 20.4/XVII. If this had been left inside the main hall after the burial of a bull, and by accident or design incorporated into the later bull's assemblage, it may suggest that an Apis 19.9 was buried (perhaps in chamber 2)[17] in the first year of Siptah's reign, given the forms of the king's name used.

This still leaves a thirty-five year gap until Apis 20.2/XV's death: either the latter was an exceptionally aged bull, or there was another incumbent which died in the early part of Ramesses III's reign. Interestingly enough, a chamber (3) directly opposite L, used for Apis 20.2/XV's burial, is without a known occupant, in which case it may have held an Apis 20.1, unless this shared a vault with its predecessor or successor.

Very little information exists on the Apis of the Twentieth Dynasty (Mariette 1882: 146–152), and the source of Mariette's 'Year 26' for Apis 20.2/XV's death is unknown—presumably a graffito or a now-lost stela.[18] The existence of a Apis 20.3/XVI is dated to Ramesses VI's reign by a jar, but its burial place is unknown, perhaps sharing the very large room L with Apis 20.2/XV.[19]

Besides Apis 20.4/XVII of Ramesses IX's reign, which was accompanied by a large number of votive shabtis of Second Prophet of Onnuris, Bakenptah, a vase of the king, and a faïence djed-pillar amulet, room M seems to have held Apis 20.5/XVIII of Ramesses XI's time. Bakenptah also appeared on an ink drawing on the wall of the chamber, wearing a panther skin, and following an image of the king (Mariette 1882: 151, n.1). Three more bulls were dated to the same king's occupancy of the throne in room N by Mariette.

An ink-drawing in Ramesside style, showing a High Priest worshipping Apis, was subsequently found on the wall adjacent to this chamber.[20] Unfortunately, the name of the pontiff has been damaged, with the traces extremely uncertain. However, *if* the first sign could be read as ▱, he might be Nebmehyt, regrettably unplaced in the pontifical succession.[21]

Only a few bull-headed shabtis seem to be assigned to these burials, and Mariette's dating criteria are unclear. In any case, four bull-deaths in the king's maximum of thirty regnal years fits uncomfortably with the sixteen or seventeen years average (and twenty-six year maximum) life-span of an Apis derived from later data. It is thus likely some or all of the chamber N bulls may belong to the succeeding Twenty-first Dynasty, which is otherwise apparently unattested in the Serapeum, since the next firmly dated stela comes from Year 23 of Osorkon II, over two centuries after Ramesses XI's accession. The gap may, however, be reduced if a block formerly attributed to Takelot II is assigned to Takelot I,[22] conceivably referring to a burial of Year 14[23] (Apis 22.x+1/XXVIII).[24]

Three burials alleged by Mariette to lie in chamber O were allocated by him to the Twenty-first Dynasty,[25] and if one assumes that Apis 20.5/XVIII, inducted under Ramesses IX, died around the end of the first decade of Ramesses XI's reign, we would have seven to eight bulls covering approximately two-and-a-quarter centuries—giving an average life span that is greater than twenty-eight years—well in excess of what is possible. There are accordingly bulls missing from the record, and it seems unlikely that they were buried in any of the currently-known chambers. It is possible that further rooms open from chamber O, but until this has been properly investigated nothing can be said. It is also possible that there was a temporary move of the bull cemetery during the earlier part of the Third Intermediate Period. Although no specific bull is attributed to Shoshenq I's reign, a block reused in early Roman times in the Apis complex at Mit Rahina mentions that king building a *wʿbt* for Osiris-Apis (Porter and Moss 1974–1981: 841–842; Jones 1990: 141, pl. VI), indicating that he maintained the cult and burial of the bull in the Memphite region.

Nothing is known of the location of the burial of Apis 22.x+2/XXVII, its stela having been found loose at the southern end of the Lesser Vaults. It could have conceivably lain in the largely-destroyed chamber 3. However, Apis 22.x+4/XXIX was buried in Year 28 of Shoshenq III in a room directly north of the place in which Apis 20.2/XV had been interred under Ramesses III. Subsequent Third Intermediate Period burials were made in chambers cut successively along the old Ramesside corridor, with most burials now well-attested by stela.[26] However, no other material relating to these burials seems to have survived; it is unclear whether this reflects simpler provision for the bulls, or particularly comprehensive plundering.

One of the most interesting burials is that in chamber S, dated to Year 6 of Bakenrenef by a number of stelae (Malinine, Posener, and Vercoutter 1968: 91–107). The room also contained an ink inscription of Shabaka, suggesting that the latter's deposition of Bakenrenef took place while Apis 24.1/XXXIV=XXXV was still in burial (cf. Vercoutter 1960: 65–69). Two succeeding burials have been identified on the basis of stelae lacking a royal name, but plausibly attributable to the middle to the dynasty (Vercoutter 1960: 68–71): Shabaka Year 14 and Taharqa Year 4. They are most likely to have taken place in the otherwise-unfilled chambers 4 and 5 (Apis 25.1 and 25.2), which have the further advantage of being appropriately placed.

The last burials to be carried out in the Lesser Vaults were placed in chamber T. The first was installed by Taharqa in his Year 24, with a second bull placed there in Year 20–21 of Psametik I (Apis 25.3/XXXVI and 26.1/XXXVII). The blocking placed there by the latter was still in situ when examined by Mariette—the only example to survive: plunderers had removed only one stone to gain access. A stela had been mounted in the center of the wall, bearing the bull's official epitaph (Mariette 1882: 190):

> Year 20, IV month of Summer, day 20, under the Person of the Dual King, Wahibre, Son of Re of his body, Psametik; went forth the Person of the Living Apis to Heaven. This

god was dragged in peace to the Beautiful West in Year 21,
I month of Inundation, day 25. Now, he was born in Year 26
of King Taharqa, and received into Memphis in the IV
month of Winter, on day 9; this makes 21 years, 2 months
and seven days.

The Greater Vaults

For the bull that died towards the end of his own long reign, Psametik I
abandoned the ancient galleries of Khaemwaset, and began a new
sequence of chambers. These were entered through a doorway in the
right-hand wall of the vestibule that preceded the pillared hall of the
Lesser Vaults, a burial chamber being constructed directly opposite this
entrance, beyond a vestibule (U). The burial chamber was equipped
with a cutting in the floor, about a meter deep, to receive the coffin of
Apis 26.2/XXXVIII (Mariette 1882: 201–202). Unlike its predecessor,
there is no 'official' stela for this bull, only one recording works associated with his interment (Devauchelle 1994b: 100).

Although some other bulls have their 'official stelae,' as well as
private examples (cf. Porter and Moss 1974–1981: 797–804), some are
attested only indirectly, through the dates of their firmly documented
predecessors and successors. Following Apis XL, which died in Year 12
of Wahibre there is no documented bull until Apis XLI, which died in
Year 23 of Ahmose II, at the age of 18 years, 1 month and 6 days, having
been born in Year 5. The 13 year 'gap' corresponds to a shorter-than-usual,
but perfectly acceptable bull-life; now, in the Twenty-sixth Dynasty
part of the Greater Vaults is the unattributed Chamber W, which might
thus be attributed to an Apis 26.5 (Vercoutter 1962: 20–26); in addition,
a number of stelae of Ahmose II's reign are not certainly attributable to
Apis 26.6/XLI (cf. Porter and Moss 1974–1981: 798).

A major innovation is found in Apis 26.6/XLI's Chamber Y, which
is for the first time equipped with a stone sarcophagus, decorated both
with texts and carved paneling (Gunn 1926a: 82–84). The need to maneu-
ver such a great monument seems to have resulted in the removal of a
number of stelae from their locations, a number being buried under the
floor of the galleries and others doubtless lost (Devauchelle 1994b: 102).

Stone sarcophagi continued to be used following the Persian invasion,
the first being Apis 27.1/XLII under Kambyses. This bull had been

born in Year 27 of Ahmose II—four years after Apis 26.6/XLI; it remains a moot point whether this reflected an unattested intervening ephemeral bull, or an exceptionally long search to find a new one. It is uncertain as to where Apis XLII was intended to be buried, as the sarcophagus, with an inscribed lid, was found in the vestibule between the entrance and Chamber U. Whether a chamber had been begun deeper in the galleries is unknown, although the position of chamber A'—adjacent to the chambers of Ahmose II—is suggestive. It remains unclear how this may fit in with Herodotus' story of Kambyses mistreatment of the Apis (III: 29, 64), although it may be noted that Apis 27.1/XLII's age at death (23) is consistent with a natural demise (cf. Devauchelle 1995; Ray 1988: 260).

Apis 27.2/XLIV, of Year 4 of Darius I, had an extremely short life, and was apparently buried in Chamber B'. The introduction of his sarcophagus necessitated some major surgery, as access to the Greater Vaults had been essentially blocked by the presence of the Kambyses lid just inside the entrance to the galleries. Accordingly, a new entrance had to be cut further to the west, its approach necessitating cutting away part of the east–west section of the old Nineteenth Dynasty stairway. The new entranceway was thus led northwards, before turning west to meet the north–south section of the original entrance approach (Ibrahim and Rohl 1988: 13–14).

This arrangement seems to have been regarded as makeshift only, as stela IM 4039, of Year 34 of Darius I (Apis 27.4), talks of extending the access passage into the Vaults (Vercoutter 1962: 75–76). The main ramp was extended beyond where the old entrance stair turned off, and after some 17 m reached a new doorway in the rock, beyond which a passage ran southwards, joining the Psametik I gallery just beyond chamber B'. The new approach was of considerably larger dimensions than the old one, and was later used to insert considerably larger sarcophagi than hitherto.

The location of the Apis of Darius I presents certain problems, exacerbated by the possibility that a third bull (Apis 27.3), dying in Year 31 (Porter and Moss 1974–1981: 800; Ibrahim and Rohl 1988: 12–13; Devauchelle 1994b: 103–104), existed alongside the well-documented Apis 27.2 and 27.4, making the latter also ephemeral. Mariette's plan attributes chamber A' to Darius I (Apis XLIII), with B' and C' belonging to Darius II (Apis XLIV and XLV). Given the lack today of material relating to the second Darius, it is possible that the ordinals given by Mariette are mistaken. On the other hand, a Ptolemaic stela (Louvre IM 3355) suggests that a bull was interred in Year 11 of a King Darius, most likely Darius II, given the number of bulls already attributed to Darius I (Devauchelle 1994b: 104–6 = Apis 27.[?]). It has also been suggested that no Apis burials took place in the troubled reigns of Xerxes I and Artaxerxes I (cf. Vercoutter 1958: 343–344).

If chambers B' and C' do indeed belong to the first two Apis of Darius I, chamber A' is left to the ephemeral Apis of Year 34. This fits in well with the first two possessing sarcophagi, in contrast to the latter. It has been noted above that the position of chamber A' might suggest its original inception for Kambyses' Apis 27.1/XLII.

The next dated material comes from Year 2 of Nefarud I, some fifteen years after the apparent death of Apis 27.[?] (Porter and Moss 1974–1981: 804; Ibrahim and Rohl 1988: 13; Devauchelle 1994b: 106). This bull, Apis 29.1, was apparently followed by another in Year 3 of Hakor, or the basis of the Ptolemaic inscription noted in connection with Apis 27.[?], above. A burial of the third year of Nakhtnebef is attested by two stelae (Devauchelle 1994b: 106–107 = Apis 30.1), while another of the time of Nakhthorheb is also documented (Devauchelle 1994b: 107 = Apis 30.2).

Unfortunately, none of these bulls are allocated numbers or chambers by Mariette. However since the 'Ptolemaic Section' (chambers K' to W') seems to hold precisely the number of chambers required to hold the Ptolemaic bulls (cf. below), with Apis 31.1/XLVI, buried by the mysterious King Khabbash, generally placed as a contemporary of the end of the reign of Artaxerxes III, in the anomalous chamber D' (q.v.), chambers E' to J' should date to the late Twenty-seventh/Thirty-first Dynasty. Assuming that the bull that died in Year 3 of Nakhthorheb (30.2) was laid to rest in J', and placing its predecessors in the chambers to the east, we find that there is one unallocated chamber between that of Darius I's last bull (27.4/XLIII) and the putative bull of Darius II (27.[?]). This supports the idea of a hiatus under Xerxes I /Artaxerxes I, although perhaps only after the death of the bull which will presumably have been installed in Year 34 of Darius I.

A curious feature of the Late Period section of the Greater Vaults is the tunnel that runs from the back of chamber D'. On the basis of its orientation, it would seem to be linked with the entrance ramp of Year 34 of Darius I. The original intention was perhaps to replicate the orientation of the Lesser Vaults, before a decision was made to revert to the Saite axis. The new gallery seems to have been left unused, save the placement of a sarcophagus in its mouth by King Khabbash. This sarcophagus, with an inscribed lid, is remarkably small by Apis standards, leading Gunn to suggest (1926a: 86) that it had "been made for an Apis who died while yet a calf." However, the previous known Apis (30.2) had died approximately two decades earlier, leaving two alternatives. One is that the bull presumably installed in Year 3–4 of Nakhthorheb had died just before the Khabbash rebellion and had either not received a proper burial from the Persian authorities or was buried in a location now unidentifiable. In this connection it may be noted that Artaxerxes III is alleged to have killed and feasted on the Apis (cf. Brugsch 1886: 39–40; Schwartz 1949; Dandamaev 1989: 311). Khabbash's Apis 31.1/XLVI could thus have been indeed ephemeral, perhaps even installed only after the king's seizure of power from the Persians. Alternatively, this bull might indeed have been born early in Nakhthorheb's reign, and had had to be somehow fitted into a human's sarcophagus owing to the rigors of the time.

Another issue concerns what happened after the burial of Apis 31.1/XLVI, Apis Ptol.1, which had died in the twenty-second year of its age in Year 6 of Ptolemy I (Devauchelle 1994a: 83–84). This life span implies its installation around the seventh year of Alexander the Great, leaving a ten-year gap: was the Apis-stall left vacant, or did an unattested bull intervene? Given the political circumstances of the reign of Darius III, it is perhaps likely that any bull installed by Khabbash will have been allowed to serve, although it might appear surprising that seven years elapsed before a new bull could be identified.

Whatever the precise circumstances that surrounded the lives and deaths of the last Apis of dynastic times, there is a clear architectural distinction between the Saite/Late Period portions of the vaults and that used in Ptolemaic times. Firstly, the main axis was extended over 50 m beyond Chamber J', after which a new stretch of burial chambers was begun. Also, just inside the gateway of the Darius I entrance, a doorway was opened in the north wall, leading to a vestibule and a new passage leading west, turning south to join the main axis a dozen meters beyond Chamber J'. These changes clearly indicate a decision to make a fresh start, with all the earlier portions of the vaults effectively bypassed.

An apparently complete list of Apis of the Ptolemaic Period can be compiled from a variety of contemporary documents (Thompson 1988: 284–296; Devauchelle 1994a: 83–85; Farid 2000). Some refer to the bulls themselves, others to their mothers, the names of which start to be recorded during the Saite Period (see below). However, there is an almost complete lack of direct data as to which chamber belonged to which bull. Only two 'official stelae,' referring to Apis Ptol.7 and 9 (LV and LVII) were found in the galleries, of which only the former was apparently allocated to a chamber by Mariette (cf. Porter and Moss 1974–1981: 804). It remains uncertain as to the basis on which this was done, particularly as the chamber in question is not in its logical place, and no extant MS records support the allocation.[27]

Nevertheless, as was briefly noted above, the thirteen chambers of the Ptolemaic Section correspond remarkably well with the thirteen bulls, which seem to be attested from the death of Apis 31.1/XLVI, to the bull which Octavian refused to visit in 30 B.C. (Thompson 1988: 296).[28] The main area of doubt would seem to surround Chamber K', apparently the first in the new series, yet lacking the expected sarcophagus. However, it may be noted that this room is smaller (only 3.6 m wide, as against in excess of five meters for most of the Late/Ptolemaic Period chambers), and awkwardly placed and angled, which might suggest that it was actually the *last* of the series, directly preceding the abandonment of the Serapeum at the beginning of the Roman Period. Interestingly, this last bull is only known by inference from the inscriptions of its mother (Thompson 1988: 296).

On this basis, one would assign Chambers L' to W' to each bull burial in order, starting in Year 6 of Ptolemy I for Apis Ptol.1. It would also ascribe the only inscribed sarcophagus, in Chamber V' (Gunn 1926a: 87–91), to Year 7 of Ptolemy XII. This monument has blank cartouches, which might rather have suggested a date at which there was some dispute as to primacy on the throne—most obviously in Year 3 of Kleopatra VII and Ptolemy XIII, when Apis Ptol.12 was interred.

If correct, it would imply that our speculation regarding the date of Chamber K' is incorrect, and that this was after all the earliest of the Ptolemaic series. On the other hand, there are many examples of the omission of royal names for other reasons, making any definitive statement difficult.[29]

Following the end of the Ptolemaic Period, the galleries seem to have fallen out of use; certainly, nothing deriving from any Roman Period interment has been recorded. References to the cult of the Apis are to be found in the works of various classical authors (cf. Mariette 1856b), but little survives to allow us to take the history of the Serapeum and its occupants beyond the demise of Kleopatra VII and Egypt's ancient independence.

The Mothers of Apis
A separate catacomb (the 'Iseum') in which the cows that bore the Apis bulls were interred in a mixture of granite and wooden sarcophagi lies just under a kilometer to the northeast of the Serapeum. Its design is highly reminiscent of the earlier structure, although details are obscured by the collapses that brought its clearance to a premature conclusion. Twenty burial places have been provisionally identified in the main vaults (Emery 1971; Smith 1972; 1974: 37–41; 1976), with the earliest certain burial dating to the reign of Hagar, the latest to that of Kleopatra VII.

A second much smaller complex lies just south of the entrance, and may have held three burials, which corresponds well to the possible three cows buried under Darius I—perhaps at the same time (Smith 1972: 180). No evidence for the treatment of the Mother of Apis cows exists prior to late in the reign of Ahmose II, and it may be that their formal interment at Saqqara was instituted in connection with the major reconstruction work within the Serapeum in Darius' Year 34 (see above).

The Apis remains the archetypal bovine deity, and the one whose history is both the longest, and best attested. It is interesting, however that the monumental attestation of the bull terminates with the end of Egyptian independence. However, other such bulls, in particular the Buchis of Armant, continued to be buried ceremonially into Roman times.

Table 1. Conspectus of Apis Bulls

Apis Number		Tomb	Date	Mother	Date
18.1	I	A	Amenhotep III		
18.2	II	B	Amenhotep III/IV		
18.3	III	C	Tutankhamun		
18.4	IV	D	Horemheb		
18.5	V	E	Horemheb		
19.1	VI	F	Seti I		
19.2	VII	G	Ramesses II – Yr 16		
19.3	IX	G	Ramesses II – Yr 30		
		H	Canopic room of Apis 19.3/IX		
19.4	X	I	Ramesses II		
19.5	XI	I	Ramesses II		
19.6	XII	1 (?)	Ramesses II		
19.7	XIV	K	Ramesses II – Yr 55		
19.8	XIII	K	Ramesses II – c. Yr 65?		
19.9		2 (?)	Siptah – Yr 1?		
20.1		3 or L (?)	Ramesses III?		
20.2	XV	L	Rameses III – Yr 26		
20.3	XVI	L (?)	Ramesses VI		
20.4	XVII	M	Ramesses IX		
20.5	XVIII	M	Ramesses XI		
?	XXI	N	Ramesses XI (?)		
?	XXII	N	Ramesses XI (?)		
?	XXIII	N	Ramesses XI (?)		
?	XXIV	O	?		
?	XXV	O	?		
?	XXVI	O	?		
22.x+1	XXVIII	?	Takelot I? – Yr 14?		
22.x+2	XXVII	3?	Osorkon II – Yr 23		
22.x+3		3?	Shoshenq III – early?		
22.x+4	XXIX	P	Shoshenq III – Yr 28		
22.x+5	XXX	P	Pimay – Yr 2		
22.x+6	XXXII	Q	Shoshenq V – Yr 11		
22.x+7	XXXIII	R	Shoshenq V – Yr 37		

Apis Number		Tomb	Date	Mother	Date
24.1	XXXIV= XXXV	S	Bakenrenef – Yr 6/ Shabaka Yr 2		
25.1		4?	Shabaka – Yr 14		
25.2		5?	Taharqa – Yr 4?		
25.3	XXXVI	T	Taharqa – Yr 24		
26.1	XXXVII	T	Psametik I – Yr 20/21		
26.2	XXXVIII	U	Psametik I – Yr 52		
26.3	XXXIX	V	Nekho II – Yr 16		
26.4	XL	X	Wahibre – Yr 12		
26.5		W	Ahmose II – Yr 5		
26.6	XLI	Y	Ahmose II – Yr 23		
27.1	XLII	Z	Kambyses – Yr 6		
27.2	XLIV	B'	Darius I – Yr 4	Isetreshy (?)	Darius I – Yr 3
27.3	XLV	C'	Darius I – Yr 31	Tent[. . .]	Darius I – Yr 33
27.4	XLIII	A'	Darius I – Yr 34	Neitiyti	Darius I – Yr 33
27.5?		E'	Xerxes I or Artaxerxes I?		
27.?		F'	Darius II – Yr 11		Artaxerxes I?
29.1		G'	Nefarud I – Yr 2		
29.2		H'	Hagar – Yr 3	Tentamun	Hagor – Yr 2
30.1		I'	Nakhtnebef – Yr 3	Ihyrudj I	Nakhtnebef – Yr 9
30.2		D'	Nakhthorheb – Yr 3	Ihyrudj II?	Nakhthorheb – Yr 9
31.1	XLVI	J'	Khabbash – Yr 2	Tentiset	Alexander III – Yr 5
Ptol.1		L'	Ptolemy I – Yr 6	Tentwery	Alexander IV – Yr 9
Ptol.2		M'	Ptolemy II – Yr 5	Wadjeyiyti	Ptolemy I – Yr 17
Ptol.3		N'	Ptolemy II – Yr 29		
Ptol.4		O'	Ptolemy III – Yr 15	Tentrenutet I	Ptolemy II – Yr 32
Ptol.5		P'	Ptolemy IV – Yr 12	Gereget I	Ptolemy IV – Yr 2
Ptol.6		Q'	Ptolemy V – Yr 19	Tentamun	Ptolemy IV – Yr 8
Ptol.7	LV	R'	Ptolemy VI– Yr 17	Tentrenutet II	
Ptol.8		S'	Ptolemy VIII – Yr 27	Tenthor	
Ptol.9	LVII	T'	Ptolemy VIII – Yr 52	Gereget II	
Ptol.10		U'	Ptolemy IX – Yr 31	Gereget-Mutiyti	
Ptol.11		V'	Ptolemy XII – Yr 7	Tentamun- Taigesh	
Ptol.12		W'	Kleopatra VII – Yr 3	Tentbastet	
Ptol.13		K'	Augustus?	Tentleby	

Mnevis (, *Mr-wr*)

The 'Bull of Heliopolis,' later known as the Mnevis, appears in the Pyramid Texts of Teti (§716), but as with the Apis, most of the substantive material relating to the bull is of much later date. Classical accounts indicate that the Mnevis of Heliopolis, the *whm-R'*, 'Herald of Re,' and closely linked with Re and Atum (cf. Otto 1938/1964: 34–40), was a black beast. Its iconography is at the outset distinct from the Apis, with curved horns enclosing a sun disk.[30] As with the Apis, Manetho attributes the institution of the Mnevis-cult to the second king of the Second Dynasty, but is in any case mentioned as the 'Bull of Heliopolis' as far back as the Pyramid Texts of the Old Kingdom. Rather more detailed information is forthcoming in the Eighteenth Dynasty, with Thutmose III donating fields in favor of the mother of the Mnevis (Helck 1955: 1372–1373). In addition, a canopic jar of a Mnevis is in Geneva, and has an additional inscription containing the name of Hatshepsut.[31] Perhaps relating to another Eighteenth Dynasty burial is a stelae of Prince Ahmose, probably a son of Amenhotep II, who served as Heliopolitan High Priest at the end of his father's reign.[32]

Evidence of the bull-cult in Akhenaten's time is provided by the direction in the earlier Amarna Boundary Stela that the Mnevis should

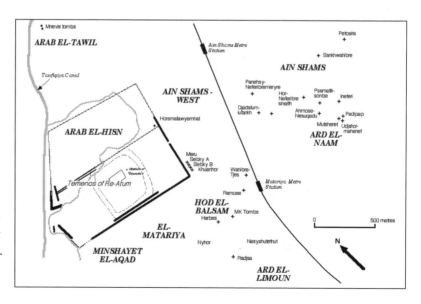

Fig. 4.5 Heliopolis, showing the location of the pricipal monuments. Map by Aidan Dodson.

henceforth be buried at that city.[33] However, it is with Ramesses II's reign that we have the definitive remains of a burial, in a cemetery that lies today under the village of Arab al-Tawil, just under a kilometer and a half northeast of the obelisk of Senusret I at Matariya. Work here has been limited to the end of the nineteenth century and early twentieth century, with modern construction making further investigations highly problematic.

The earliest dated sepulcher dates to the time of Ramesses II (Châaban 1919; Daressy 1919c). Unlike the quarried chambers of Apis, the flat ground around the City of the Sun meant that an alternative approach had to be taken; accordingly, the tomb took the form of a stone structure built in a pit in the ground. Exactly the same type of construction was employed for the royal tombs at Tanis and Mendes, and many private tombs at such northern sites.

The tomb was rectangular, 5.3 m long, 3.05 m wide, and 3.1 m high. The entrance, in the south side, and presumably originally reached by a temporary ramp, gave access to a large room, decorated with badly damaged reliefs of the king and the gods. Many of the blocks had been taken from a construction of Tutankhamun and Horemheb. Stelae at either end of the tomb dated its construction to Ramesses II's Year 26—presumably for the bull whose death is recorded in the previous year on the Serapeum stela of Apis IX;[34] brick walls on the surface may indicate that a chapel and/or temenos-wall once stood above.

The tomb was flooded by ground water, destroying much of its contents. However, canopic jars were present, some shabtis, amulets, and vases, plus the bull's heart scarab and bronze elements from a bier upon which the bull seems to have lain. No fewer than four full or partial sets were found in the Mnevis tomb.[35] Interestingly, their design and texts both differ completely from the allegedly contemporary Apis canopics (Dodson 1999: 65, 69–70 n.78), and if they had not been found in an allegedly secure Ramesside context, on stylistic grounds, one would have refused to place any in the New Kingdom at all. Most significantly, they also differ completely from a Mnevis canopic jar in Madrid, which is reminiscent of that of Apis IX.[36] Given the water-damaged nature of the deposit, it seems not unlikely that what was found may represent at least three, if not four (perhaps successive) intrusive interment(s) in the original Ramesside tomb.

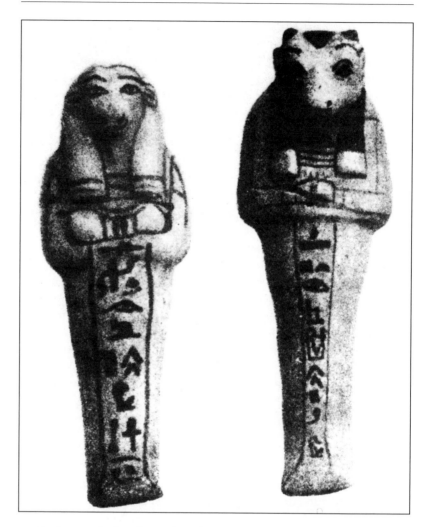

Fig. 4.6
Ramsesside
bull-headed
shabtis from
the Serapeum,
now in the
Louvre
Museum. From
Mariette 1857.

Perhaps pointing in such a direction is the fact that the bull was found lying simply upon a bier, reminiscent of the burials in the Bucheum (q.v.). In contrast, in the reign of Merenptah, the Mnevis seems to have had a limestone sarcophagus, excavated at Heliopolis by one P. Philipp in 1892–1893.[37] Unfortunately, nothing is known of the context in which the piece was found. It is small (136.4 x 79.8 x 58.3 cm) and cannot have held a proper bull mummy. Indeed, there is no unequivocal evidence that this piece is indeed a bull sarcophagus, certainly not from its texts. If indeed a sarcophagus, some kind of arrangement as found with the earlier Apis interments seems likely.

Another fragment from the area of the bull necropolis may refer to a burial under the auspices of the Chancellor Bay in the time of Siptah and Tausret (Griffith 1888: 67, pl. XXI [21]). A heart-scarab of a bull is now in Toledo, Ohio (Spiegelberg 1928b). A second surviving tomb dates to the reign of Ramesses VII (Kamal 1903; Daressy 1919d). Blocks from its walls, in poor condition, were taken to the Cairo Museum. Their decoration shows the king offering to the deceased bull and various gods. Its contents included seven canopic jars of large size (Cairo JE 35737–8). As with those from Ramesses II's Apis tomb, they present certain problems as to dating, and their number once again suggests successive burials in the same tomb. The remains of the bull had suffered badly from the flooding of the chamber, but it proved possible to salvage the bones. Fragments of the coffin also survived, although only bronze fastenings could be retrieved for the museum.

Mnevis burials continued into the Late Period, although only odd fragments survive, including one from the reign of Apries (Griffith 1888: 67, pl. XXI [22]). From early Ptolemaic times comes part of a statue of a Priest of the Mnevis, one Ankh-Psametik, called Ankhmerwer (Touraeff 1917). As with the Apis, literary allusions to the cult continue much later, and it appears that, like other animal cults, the Mnevis continued into the Roman Period (cf. Kákosy 1982), but without any archaeological material now surviving.

Buchis (⳻ Bḫ[38] ⳻ B3-ḥr-ḫ3t)[39]

The cults of the Apis and Mnevis bulls can be dated back to the very dawn of pharaonic history, with evidence for their interment being found in the New Kingdom. In contrast, the black-headed white Buchis bull of Armant appears as such only at the very end of the Late Period, under Nakhthorheb, in the form of its burial. However, in earlier times there are references to four bull-forms of the ancient southern Egyptian war-god Montu, one for each of his places of worship—Armant, Medamud, Tod, and Thebes—and it seems likely that the Buchis united in himself these more ancient divine bovids.

In spite of its close affiliation with Montu, the Buchis was closely linked with Re, holding the title of *wḥm-Rʿ*, identical with that of the Mnevis, and akin to that of the Apis apropos Ptah, as might be expected from the bull of the Upper Egyptian Heliopolis (*jwnw sm3w* = Armant). Indeed, it is possible that the bovid of the Thebaid were originally solar deities, only secondarily assimilated with Montu. He also had other divine links, being closely associated with both Amun and Min, and a participant in the various festivals of the Thebaid (Fairman, in Mond and Myers 1934: II, 40–43).

The bulls were generally installed at Thebes and then taken in a sacred bark southwards to Armant; in at least two cases, however, the ceremony took place in Armant. While principally resident there, the Buchis is known to have traveled among the towns of whose bulls he was the incarnation (Mond and Myers 1934: I, 11–25; II, 45–50).

Like the Apis, the life spans of the Buchis varied considerably, but averaged out at around twenty years.[40] The earliest known burial dates to the reign of Nakhthorheb, on the edge of the desert, are due north of the modern town of Armant. The Bucheum, as the complex of tombs that subsequently developed is known, was excavated under the patronage of Sir Robert Mond and the Egypt Exploration Society in 1927–1932, and proved to be in relatively poor condition, having been extensively robbed, as well as damaged by rising groundwater.[41]

As with many sacred animals of Greco–Roman times, the bull mummies had been adorned with gilded headpieces. The Buchis themselves had been so badly damaged that little detail could be discerned by the excavators. However, the nearby cemetery of the bulls' mothers (see below) revealed more complete burials which allowed detailed examination.[42] These showed that the bovids had been forced into a 'canine' repose-position, probably by cutting tendons. The head was supported by a wooden chin-rest, the whole mummy being fastened to a base board with bronze or iron clamps.

The first interment (10), comprised a vaulted limestone chamber, sunk into the bedrock, containing a granite sarcophagus. A mud-brick vaulted chamber adjoined it to the west, probably serving as a store-room for offerings. Although later building work has made assessment difficult, it seems as if overall access was from the north, with a passage leading to a winding stairway. The latter was later largely quarried away when the later phases of the Bucheum were constructed.

Following the construction of this isolated tomb, the precise sequence of interments is not totally secure,[43] but seems to begin with G, directly to the east. It is approached by a brick-paved ramp, but is much simpler than tomb 10, lacking a sarcophagus and comprising but a single room. The lack of a sarcophagus has been ascribed to the poor state of the country under Alexander the Great, a lack which also continues in tomb 16, cut to the north of G during the reign of Alexander IV. This tomb lacks the brickwork of its immediate predecessors, and is built on three descending levels.

A sarcophagus returns with tomb 18, built during the reign of Ptolemy I. It is a compact sepulcher, with a brick-paved ramp, and a burial chamber closely fitting the sarcophagus. Both it and tomb 16 were reached by a rock-cut passage, north of what seems to have been the stair down to the level of 10 and G, thus becoming the first part of the Bucheum catacomb. For the next burial (14), it seems that major changes were made, with the old stairway removed and the area converted into a burnt-brick vaulted vestibule, approached by a ramp from the east. The latter ran alongside tomb 10, and was lined and vaulted in the same burned brick as the vestibule. The west wall of the latter concealed tomb 14, and the next tomb, H, lying directly to the south; together with the approach to tomb G, the area was also vaulted over to create the South Passage of the new catacomb.

At what became its southern extremity, a new tomb, S, had been begun, but abandoned unused, perhaps owing to its proximity to the water table. It was later largely obliterated by the building of tombs A, D, E, and 21. S seems to have been replaced by either 14 or H.

The attribution of tombs to the bulls known to date to Ptolemy III–V has been through a process of elimination, working back from later better-dated bulls. On this basis, and some architectural grounds, three chambers on the further-extended North Passage (L, M, and 17) have been dated to this period. M's granite sarcophagus is thus the last of its type. All subsequent such containers were built up from a number of blocks, the prototype being found in the immediately-preceding L. The poor tomb 17, with only a cutting in its floor for a sarcophagus, may be attributed to the rebellion against Ptolemy V, which disrupted the Thebaid, and consequently effected the burial of this Apis bull.

In contrast, Tomb F was occupied following the end of the rebellion. It was placed near the then-end of the South Passage, and consisted of a simple chamber, containing a built sarcophagus, closed by a mud-brick wall into which the stela was originally fixed.[44] This end of the Bucheum was also used for the next five bulls, chambers A, D, E, and 21 being cut in the east and west walls of what had once been chamber S, and K in a further southern extension of the latter. Chamber K is very poor, lacking a sarcophagus; this may result from the political problems between Ptolemy VIII and Kleopatra II that had affected Armant.

For the second bull of Ptolemy XI, however, it seems that a more northern location was chosen, given the discovery of its stelae in the North Passage. The bull therefore seems to have been interred in chamber 15, placed between the earlier chambers of Alexander IV and Ptolemy II (14 and 16). However, a return to the other end of the catacomb occurred under the early Roman emperors, where the South Passage was gradually extended to accommodate chambers B, 22, and C. The first and last of these are securely dated by the survival of their stelae in situ. These were the last burials in the southern extension of the Bucheum, the end of the passage being finished off by a brick wall. No further extension of the North Passage being apparently contemplated, the next five chambers (11–13, N, and O) were cut into the west wall of the gallery, essentially completing the set of burials in the main body of the Bucheum.

For the subsequent interments, new sets of chambers were prepared west of tomb 10, accessed from the main approach ramp. The first lay on the west side of a passage running north (chambers 1 and 2), being followed by a pair of chambers directly west of tomb 10, and opening directly from the ramp (7 and 8); oddly, 7 has a rear extension (7a) that held its stela and offering table. Chamber 6 was built under Antoninus Pius opposite 1 and 2, being the last Buchis burial certain to incorporate a sarcophagus. Later destruction has made it impossible to determine whether the remaining chambers in this part of the complex (3–5) included such features.

These rooms are the latest 'proper' burial places in the Bucheum. The remaining five known bulls seem to have been placed in a room built into the offering chamber of tomb 10 (9), in the South Passage (19 and 20), and in the entrance of chamber 6 (23). These take the story of the Bucheum down to the time of Diocletian; it is uncertain how much longer the bull-cult survived after this (Mond and Myers 1934: I, 171).

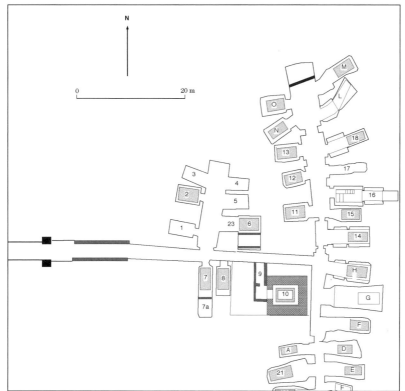

Fig. 4.7 The vaults of the Bucheum. Plan by Aidan Dodson after Myers.

The Mothers of Buchis

Like that of the Apis, the Buchis' mothers received ceremonial burial in Late/Greco–Roman times. At Armant, this tomb (the Baqaria) lay a few hundred meters north of the Bucheum, and closely resembled it.[45] The earliest interments were individual tombs, with large sarcophagi, built as open cuttings, roofed with brick vaults, and approached by ramps from the west (tombs 30 and 31) or fully rock-cut (33). Later, however, they become small rectangles, roughly-cut in the desert conglomerate, with brick vaults, that were incorporated into a 'T'-planned catacomb from the reign of Ptolemy III onward. A victim of collapse and reconstruction during its period of use, the Baqaria came to an end under Diocletian, when the last known cow-burial took place in a separate grave, approximately 100 meters south, on the opposite side of the adjacent Roman village.

Table 2. Conspectus of Buchis Bulls

Tomb	Date	Mother Date	Tomb
10	Nakhthorheb – Yr 14		30
G	Alexander III – Yr 4		31
16	Alexander IV		33
18	Ptolemy I – [Yr 14]		11
14	Ptolemy II – Yr 13		12
H	Ptolemy II – Yr 31		13
L?	Ptolemy III – Yr 13		1
M	Ptolemy IV – Yr 8		2
17	Ptolemy V – [Yr 11]		3
F	Ptolemy V – Yr 25		8
D	Ptolemy VI – Yr 19		9
E	Ptolemy VI – Yr 36		10
K	Ptolemy VIII – Yr 45		5
A	Ptolemy IX – Yr 16		6
21	Ptolemy XII – Yr 4		32
15	Ptolemy XII – [Yr 28]		7
B	Augustus – Yr 1		17
22	Augustus – Yr 24		14
C	Tiberius – Yr 6		4
11	Tiberius		16
12	Caligula – A.D. 36		18
13	Nero		23
N	Vespasian		19
O	Domitian		20
1	Trajan		24
2	Hadrian		25
8	Antoninus Pius – [Yr 4]		26
7	Antoninus Pius – Yr 7		21
6	Antoninus Pius		27
3	Marcus Aurelius (?) – [Yr 33]		22
4	Commodus (?) – Yr 31	Commodus – Yr 30	28
5?	Caracalla		35?
23?	Maximinus		36?
9	Valerian – [Yr 7]		37?
19	Probus (?) – Yr 4		38?
20	Diocletian – [Yr 12]		29

Regnal Dates of Rulers

Horus Aha 32nd–31st cent. BC
Horus Den 32nd–31st cent. BC
Horus Anedjib 32nd–31st cent. BC
Thutmose III 1479–1424 BC
Hatshepsut 1772–1457
Amenhotep II 1424–1398
Amenhotep III 1388–1348
Amenhotep IV 1360–1343
Tutankhamun 1343–1333
Horemheb 1328–1298
Seti I 1296–1279
Ramesses II 1279–1212
Merenptah 1212–1201
Siptah 1195–1189
Tausret 1189–1187
Ramesses III 1185–1153
Ramesses VI 1141–1133
Ramesses VII 1133–1125
Ramesses IX 1123–1104
Ramesses XI 1094–1064
Shoshenq I 948–927
Takelot I 892–877
Osorkon II 877–838
Takelot II 841–815
Shoshenq III 838–798
Pimay 786–780
Shoshenq V 780–743
Bakenrenef 727–721
Shabaka 721–707
Taharqa 690–664
Psametik I 664–610
Nekho II 610–595
Wahibre 589–570
Ahmose II 570–526
Kambyses 525–522
Darius I 521–486
Xerxes I 486–465

Artaxerxes I 465–424
Darius II 423–405
Nefarud I 399–393
Hagar 393–380
Nakhtnebef 380–362
Nakhthorheb 360–342
Khabbash c. 340
Darius III 335–332
Alexander III 332–323
Alexander IV 317–310
Ptolemy I 310–282
Ptolemy II 285–246
Ptolemy III 246–222
Ptolemy IV 222–205
Ptolemy V 205–180
Ptolemy VI 180–164
Ptolemy VIII 170–163
Ptolemy IX 116–110, 109–107, 88–80
Ptolemy XI 80
Ptolemy XII 80–58, 55–51
Kleopatra VII 51–30
Augustus 31–AD 14
Tiberius 14–37
Caligula 37–41
Nero 54–68
Vespasian 69–79
Domitian 81–96
Trajan 98–117
Hadrian 117–138
Antoninus Pius 138–161
Marcus Aurelius 161–180
Commodus 180–192
Caracalla 211–217
Maximinus 235–238
Valerian 253–260
Probus 276–282
Diocletian 284–305

Notes

1   §1279, 286, 1313, 1988; owing to the lack of determinatives, it is possible that some mentions may actually be of the funerary genius, Hapy.

2   Cf. the careful distinction between the horns of the Apis and the Mnevis on a stela of Ramesses II's reign (Malinine, Posener, and Vercoutter 1968: cat. 4). For an anomalous depiction, see Gunn 1926a: 87.

3   Lucas 1719: 96–101; the significance of his discovery is considered in Aufrère 1997; Dodson 1999: 67–69; 2000; see further below.

4   On the woefully incomplete nature of the surviving documentation from Mariette's work, cf. Malinine, Posener, and Vercoutter 1968: viii–ix. The poor luck that accompanied Mariette's attempts at publishing his work struck early on when, after the publication of the first parts of Mariette 1855, the journal used ceased publication (after only 38 of the promised "64 Apis trouvés dans les souterrains du Sérapéum"), with the MS for the outstanding parts never recovered from the proprietors (Maspero in Mariette 1904, 255 n.1).

5   A number of different chamber-designations have been used by different authors (cf. Porter and Moss 1974–1981: 940–941; Vercoutter 1960: 67; Ibrahim and Rohl 1988: 13, 15); for the purposes of this paper, I have used the ultimate notation of Mariette (Malinine, Posener, and Vercoutter 1968: plan A), extended beyond D' to cover the remaining chambers of the Late and Ptolemaic sections (thus E' to W'), with unlettered rooms of the Lesser Vaults numbered after Malinine, Posener, and Vercoutter 1968: plan B.

6   Mariette 1882: 117, fig.1. A fragment of a scene described by Mariette is almost certainly now Munich Gl.93 (published by Schoske 1990: 59 [4]).

7   Mariette first numbered the bulls in dynastic series (e.g., 'XIXe Dyn._Apis IX'), before changing to a unified series while working up his findings, the last mentioned bull becoming 'Apis XIV.' The latter are those used in Porter and Moss 1974–1981: 780–804. It has now been recognized, however, that some bulls were misplaced or omitted by Mariette: a new notation, employing Arabic numerals and once again based on dynastic series is used by Didier Devauchelle in Devauchelle 1994b. For clarity, I employ a compound of the latter numeration and the ultimate one of Mariette—the aforementioned bull is thus 'Apis 19.9/XIV.' Where no roman numeral is given, it indicates that the bull was not recognized by Mariette (cf. Table 1).

8   When first discovered, a cartouche on a stela (Malinine, Posener, and Vercoutter 1968: cat. 1) was read as that of Akhenaten, thus contributing to the bull's historical placement; however, it is now quite clear that the king shown offering flowers to Osiris is actually 'the Son of Re, Teti.'

9   Apis VIII did not exist: a stela of Apis IX shows two other bulls, Apis VII and another which was dubbed Apis VIII by Mariette. However, this bull is clearly a Mnevis, embalmed by the stela's dedicator, an embalmer who was commemorating his bovine handiwork!

10   This approach was later partly cut away and modified in the Late Period to facilitate access to the new Greater Vaults: see p. 85.

11   For example, using a numbering system for the chambers in his text, which does not appear on his only surviving plan of the vaults!

12   It should be noted that these Apis must have had very short lives, if correctly

dated by Mariette—an average of only seven years, as compared with the six-teen/seventeen year average in later periods (q.v.). One might thus at first sight question the existence of some of these bulls. On the other hand, the number of canopics probably datable to the reign is consistent with such a number of burials: cf. below and Dodson (in preparation).

13 This is one of the points where Mariette's description (1882: 58) is not as exact as it might be—infuriatingly, given the importance of the material found in what seems to be this area!

14 Mariette 1882: 146; the jewelry is published in Mariette 1857. This is the so-called 'mummy of Prince Khaemwaset,' but was in reality the burial of a bull, prepared in the same way as Apis V, VII, and IX. Unfortunately, none of the bovid bones found by Mariette in the Serapeum appear to survive; although a skeleton and a head now in the Agricultural Museum, Doqqi (CG 29518 and 29526) have been called Apis remains, Gaillard and Daressy state explicitly of the Serapeum "qui n'a du reste rien donné à [the Cairo Museum], puisque Mariette l'avait fouillé avant la fondation de Boulaq et qu'il n'y avait trouvé, dans les tombes des Apis, que des débris d'os qui nont pas été conservés" (1905: [i]).

15 On the relative order of Apis XIII and XIV, see Dodson 1995: 26–27.

16 Dodson 1999: 66–69; to the thirteen (or possibly up to sixteen) items noted there might be added a further example recorded by Bernard de Montfaucon in 1719 (Aufrère 1997: 56–57); on the other hand, the similarities in the texts recorded for the latter with those on one found by Lucas suggests that the objects may be one and the same. For Aufrère's suggestion that the jars actually belong to the Ptolemaic Period, see below.

17 Later enlarged to provide for a projected extension? Cf. Ibrahim and Rohl 1988: 16.

18 Over 350 stelae were destroyed by flooding of the old Bulaq Museum.

19 The existence of Apis XVI is assured by the death-date of Apis XV: if buried under Ramesses VI, Apis XVI will have had a life of between 18 and 24 years.

20 As yet unpublished; cf. Ibrahim and Rohl 1988: 16. My thanks go to Bill Manley for his comments on the position of this representation, and to David Rohl for the loan of a transparency of it.

21 Cf. Kees 1953: 64.

22 SN 82: Malinine, Posener, and Vercoutter 1968: 18 [19], referring to a Hedjkheperre Takelot—bearing a prenomen common to both Takelot I and II (Jansen-Winkeln 1987). If David Aston's reassessment is correct (1989), Takelot II would have been an Upper Egyptian ruler unlikely to have been concerned with the Apis.

23 Malinine, Posener, and Vercoutter 1968: 18 [19]. This block was found among the remains of the temples on the surface, not from the catacombs themselves.

24 On these various points, see Dodson, in preparation.

25 On this anomalous chamber, never properly explored owing to its dangerous condition, cf. Ibrahim and Rohl 1988: 13, 17, 19.

26 Some problems arise from confusions in Mariette's various records, including changing the numbering of some bulls: cf Vercoutter 1962. There is also a contradiction between Mariette's final plan (published in Malinine, Posener, and Vercoutter, 1968) and that of Rhoné 1877 (Vercoutter 1962: 12, n.5): in

the former, Apis XXX is shown in the same chamber as Apis XXIX (chamber P), but in Rhoné's, the first three bulls of the Twenty-second Dynasty (Apis XXVIII, XXVII, and XXIX) are all in Q, with Apis XXX, XXXI, and XXXII in P. It is notable that none of the stelae of Apis XXXII found with those of Apis XXX, suggesting that the bulls did not share a chamber. It now appears that Apis XXXI did not exist (Porter and Moss 1974–1981: 787).

27 The Apis LV stela is registered in the Louvre under the numbers N 409 and E 3866. The former simply records it as being "une stele de Serapeum en granit," while the latter has the following notation: "Porte ici pour memoire. Partie inferieure d'une epitaphe officielle d'Apis, datée de l'an VI de Ptolemée Philometor I, et dont le musee possedait deja la partie superieure. Ce fragment de granite noir porte 10 lignes de texte hieroglyphique gravees en creus; il a ete decouvert par M. Mariette en 1859 dans les deblais du Serapeum de Memphis et apporte a Paris en 1862 par MM. Mariette et Deveria, il est maintenant reuni a l'autre fragment dans la salle du Serapeum. (Don de Said Pacha, vice-roi d'Egypte)." As always in such matters, I am indebted to Mlle Bridonneau for this information.

28 This fact alone would argue against Aufrère's suggestion (1997) that Ptolemaic bulls might have been buried elsewhere, in the Sacred Animal Necropolis, even if it were not clear that his principal evidence, the series of Apis canopic jars recovered early in the eighteenth century, is certainly not of this date; cf. above, and Dodson 2000: 53 n.10.

29 It is possible that detailed architectural examination might establish the true relative date of K'.

30 Both bulls are conveniently shown together on a stela from the Serapeum (Malinine, Posener, and Vercoutter 1968: cat. 4). Later on, however, a sun disk is shown on depictions of the Apis as well.

31 Geneva 19488 (Guarnori 1982: 20–22), bought in 1955 from the V. Oryng collection (lots 019487–019489, information courtesy of Jen-Luc Chippaz); it is a human-headed Hapy jar, 69 cm high. The writer will be discussing this piece further, together with the other Mnevis funerary material, elsewhere.

32 Bryan 1991: 67–68; on his parentage and the probability that his known monuments should be placed in Amenophis II's reign, rather than Thutmose IV's, see my review of Bryan's book (Dodson 1994).

33 The discovery of bovid bones, and a skull, in the royal cemetery area at Amarna might represent such an interment; on the other hand, the remains may more likely be the debris of a food-offering, whole oxen being known from at least two Kings' Valley tombs. Cf. Khouly and Martin 1987: 12, 13, 16.

34 Cairo TR 2/2/21/1 (el-Alfi 1972).

35 Cairo 14/7/18/1 (jackal head, height: 44 cm); 14/7/18/2 (falcon: 60 cm); 14/7/18/3 (human: 62 cm); 14/7/18/4 (baboon: 61 cm; 14/7/18/5 (hawk; 70 cm); 14/7/18/6 (hawk: 68 cm); 14/7/18/7 (human: 76 cm); 27/37/18/1 (44 cm); 27/37/18/3 (62 cm); 27/37/18/4 (47 cm); 27/37/18/5 (60 cm); 27/37/18/6 (70 cm).

36 Museo del Arqueológico Nacional 44/1973 (Perez Die 1983: 240–244). This human-headed Duamutef jar (height: 75 cm) had left Egypt in antiquity, having been found on the Iberian peninsula.

37 Brussels E.3058; KRI IV 1981: 51 [24A]. I am indebted to Luc Limme for

information on this object, and the ability to study it. The location of Philip's discovery in uncertain; of uncertain significance is the fact that he also found the Saite tomb of Udjahormhenet, which lies 2.5 km south–east of the known Mnevis-tombs (see Bickel and Tallet 1997).

38 Secular name of the bull.
39 Secular name, only found in funerary inscriptions; for the names and titles of the bull, see Fairman in Mond and Myers 1934: I, 38–44.
40 Excluding one premature demise.
41 It should be noted that some of the material allocated to the Wellcome Historical Medical Museum (see distribution lists in Mond and Myers 1934, passim) is now in the Egypt Center, University College Swansea. For the following list I am indebted to Carolyn Graves-Brown: coffin clamps from Buchis 13: 2080?–2086?, W968–W983 (ex-Wellcome 153965, 153958, 153966, 153952, 153970, 153957, 153967, 153951, 153950, 153946, 153945, 153964, 153963, 153948, 153962, 153959, 153953, 153954, 153943, 153945, 153944, 153961, 153960); ceramics: W492 (Baqaria 3: ex-153469), W493 (ex-153469 QQ), W494; stela of Commodus cow: W946 bis (ex-153443); The skeleton from Baqaria 7, although explicitly stated to have gone to the Wellcome seems now to be lost, as Craig Brierley of the Science Museum, London, informs me as follows: "I have searched through our records and discussed the matter with Dr. Tim Boon, Curator of the Public Health Collection, who did work on the acquisition of objects to The Science Museum from the Wellcome Trust. Unfortunately, I can find no record of the said object ever coming into our collection" (personal communication, June 7, 2000).
42 Mond and Myers 1934: I, 57–73. One complete cow is now in the Cairo Museum JE 55619 = CG 29859; another was sent to the Wellcome Historical Medical Museum in London (see note 41) .
43 The chronology of the Bucheum is reconstructed in Mond and Myers 1934: I, 169–178, and is essentially followed here.
44 The stela of Ptolemy V was found outside, but had clearly been moved, making the attribution not 100 percent secure, but likely (Mond and Myers 1934: I, 173).
45 This monument is discussed in Mond and Myers 1934: I, 37–44 (architecture) and 175–178 (chronology).

5

The Cats of the Goddess Bastet

*Alain Zivie and Roger Lichtenberg**

Among all the 'sacred animals' that were mummified and buried in vast quantities by the ancient Egyptians during the last centuries of their long history, cats held a special place and were accorded a special respect. However, uninformed people misunderstand the true state of affairs in ancient Egypt with regard to animal worship. They believe that in ancient Egypt all cats were worshipped, mummified, and interred, as were dogs, both the favored animals of the Egyptians par excellence. Moreover, cats were put into a separate category from dogs as they were regarded as 'special' and mysterious animals, almost divine, beloved and feared at the same time. But this attitude is a projection of a modern point of view that has its roots in the Middle Ages, and one that is above all occidental and anachronistic.

In actuality, the ancient Egyptians regarded the cat as they did other animals that were also revered and mummified. Moreover, one should remember that for the cat, like other animals deemed 'sacred' (and many species can be thus described), above and beyond the animal itself, stood the divinity. This should be remembered even in those few cases when the divinity behind the animal was nearly forgotten and the focus placed on the beast. The animal is only a sort of hypostasis of the god or goddess, or at the least, an intermediary between the divinity and the believers. The animal is sacred through delegation and association rather than on any other merits.

In conjunction with the cult for the lioness goddess, and above all, the cat goddess Bastet, important cat necropoleis have been active at

---

* Translation by S. Montgomery.

Fig. 5.1
Small cat coffin in
stuccoed wood.
Photograph by P.
Chapuis/ MAFB. ©
Hypogées.

Bubastis in Lower Egypt, at Speos Artemidos in Middle Egypt, and finally at Memphis (Saqqara). These three towns have witnessed the development of important cemeteries that were used for several centuries, with each one catering to hundreds of thousands of cats. It is the remains from these three locations that, despite the vicissitudes of time, tomb robbers, and seekers of fertilizer (see below), have furnished a vast number of specimens of cat mummies and associated objects (sarcophagi, statues, etc.) that are found in museums and collections throughout the world. One must, however, remember that cat mummies are also found in many other Egyptian sites. The catacombs often contain a 'mixed' population, with other animals mixed in with the cats. These interlopers are frequently not felids of any sort, but are buried among them nonetheless. This practice is commonly found throughout Egyptian animal necropoleis, and although the reason for this is still unknown, albeit discussed frequently.

Opposite: Fig. 5.3 Bronze statuette of cat (coffin ?). Photograph by P. Chapuis/ MAFB. © Hypogées.

The present contribution is dedicated to the catacombs and cat mummies found at the Bubasteion of Saqqara (Zivie 1982, 1983a, 1983b, 1985, 1988b, 1990a, 1990b, 1995, 1999). This site has been excavated and studied for some twenty years by the Mission Archéologique Française du Bubasteion (MAFB), directed by A. Zivie, sponsored by the Ministry of Foreign Affairs and the Centre National de la Recherche Scientifique (CNRS), in close cooperation with the Supreme Council of Antiquities of Egypt, and with the sporadic support of certain French companies).

Fig. 5.2 The south face of the cliff of the Bubasteion and its tomb entrances. Photograph by A. Zivie/MAFB. © Hypogées.

The term Bubasteion is the Greek designation for the temenos consecrated to the goddess Bastet, which is situated at the entrance to the Memphite necropolis. This term, dating to the Ptolemaic Period, refers to a more ancient reality at Saqqara: a sanctuary consecrated to a cat goddess (in her inception primarily a lioness), Bastet, lady of Ankh-tawy (this is the name of a quarter of Memphis), one of the great divinities of Memphis, which appears to have already existed in the New Kingdom. However, it is only during the second half of the first millennium B.C.

that these catacombs were filled up with cat mummies, making this site almost as important as the celebrated cat cemetery of the metropolis of Bubastis, the Delta town dedicated to Bastet.

The escarpment where at least a section of the catacombs is arranged is situated within the interior of the temenos of the Bubasteion. The Bubasteion was a huge sacred complex dedicated to the goddess Bastet from the Late Period onward. The Late Period buildings can be identified thanks to a gigantic enclosure wall made of mud brick that is still visible in certain areas, the south and the west above all. A whole ensemble of sanctuaries built on the plateau, of which nothing remains, must have constituted the heart of the complex. A little to the east, the other great ensemble was the Anubeion, consecrated to Anubis, and equipped with catacombs for canids. The location of the Asklepeion complex is still debated.

The divinity represented by the cat was a goddess: Bastet or Bubastis, as she was called in Greek, a corruption of her Egyptian name. She was usually represented as a cat, or more often, as a cloaked woman with a cat's head, generally standing straight, and carrying a basket. Thus far, things are simple. However, they become less so when one remembers that Bastet was not always a cat or an ailurocephalic goddess (if one can risk this neologism based on 'ailouros,' the Greek name for cat). Initially, and even through the Late Period in some manifestations, she was a lioness or a woman with a lioness's head.

The majority of the animal necropoleis at Saqqara are situated to the north of the site. The ensemble is known as the 'Sacred Animal Necropolis,' discovered and excavated, and studied by the Egypt Exploration Society (see Nicholson, this volume). The cat cemetery is located at the southern end of the grouping, not far from the access to the site, below the modern rest house of the Antiquities Service. If the animal necropoleis of North Saqqara were carved especially for the burial of animal mummies, the cat cemetery is unique in its reuse of the tombs of the New Kingdom (1549–1069 B.C), dating to the middle of the first millennium before our era. The most striking case being that of the tomb of the Lady Maïa, the wet-nurse of Tutankhamun (1343–1333 B.C.). For several decades this zone has been called in Arabic Abwab al-Qutat, 'The Doors of the Cats.' This is due to the systematic pillage of the area that has revealed the presence of vast numbers of mummified cats buried in pits and tombs dug into the flank and sum-mit of the cliff.

These mummies, like other animal mummies of Saqqara and else-where, were exported on a huge scale, by boat, to Europe, especially Britain, where they were used as fertilizer until it was decided that such an unusual material should not be used. This modern industrial exploitation was practiced mainly during the middle of the second half of the nineteenth century.

The study of the cats of the Bubasteion unfolded under the umbrella of the exploration of the group of New Kingdom tombs that were established on the eastern edge of the Saqqara plateau. However, this study became an integral part of the excavations as most of these tombs had been reused as catacombs for cats. Thus, quite early on in the project's history, many cat mummies were discovered in these reused tombs of the New Kingdom. This additional responsibility added greatly to the project, and increased its scientific interest. It has been with pleasure that we have pursued this alternate research into the mummies, together with the planned excavation work, and enjoyed the challenges that it has presented. Excavating and studying the cats of the Bubasteion is, in effect, to enter completely and wholeheartedly into archaeozoology, as well as into the study of Late Period religious beliefs and practices, especially as they relate to animal cults. The study of the feline necropolis of the Bubasteion contributes to a better under-standing and a deeper knowledge of animal necropoleis at Saqqara, and in Egypt in general.

This has been a long task and we are still not at its end, even if we can now retrace the main stages of these burials. Effectively, for many years the Bubasteion material had vanished due to pillaging and very little remained in situ. However, by coincidence, the main tomb exca-vated by MAFB, that of the Eighteenth Dynasty Vizier 'Aper-El (Bubasteion I.1), did not contain any cat mummies, with a few excep-tions in the topmost levels. In contrast, we have the group of relatively unexcavated tombs to the east of 'Aper-El's, which have been called by the MAFB the "Eastern Tombs." These tombs are connected to that of the vizier, and contain many cat mummies in different degrees of preservation (Verdel et al. 1995). Some are destroyed, and almost reduced to burnt bones. Certain other tombs, placed more to their west, are also similarly filled. Further deposits of cat mummies, found more or less *in situ*, were located at the exterior of the southern face of the cliff.

The earliest cat remains (mummies, and above all bones) discovered by the Bubasteion Mission were examined during the 1980s, by Leonard Ginsburg (Museum of Natural History, Paris). During the course of several brief missions he undertook a systematic examination of a certain number of cat skeletons, particularly their skulls. Measurements of bones, and especially the cranial capacity of the animals was a priority (Ginsburg 1999). These measurements provide important information concerning domestication, and the basis for establishing solid criteria for distinguishing between examples of *Felis sylvestris libyca sive maniculata* and wilder types of cats *(Felis chaus)* (Ginsburg et al. 1991). The statistics were based on the measurements on these mummies' bones, especially from those animals found in the tombs that lie to the east of 'Aper-El. Other observations concerning mummification methods and types and designs of bandaging, etc. were also made during the course of his analysis (Zivie 1988a; Zivie and Ginsburg 1987).

This phase was completed with the discovery of the burial chamber of 'Aper-El and his family. This necessitated the MAFB to concentrate its efforts on the study and preservation of their rich funerary material. A few years later an important new step in the study of the cat catacombs took place. First, there was a surprise in 1993: the discovery of a niche in a previously inaccessible portion of 'Aper-El's offering chapel, blocked behind a masonry wall. This contained several cat burials that were in situ, one still in its stone sarcophagus. A large number of New Kingdom tombs were, in effect, closed off or redesigned at the end of the Late Period or later to contain these cat burials and/or to maintain the integrity of the area that was becoming riddled with burials and perhaps affected by the resulting instability of the site (earthquakes?). The continuation of the excavation of the tombs situated immediately to the west of that of 'Aper-El also yielded a new and rich source of felid remains.

The discoveries necessitated a new approach to all this material. The discovery of mummies in a better state, in great numbers, made a more systematic study of these cat mummies possible than had ever been before, and took on new directions. In particular, radiological studies of

Fig. 5.4
Excavation, study,
and conservation
of a cat sarcophagus
found in Maïa's
tomb. Photograph by
P. Chapuis/MAFB.
© Hypogées.

these mummies became possible and were carried out in the laboratory and magazines of the MAFB at Saqqara. This study was carried out by Roger Lichtenberg, radiologist, and specialist of human mummies, assisted by his colleague and wife, Martine Fayein-Lichtenberg. During the campaigns of the 1990s, they x-rayed and examined a vast number of felid remains, which yielded rich statistics (see below).

In 1996 the direction of this study was once again altered with the discovery of the tomb of Maïa, wet-nurse of Tutankhamun (Bubasteion I.20). In effect, much later in its history this tomb was transformed into a massive repository of the cats associated with the Bubasteion, on a scale unlike that of other tombs hitherto found in the area. Moreover, a violent fire had reduced many of these cats to ashes. Nonetheless, other rich sources for their study had accompanied these burials: votive objects, amulets, sarcophagi, coffins, etc. The lower levels of Maïa's tomb, discovered toward the end of 1998, were reused and contained several dozen human mummies in addition to those of cats, with their usual complement of associated objects: coffins, sarcophagi, statues, amulets, etc. However, on these levels neither the human nor the animal burials had suffered from fire, but instead, the humidity had transformed the majority of the cat mummies into blackened powder surrounding bones, which had been further disturbed by the robbers who had violated the area in antiquity (Lichtenberg and Zivie 2000; Zivie and Lichtenberg 2003).

The last excavation season (autumn 2001 and autumn 2002) has allowed MAFB to work in and to clear the lower levels (levels –1 and – 2) of the tomb, below the level 0 (the chapel). Level –1 had been completely reused as a cat burial ground (after previous periods when human beings had been buried there). Level –2 appears to be smaller in area than the preceding floors, and was not used for the burials of cats. The excavation of the lower levels has been conducted by the archaeologist Anaïck Samzun (National Institute of Preventive Archaeological Research, Paris) and the study of the animal material was greatly enhanced by the presence of the archaeozoologist Cécile Callou (National Museum of Natural History, Paris), both members of the MAFB team. A very systematic archaeozoological study of the material found was started by her and continues until the present time. It is still too early to include the initial results in this contribution. However, one can already say that these burials are much less disturbed than others found before, and that their location and the nature of deposition is of particular interest and importance. The excavation of level –1 of the tomb of Maïa, carried out during the autumn of 2001, has already yielded an astonishing discovery: a skeleton of a lion, originally most certainly a mummy, and now reduced to bare bones, found in association with the other animal burials (Callou, Samzun, and Zivie 2004). Thus, here at the Bubasteion we have found united for the first time in the same place the two faces of the goddess Bastet: cat and lioness.

Study of the Material Found at the Bubasteion: Methods and Results

Between 1991 and 1999, 272 'packets' were examined. The term 'packets' and not 'mummies' is used here as an effort to be precise as certain packets only contained mud, some clay, or a few pebbles, and as such, can be considered fake mummies. Others only contained a few unrelated cat bones, while others, and these are the most numerous, contained the mummified remains of cats. Finally, some rare 'packets,' the largest, in fact, held two to six cats! The fake mummies generally measure 20 cm or so in length, and thus can be recognized almost immediately.

The total results of the material:

184 cats	68%
84 fake mummies	31%
11 'packets' containing a few cat bones	4%
1 fish mummy	0.4%
2 empty 'crowns,' in textile	0.8%

Eleven crania of cats were radiographed, while wrapped, in an extremely rigorously controlled manner in order to determine a methodology for establishing precise craniometric measurements on x-rays.

Radiographic and Photographic Study

The technique used to study the cat mummies is the same one that was established and used in Kharga Oasis for the study of human mummies. The 'packets,' when they were of a small size, were x-rayed in groups of three, four, or six. The larger mummies that measured over 60 cm in length, necessitated a more complicated technique using several x-ray films joined together. Thus, large radiographic cassettes (36 x 43 cm) had to be used. The x-ray machine used was a portable type, generally used on people who were confined to their homes (a Massiot-Philips 90–20, provided by Philips). Its limited strength was, for the most part, sufficient for the work at hand. The x-ray films were

Fig. 5.5   Field x-ray laboratory used by the MAFB at Saqqara. Photograph by R. Lichtenberg/ MAFB. © Hypogées.

developed at Saqqara in manual baths, with the films and developing chemicals generously supplied by Kodak.

Every mummy that was x-rayed was also photographed. The images were obtained using a lens of 105 mm focal length, designed to remove all distortion. Generally the mummies were photographed so that special details were obvious and could be more closely examined.

Results

Position of the Paws

The position of the paws of the cats allows one to classify the mummies into two categories. Type 1: the forepaws are extended along the trunk, and the hind-legs are folded up along the abdomen. The tail is pulled through the hind-legs and rests along the belly. The mummy resembles a sort of cylinder of bandages surmounted by the head, which is also wrapped and provides a crude silhouette of the animal's head. We have nicknamed these mummies "skittle mummies." They are often coated with resin and their bandages are treated with various materials. Two such mummies were found in a white limestone sarcophagus. Sometimes the body or just the head was covered by decorated cartonnage. Type 2: the mummy is more suggestive of the animal. The head, the limbs, and the tail are separately bandaged, giving the silhouette of a cat. The head is often decorated with painted details such as the eyes and nose. Sometimes ears and eyes made of cloth are also added on to provide additional life-like details.

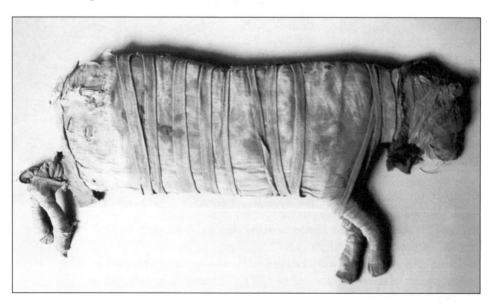

Fig. 5.6 Intact cat mummy with individually bandaged legs, discovered in the Eastern Tombs. Photograph by A. Lecler (IFAO)/MAFB. © Hypogée

Although the second type of mummy is well represented in the collections of the Louvre Museum, it does not appear in the collection of cat mummies in the British Museum studied by P.L. Armitage and J. Clutton-Brock. The Bubasteion series is, in this regard, heterogeneous, as among the mummies coming from the Eastern Tombs, of which the total is 93, 45 are of Type 2, while 48 are of Type 1. Among the mummies found outside the tombs, 53 out of 57 have their hind limbs bent (Type 1). These differences might indicate chronological differences, or reflect the existence of many different embalming ateliers.

Mummification

The style of mummification at the Bubasteion appears to be quite simple. There is no evidence of evisceration, for example. The bodies appear to simply have been desiccated, and internal organs have never been identified, as is often the case with human mummies, especially since radiographs only provide evidence for the skeleton. The state of the mummies has often been altered—the mummies have often been brutally damaged by ancient robbers. In this regard, the "skittle" cats enjoy a better fate due to the rigidity conferred by the resin and their compact shape. Often the mummies have been totally destroyed by the infiltration of water, as was the case with several cat mummies that were reduced to a mass of bones in the tomb of Maïa.

Very few mummies were decorated with elaborate bandaging, or appliqués such as those often found displayed in museums. However, some mummies were found in stone or wooden sarcophagi. One might hypothesize that these mummies were the animals viewed as the particular manifestation of the goddess Bastet herself, and thus given special, elaborate funerary equipment.

Cause of Death and Age at Death

During the course of the radiographic study, it rapidly became apparent that the cats were, for the most part, young, or sub-adults. Very frequently they showed signs of violent death in the form of cranial fracturing, most often in the occipital region, or in the dislocation of their cervical vertebrae, a sign consistent with strangulation. In only a certain number of cases were both a dislocation in the cervical vertebrae and a cranial fracture found. The blows to the head were sometimes so violent that the bones were literally dislocated.

It is difficult to determine the age of the animals solely from radiographic analysis. However, one can divide the 'subjects' into three categories: juveniles, identified by the visible separation of epiphysis; the sub-adults, whose epiphyses are in the process of fusing; and the adults with fully fused long bones. On the whole, only one cat out of three was an adult.

The cause of violent death was identified in two out of three cats. That, together with the age at death range of the cats leads us to the inescapable conclusion that the Egyptians raised cats that were specifically destined to end their lives as mummies to be sold to pilgrims. The number of 'fake' offerings would suggest an excessive demand and an insufficient supply of cats, rather than a desire for deliberate trickery on the part of the priests. However, a certain amount of trickery is apparent with certain cat mummies, for example, the mummy whose exterior dimension is 43 cm, while the cat itself really measures only 26 cm. Thus, one can consider these cat mummies as ex- votos, purchased by pilgrims and destined to be offered to the goddess Bastet (the same phenomenon is attested for other large groups of animal burials: ibises, falcons, etc.).

The Different Species of Cats

It is known that two species of cats flourished in ancient Egypt: wild cats, *Felis chaus*, and domestic cats, *Felis silvestris libyca*. It is very difficult to determine the species of mummified cats for two reasons. First, in an archaeological context, and out of respect for the object, the mummies cannot be unwrapped, and thus the bones cannot be carefully measured and studied. Second, it is very difficult to confidently identify the species of juvenile animals. One can only hypothesize that the very large specimens, that measure more than 60 cm, excluding the tail, are probably wild cats. However, the existence of vast quantities of cats fed in the precinct of the temple (before being ritually killed and eventually buried in dedicated catacombs) tends to prove that the majority of these cats were domestic animals, with the wild cats being an anomaly.

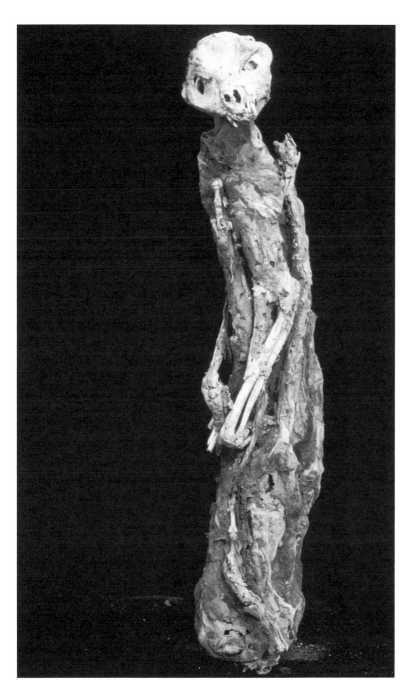

Fig. 5.7 Cat mummy (ref. 503), just as it was discovered during the excavation of the chapel of the tomb of 'Aper-El. Photograph by R. Lichtenberg/ MAFB. © Hypogées.

6

Tuna al-Gebel
Millions of Ibises and Other Animals

—— *Dieter Kessler and Abd el Halim Nur el-Din* ——

The Site of the Animal Cemetery (Tuna-South)

The modern village of Tuna al-Gebel is situated in Minya province, six kilometers to the west of the village of al-Ashmunein, the ancient town of Hermopolis (Magna) with its famous temple to Thoth, the moon god. The village gives its name to the western cemetery of Hermopolis, an archaeological zone of about seven kilometers in length that lies along the western desert edge, beginning one kilometer to the north of the village of Tuna al-Gebel and ending six kilometers south of the village in a broad desert valley. The name, Tuna al-Gebel, derives from an ancient toponym Thone, meaning 'the swamp.' It refers to a natural low-lying basin that was originally regularly filled with water by the inundation of the river-canal of the Bahr Yusuf. The depression of the Tuna basin, today dry, stretches more than six kilometers to the south.

During the New Kingdom the remote western desert edge was surely connected with the town of Hermopolis by a dam raised above the floodplain. A cemetery of New Kingdom date was founded one kilometer to the south of the village of Tuna. Objects dating to the reigns of Amenhotep III (1388–1351 B.C.) and Ramesses II (1279–1213 B.C.) have been later reused in the animal cemetery, indicating a royal temple, perhaps associated with a necropolis, located nearby in the surroundings of Tuna. After the New Kingdom, groups of human burials were dug behind and to the southwest of Tuna into the limestone cliff near the mouth of two small desert valleys.

A shift to a semiarid climate, resulting in higher Nile floods dramatically altered the floodplain after the New Kingdom. It seems that the lake of Tuna and its southern tip favored an intensified traffic with the administrative center, Hermopolis, probably by using the navigable river Bahr Yusuf. The improved agrarian base of the villages along the Bahr Yusuf caused more people to settle in the area of Tuna-South. The donkey track, wending its way through the desert valley of Tuna-South to the desert plateau, and leading further on to the oasis of Bahariya, must have been controlled by a military garrison.

The supposed early Saite settlement located at the mouth of the great desert valley of Tuna-South is yet to be found. The earliest extant archaeological structures known at the site until now do not lie on the surface, but underground, consisting of the vast subterranean world of the animal galleries of Tuna al-Gebel. These are the burial place of ibises, baboons, falcons, and other sacred animals, at the foot of the western limestone cliff immediately to the north of the desert wadi.

The Foundation of the First Egyptian Ibis Burial Place

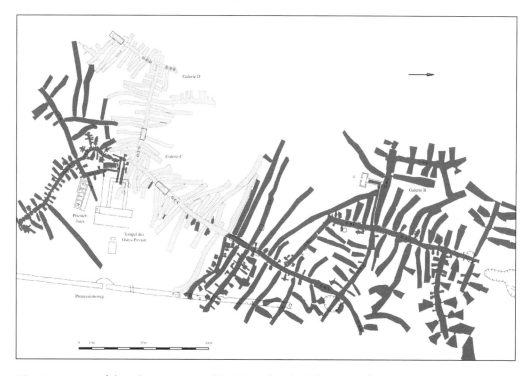

Fig. 6.1 A map of the subterranean world at Tuna al-Gebel. The pre-Ptolemaic parts of the galleries are indicated by lighter coloring. Courtesy of Dieter Kessler.

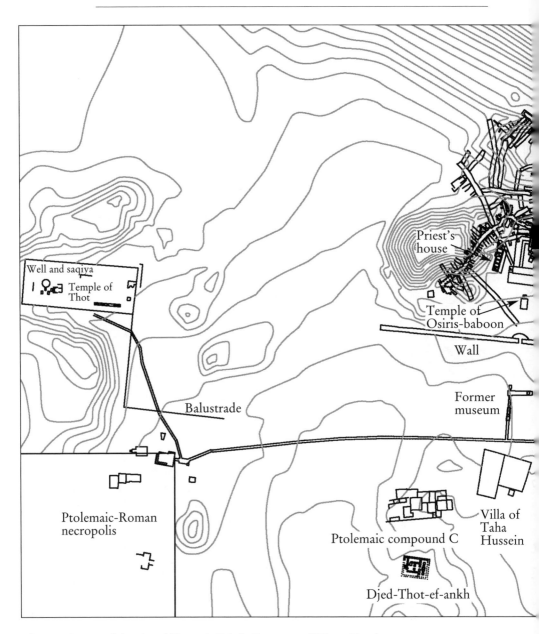

Fig. 6.2 A map of the site of Tuna al-Gebel. Courtesy of Dieter Kessler.

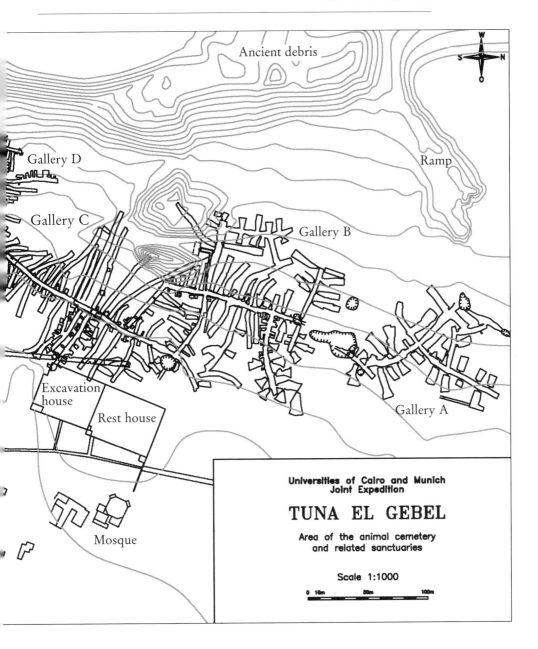

Ancient debris

Gallery D

Ramp

Gallery C

Gallery B

Excavation house

Gallery A

Rest house

Mosque

Universities of Cairo and Munich
Joint Expedition

TUNA EL GEBEL

Area of the animal cemetery
and related sanctuaries

Scale 1:1000

0   10m   50m   100m

About 450 B.C., when Egypt was under Persian rule, the Greek historian Herodotus traveled to Egypt. In the Lower Egyptian town of Bubastis talkative priests tried to explain to him the ideas behind the Egyptian sacred animals. It is doubtful that he understood the mysteries completely, but apparently he correctly reports those facts that he had heard. As he writes in his *Histories* (II, 67), the Egyptians brought all sacred ibises to the Upper Egyptian town of Hermopolis, i.e., to the animal necropolis of this town. It is possible that a second early ibiotapheion existed in the Lower Egyptian town of Hermopolis, known today as Tell Baqliya, which was the religious counterpart to Hermopolis Magna, although no firm evidence has yet emerged.

A long time before Herodotus's visit, probably *all* dead sacred ibises, and not only those that were used during prominent rituals in the Egyptian temple precincts, but also those kept together with other sacred birds at a special local breeding site, called the ibiotropheion by the Greeks, were brought to the burial place of ibises (Greek: ibiotapheion, in Egyptian: resting place of the ibis) at Tuna al-Gebel. Judging by clay seals found inside the animal galleries the decision for a central Egyptian ibiotapheion was made during the reigns of the pharaohs Psametik I (664–610 B.C.) and Amasis (570–526 B.C.). This was surely ordered by a royal decree, which also announced the death penalty for anybody killing, deliberately or accidentally, a sacred ibis or a sacred falcon (Herodotus II, 65). Furthermore, the group of protective gods in the shape of animals either standing as statues in the forecourts of the Egyptian temples or being carried during processions as sacred animal standards, were systematized, including probably new rules for their associated cult groups that were installed for their maintenance. The income from specials field endowments, called 'Fields-of-the-Ibis' was attributed to sustain the local institution of the ibiotropheion, and partly used for the feeding of the sacred animals, and partly for the group of priests and servants responsible for the animals' upkeep.

The early transfer of Egyptian sacred ibises to Tuna can be confirmed by objects excavated from the subterranean galleries: demotic papyri, found in jars, together with bundles containing bones of ibises and other sacred animals. Dating to the time of the Persian ruler Darius I (522–486 B.C.), these papyri record the transport of the special ibises from the Fayum region to Tuna al-Gebel with the help of certain cult servants (Zaghloul 1985), all probably belonging to the local religious organizations of 'The-Ibis.' A general was responsible for their safe transfer. In one case, a Greek called Ariston, presumably a military officer, is also mentioned.

The ibis and other animal figures that appear on standard poles were important sacred military insignia, accepted also by foreign troops, who participated in the local Egyptian temple ceremonies, but stayed in their own ethnic units. Sacred standards were kept in the guardianship of the military officers, perhaps used, for example, during the festivals for the reigning king who was also their military leader. According to the papyrilogical evidence, local ibis associations seem to have been under the control and leadership of a person, having the title of a general. In later times the title of the general was also formally transferred to the leader of every small local cult association of 'The-Ibis' and 'The-Falcon,' both often combined. Ptolemaic papyri even mention female generals (de Cenival 1972).

For the continuing habit of sending special deified mummified temple ibises, to Tuna al-Gebel after 305 B.C., there is abundant evidence in the form of demotic inscriptions (Thissen 1991). Usually one to three lines of text are found on special ibis sarcophagi made of wood, clay, or limestone. The mummies inside originate from places all over Egypt, not only from bigger towns like Aswan in the south, Ptolemais-Psois in Upper Egypt, Hermopolis or Heliopolis in the Delta, but also from smaller sites, many of which are still not identified.

The typical demotic inscription on such ibis sarcophagi or ibis jars runs, in a more extended version: Year X month Y day Z—the god of Thoth, whom NN has brought, son of NN, from the town A in the hand of the scribe NN, son of NN.

These Ptolemaic inscriptions first mention the person who brought the dead animal from his home institution, already mummified and deified, to the administrators of the temple precinct in Tuna-South. His titles are given in only a few cases, demonstrating that these messengers belonged to a special class of lower ranking cult servants. The receiving scribe must have been the scribe of the responsible organization of 'The-Ibis' in Tuna al-Gebel. Maybe the high status of such temple ibises and the financial transactions necessary for the payment of the expenses concerning their embalming and transportation led to their special treatment and exclusive burial inside the catacombs. Renewing the deification by again performing the 'Opening-of-the-Mouth' ritual, the single ibis mummy was carried down into the subterranean galleries, placed individually in a jar or a sarcophagus. The container was then deposited into a recess inside the walls of the catacombs, mostly along the main passageways. Once filled, the niche was blocked with mud brick. A few traces in the subterranean passages show that some of these brick walls were plastered and painted with a short demotic inscription in red ink that noted the delivery of the ibis.

The transfer of the special temple ibises to Tuna continues at least into late Ptolemaic times. Unfortunately the year dates on their containers frequently omit the name of the reigning Pharaoh. It can be observed that gradually, over time, the care taken over the ibis burials declined: sometimes two or three of these ibises were put into one single jar, which resulted in two or three short inscriptions appearing on its exterior.

The distant desert site chosen for the new ibiotapheion far to the south of the village of Tuna can only be explained by the presence of another, closer settlement, which may have been found now 700 m to the east, in the settlement debris of the Kom al-Loli (Hill of the Pearls) at the edge of the western desert. This flourishing settlement may have included the presence of soldiers and an adjoined royal sanctuary for their worship. We may also imagine that nearby, on the edge of the lake of Tuna, the town of Hermopolis maintained a colony of sacred ibises. These might have provided the sacred ritual animals for the temple precinct of Hermopolis, possibly already during the Third Intermediate Period. Perhaps a new necropolis sanctuary was initiated by the Pharaoh Amasis, the founder of other necropolis temples in the cemeteries like Saqqara, Tehna al-Gebel, and elsewhere. His new laws may have forced the local villagers to act as cult servants of the organization, and to participate in the hard labor of hewing out the subterranean rock catacombs. A plea of a female servant of the ibis organization to the god Thoth mentions a pre-Ptolemaic toponym "The-Place-of-the-Sand," but it is not sure if this is indeed the ancient name of this village at the desert edge. Another demotic plea from Persian times mentions the ibiotropheion including a "house for feeding the ibises," the female servant living in a village called 'The-Wall-of-the-General."

The Cultic Function of Deified Ibises
in the New Ibiotapheion

All species of animals that were buried as gods inside the animal ceme-teries, made divine by the act of the Opening-of-the-Mouth ceremony, were chosen for highly theological reasons. The listed Egyptian animal world, classified in categories, was part of the continuous renewal of all creation. A Late Egyptian papyrus describing different Egyptian snakes reveals that every kind of male and female animal, distinguish-able by a characteristic color, was schematically attributed to a certain god of the Great Ennead (Atum, Re, Horus, Osiris, Isis, Hathor, Seth/Apophis, etc.). The attribution implies, that the god could trans-form himself into the shape of the corresponding animal. Therefore animals inside an animal cemetery, even rats, worms, and pigs, were all those from the environment and landscape of the primeval hill, and all forms that were taken by the gods, who could use the special animal power (the ba-power) for their rebirth, their fight against the enemy on the primeval hill, and their transfer to heaven to the sun god. But it would be wrong to conclude from the listing that the animal forms were attributed to one special god only. When after the creation earth and heaven were separated, most animals were transferred to the heav-en as ba-forms of the solar god (Re, Amun-Re, Sobek-Re, etc., as visi-ble gods of the heaven), and only a few species like shrew, snakes, catfish, worms, etc., living in the darkness of the earth or the hidden waters, appeared as ba-forms of the hidden sun god Atum, who after sunrise greeted the distant sun god from the earth. The same transfer changed and divided the female animal group into forms of the god-desses, like Neith or Hathor. The animal forms visible as minor gods in the forecourt statues of the Egyptian sanctuaries became ba-forms of the solar god again at the time of the rising sun. The animal gods were never forms of local gods who resided inside the temple shrines, thus there exists no local ram form of Amun of Karnak or local ibis form of Thot of Hermopolis. For the cultic transformation of these minor gods into animal shape, special sacred animals were needed as their hosts/manifestations.

Certain living ibises, used during different ritual acts at the temples (see below), were selected out of a legally protected group of sacred ibises and other sacred birds, which were kept in a local animal colony

Fig. 6.3 View over the site of Tuna with the Nile Valley in the distance. Courtesy of Dieter Kessler.

near a body of water, and made more or less residential by additional feeding and care. Ibises and falcons as the most prominent birds of sacred rites in temple precincts had to be protected by prescriptions of the state. Selected according to their markings, the birds were used to announce the coronation of the king during the Egyptian coronation festivals by being released into the air. Single ibises and falcons were used in solemn temple processions in a specific role as a visible power of a god. During yearly repeated feasts like the moon festival of Thoth, the renewal festival of the king (his Sed-festival), the Osiris-festival in the month of Choiak or the following New Year festival in the Egyptian month of Tybi, the god in the form of the walking ibis on the standard-pole appeared together with other animal-gods belonging to the protecting lesser gods (dei minores) in front of a temple building. A group of living ibises, falcons, baboons, and others were shown on the days of the feasts on their window-of-appearance near the temple pylon. Other sacred animals, often chosen for their distinctive red coloring, were killed in offering rituals.

The ibis, as part of the animal group of the Egyptian feast of appearance, gradually became a major figure in the dominant cult center of the state at Hermopolis Magna, one of the main Egyptian festival towns. The mythical Hermopolis with its primeval hill was the place where the ibis-headed moon god Thoth transferred himself fully into the shape of an ibis. The famous temple of Thoth in the actual town of Hermopolis was the site of the reappearance and enthronement of the immortal Hermopolitan god in his forms as god of the sky and lord of Hermopolis, and of his juvenile forms (the gods of the city), and of the king during the New Year feast or the coronation ceremonies, performed and guarded again by the assembly of the Egyptian standard gods with their totemic animals (ibis, falcon, dog, baboon, and others), who accompanied the king's appearance since the First Dynasty. In the temple forecourt of Hermopolis stood the dominating animal statues of the ibis and the baboon, representing the visible Hermopolitan city gods Thoth-Ibis and Thoth-Baboon. The majority of the inhabitants of Hermopolis may have been members of their respective cult association. Both minor gods were never forms of the local god Thoth of Hermopolis, but offspring, i.e., active, Horus-like forms, in which the power of the sky god became visible, that of the reigning sky (moon) god Thoth, corresponding to the reigning king, who got, as a descendant of the sky god, the religious predicate of a "son of Thoth."

The permanent renewal of superior gods, minor gods, and Horus-king was a secret religious part of the king's feast and part of secret temple rites, the gods using the animal power for their transformations. The ibis and all the other animals, finally visible on standard-poles, were animals of the first creation of the world on the primeval hill, emerging out of chaos. They lived on the primeval hill, as part of the so-called Hermopolitan cosmogony. The primeval ibis eggs gave birth to the first couple of male and female ibises.

The ibises could be dangerous animals too. They slaughtered the enemy (Apophis) of the reigning primeval god, the sun god or another god of the creation, on the riverbanks of the mythical landscape. Later on—earth and heaven now separated—ibises and falcons were used to help the king to fly to heaven to the sun god. The king transformed himself into an ibis and a falcon to achieve the unification with the distant sun god. We also know the transformation of a king into a baboon since the First Dynasty (there is a baboon statue of King Narmer), and late prehistoric baboon burials were found in Hierakonpolis in Upper Egypt. Ibis and baboon probably came into the town of Hermopolis by being originally representative forms (standards and statues) of a kingly presence and protecting as residential gods the elite group of the king, who had to administer in Hermopolis the revenues of the province.

Religious secrets and public temple processions from the town to the necropolis temple and back combined the cults of Hermopolis Magna with that of the sanctuary on the western desert edge. The Great Temple of Tuna al-Gebel became the mysterious site of the primeval hill and of the renewed creation of the world, as well as the site of the appearance of the sky god Thoth-star (bull)-of-the-sky. The Osiris-sanctuary built over the animal cemetery in Tuna was the site of the reappearance of Osiris and the Osiris-gods in form of the deified animals during the Osiris-Sokar festival. The deified ibis, now inside the ibiotapheion below the temple, i.e., the god Osiris-ibis in its visible cult form of a resting ibis, was connected to the fate and resurrection of the god Osiris during the yearly processions, passing also the ibiotapheion and returning to the temple of the metropolis.

It must have been the mythical and theological importance of the sacred ibis as a temple animal in addition to the Egyptian animal-god visible in the shape of an ibis, which guaranteed through its cycle of birth, death, and reappearance the immortality of king and gods, and also the protecting role of the ibis figure in Egypt as an accompanying god for the reappearance of the king, which finally led to the decision to install a new central burial place for all sacred ibises in Egypt. The early ibis cemetery in Tuna is clearly not influenced and promoted by local worship and popular attitude. It may be that the local group of living temple baboons, belonging to the cult of the Hermopolitan city god Thoth-the-Baboon, had been buried in the early catacombs after their deification too. Perhaps they rest within the wooden chests of the Saite gallery D. But their burial was exclusive and known only to those with the title of "over the secrets."

The Great Necropolis Temple:
An Egyptian Hermaion and Greek Serapeum

To the south of the burial place of the ibises lies the cultic center of the necropolis, the Great Temple. Its scanty remains were excavated by Sami Gabra, head of the archaeological mission of Cairo University before and after the Second World War. Beside a short report, these excavations were never published. Only foundation blocks have been left. Some columns of the temple have been re-erected for tourists. Behind, further to the south, lie the remains of what might be the earliest well and *saqia* (oxen-powered water wheel) found in Egypt. The water from here supplied basins and a conchoid-rounded nymphaion. A stone trough, found on the ground, was interpreted by the excavator as a feeding place for sacred animals: either ibises or a sacred bull. However, the outer colonnades, the casemate-like southern wall, and the nymphaion have convinced us that this is not a genuine Egyptian temple, but the garden area of a Greek Serapeum, rebuilt and enlarged in Roman times, using older Ptolemaic foundations. Greek papyri of

Fig. 6.4 Entrance to gallery C with remains of the temple of Osiris-Baboon. In the foreground the priest's house.

the Hermopolite nome and an ostracon found in situ mention the existence of an already Ptolemaic "Serapeum of Hermopolis on the sand," with an adjacent Ptolemaic and Roman settlement known as "village of Serapeon" (Drew-Bear 1979: 233). This village, which we now may combine with the site of the Kom al-Loli to the east, flourished until the seventh century A.D.

The core of the Great Temple must have been a pre-Ptolemaic sanctuary with an open court, probably erected anew under Ptolemy I (304–284 B.C.). It was rebuilt in the Roman Period, maybe under the emperor Nerva (A.D. 96–98), as suggested by a single column inscription. The Egyptian temple was a sanctuary of the secret primeval hill, the place of the Ogdoad of Hermopolis and their spiritual ba-forms, where Thoth as creator god manifested himself, and where he appeared after his unification with Osiris as bull-of-the-sky, as a star god, visible during the night. The king's scribe and chief administrator of the whole necropolis area named Padikem ('whom-the-bull-has-given'), whose tomb lies to the east of that of the famous Petosiris, served as his prophet. Statues of ibises, baboons, and that of a bull probably stood in the temple's forecourt. The temple of Thoth was the equivalent of a Greek Hermaion. The Greeks combined their god Hermes only with the creator and oracular god Thoth, never with the local form of Thoth of Hermopolis. Smaller mud-brick chapels probably surrounded this temple.

After 305 B.C., Ptolemy I, following the ideas of parallel Greek and Egyptian main deities advocated by Alexander the Great, established the cult of the god Serapis in Egypt. Serapis was exclusively a god for the Greeks. Are we sure that no Egyptian would worship him? Yes, if he was not identical with the Egyptian god Osiris-Apis! He has to be seen parallel to the exclusive Egyptian oracle god Apis-Osiris in Saqqara and is essentially different from the Egyptian god Osiris-Apis (Greek: Osoroapis), represented in a statue in the shape of a reclining bull. By installing Serapis as a god of his dynasty, Ptolemaios linked the Greeks to the traditional festivals of the Egyptian state. As in Saqqara, Alexandria, and elsewhere, the Greek Serapis sanctuary was a state institution associated with an already existing central Egyptian sanctuary for the royal cult in the local necropolis, and its adjacent Osireion. Gradually the Greek architectural forms dominated the Egyptian, in Tuna changing the Egyptian temple of Thoth to a more or less Greek

Serapeum. This explains the growing attraction of the area near the Great Temple of Tuna for the burials of the area's Greek inhabitants, and also why the Egyptian administrator of the temple precinct in Hermopolis, Petosiris, living under Ptolemy I, chose a very obviously Greek style of decoration for the forecourt of his tomb-chapel.

Ptolemy I must have been actively involved in developing new rules for cultic activities and the liturgy in the necropolis areas for both ethnic groups, the Egyptians in Demotic, and the Greeks in Greek. Part of this new concept for unifying the two groups was an enormous building program that included in Tuna not only a completely new Hermaion-Serapeum, but also totally changed the structure of the old ibiotapheion. The burial place of the ibis was enlarged to make it accessible for cultic activities. A new Osiris temple was built in front of the new entrance to the galleries. Thus, in every Ptolemaic cemetery, the central cult temple of the state, the temple of Osiris and his family, and the animal cemetery nearby formed a cultic unit as part of common Greek and Egyptian festival processions from the metropolis to the necropolis and back.

The Temple of Osiris-Baboon and the Practice of Giving Oracles

The earliest entrance to the animal galleries in the Saite Period was too narrow to permit extensive subterranean development of the galleries. Between 310 and 305 B.C., Ptolemy I initiated a new access and expanded the galleries into different directions. It was now much more convenient to perform the daily cult duties downstairs in the new baboon chambers, and to convene there for the weekly oracle sessions. This entrance was integrated into a new temple building of the god Osiris-Baboon just above the ibiotapheion, clearly in cultic interdependence with the subterranean oracle gods and the new cult chambers for single deified Hermopolitan baboons. Between the temple and the main subterranean oracle room (C-C-2) there existed, parallel to the staircase, a connection formed by a rectangular hole in the rock. This favored the theologically important transition between upper-solar/light/day and lower-dark/night regions. The steps to the galleries lie exactly behind the temple, in the west–east orientation of the main axis. To the right of the entrance lay a small chamber, now often misidentified as an embalming chamber, which functioned in fact as a ceremonial room for the Opening-of-the-Mouth rites that were regularly performed. After the ceremony, the mummies were brought down into the catacombs by 'special carriers of the ibis.' The mummies were still dripping from the oils and unguents that had been quickly poured over them; these unguents still stain the stairway.

The new Osiris-Baboon temple was built on a rocky surface that had been leveled. The heavy limestone foundation blocks were laid against mud-brick walls, lining the inner sides of the rock of the foundation pit. The paved open inner space of the temple has no limestone foundation blocks but consists only of accumulated sand and limestone chips. The temple was initially examined by Sami Gabra, and more recently, between 1989 and 1994, by the Universities of Cairo and Munich. This work shows that the majority of the blocks from the building proper, above the foundation level, had been removed in antiquity.

The temple was completed before 305 B.C., and dated to the reign of the Macedonian king Alexander (IV), son of Alexander the Great and the Bactrian princess Roxane. Its ground plan consists of a broad (26 m), pylon-like entrance façade, the front part of which was open to the ceiling. It was later copied in the famous temple-like tomb-chapel of the Hermopolitan temple administrator, Petosiris. The inner part of the broad entrance hall is extremely narrow, leading to an inner open court, surrounded by symmetrically arranged, roofed chambers. The architectural plan follows the prescriptions for a so-called Egyptian *wabet*, a building for purification ceremonies that was open to the sky for secret rites with the decan stars and with the moon and sun god, and especially used in connection with the secrets of the resurrection of Osiris. We may assume that statues of the 'resting gods' Osiris-Baboon and Osiris-Ibis probably stood in the court on stone pedestals. The supposed six or eight main chambers were most probably used for the secret cults of the primeval and cosmic high gods like Osiris's family, Thoth, Re, Shepsi, and others. To the west of the paved forecourt in front of the temple façade stood an altar and a gate building. Only the foundation pit and some limestone blocks remain.

The *wabet* of the Osiris-Baboon was not a temple for individual worshippers of this god, but is comparable to the *wabet* of the god Osiris-Falcon known from a hieroglyphic statue text, which is combined with the animal (falcon) cemetery of Athribis in the Delta. The interior was accessible only for people privy to the secrets of the resurrection rites. The hypostyle hall in front of the *wabet* may have shown a representation of the king. The Athribis text mentions the presence of a royal wooden throne in this area. In Tuna the lintel inscription leading to the inner court gives the different names of Alexander IV, and contains the scene of the so-called Uniting-the-two-land *(sema-tawy)* rite.

Probably in later Ptolemaic times an annex was added to the temple, built into the foundation blocks at its southeast corner. Steps lead down to an antechamber with cultic installations of niches and offering tables. The narrow main room is dominated by a rectangular cage of about 1 x 1 m, and 2 m high. It is made of limestone blocks placed against the interior southern wall of the building. A small rectangular opening on its western side, 80 cm above ground, once lockable by a wooden bolt, suggests that this was the restricted living place of a selected sacred animal, perhaps a small sacred baboon, who might have been used in connection with the oracle service (Kessler and Nur el-Din 1999).

The priest responsible for the daily cult and the performance of the oracular readings every tenth day probably lived in the (now) heavily restored mud-brick building 6 m opposite the temple on its southern side. The priest's house was built in about 170 B.C. It consists of three separate complexes of rooms, each with a separate entrance that was fronted by a small raised porch. The priest and his family presumably were in charge of the temple building opposite. A niche, located in the west wall of the special shrine room (V) in the western part of the house, probably contained a movable cult image of Osiris-Baboon, housed in a wooden naos. A cult staircase had been built in front of the niche mirroring the cultic situation below the house. The upper floors, used for the living quarters, were accessed from a staircase located in Room IV, which also served as an antechamber to Room V. Finds of a scribe's writing palette and brick benches suggest that Room III, on the ground floor, was used as an administrative area for recordkeeping, and the reception of visitors. A chamber of the eastern wing (room I) was a kind of archive room. Fragments of a correspondence with an overseer of fields were found on its floor. Perhaps the famous Legal Code of Hermopolis, a demotic document, containing legal cases and mathematical texts on its reverse, was originally stored in this room. This papyrus was found by Gabra in a pottery jar, lying near this building. Priests needed scientific handbooks to solve legal matters posed by the oracle, questions which they took with them into the oracle chambers of the subterranean ibiotapheion to be answered by gods.

One of the compensations for a common Egyptian for his labor as a member of a religious organization was religious security. He was allowed to address the god of his institution by passing petitions to his oracle priest, probably in front of oracle statues of certain baboon- and ibis-gods. In the area of the temples of Hermopolis and Tuna the baboon-god Metasythmis (the Hearing-Ear), the ibis-god Thoth-of-the-palette and the ibis-god Teephibis ('the-face-of-the-ibis') are all well-attested. Living sacred animals belonged to the cult of oracle gods, their ritual use guaranteeing the permanence of the religious cycle of rebirth. At Tuna, the priest himself may have written down some of the questions addressed to the oracle, especially if delicate juridical matters touched on the personal interests of his superiors. He and his colleagues, who served as priests of the subterranean Osiris-Baboon-gods inside the galleries, took the petitions with them during the festivals that occurred every tenth day of the month. This process culminated in a personal meeting between the priest and the protective god, e.g., the god Thoth, who killed dangerous, evil creatures, which emerged in the darkness of the night and endangered the priest. Then—on the setting of the primeval hill—there was a personal meeting of the priest in the role as a servant subdued to his master, the judging god, who discussed and decided the petitions in the assembly of the gods, then gave his decisions. All this was an exclusive cult action of the priest, carried out in secluded chambers inside the galleries, and performed during the darkness and the dawn. Thoth's decisions and answers were given to the petitioners during the morning of the feast day. The assembly of the pastophors, perhaps in the scribe's office near the temple, would have discussed the content of the more delicate answers earlier.

Demotic oracle inscriptions written on small sheets of papyrus, linen strips, rounded pebbles, or on pottery vessels, found inside the galleries, prove that oracle petitions were given to priests by common Egyptians who had a personal relationship with the temple and its priesthood. There is no evidence at Tuna of common pilgrims from other distant towns coming to individually address the gods. A local villager would use the oracle by writing down personal matters (e.g., accusations against neighbors, relatives, or his superiors, which sometimes reveal a deep hatred and feeling of personal injustice, with a request that the great god (Thoth) bring about justice). These privately written pleas would be given to one of the lesser priests of his neighborhood, who served the subterranean gods, and it would be then taken downstairs to the more secret cultic oracular area for an answer. Official petitions on behalf of people of higher status, especially of those who participated in the important feast processions and legal decisions, had to be written on papyri, checked and sealed by the leaders of the ibis organization.

An earthquake damaged the temple and the priest's house in later Ptolemaic times, leaving both in need of repair. The unstable and weak rock formations of subterranean branches in gallery G–A collapsed. Holes to the underground region inside the house and near the temple had to be filled in with debris. A gap between the animal galleries and the priest's house on its northwestern corner had to be closed carefully with a limestone facing, thereafter allowing the direct communication between the priest and the subterranean area. The archaeological evidence shows that the house (and the temple) were still inhabited during the first half of the first century A.D. Later on, sand and rubble from the debris hill to the south and directly behind the house covered the building, luckily preserving its walls.

The Ibis Galleries, the Resting Place of the Ibis-god and Others

The official name for the subterranean ibiotapheion in Tuna may have been: "resting place of the ibis, the baboon, the falcon and the gods who rest with them." The animal cemetery was not only the depot for the deified sacred animals who were regarded as gods corresponding to Osiris, but was also, starting from the time of Ptolemy I, a place of numerous other religious activities. Unfortunately, the subterranean galleries have been robbed continuously for centuries. Objects from the catacombs are to be found in nearly every museum collection containing Aegyptiaca.

The regular excavations by Gabra and others (e.g., Ahmed Badawy, Zaki Aly) in parts of the galleries between 1933 and 1953 yielded thousands of objects, but these were never adequately published. Since 1989 the Egyptological sections of the Universities of Cairo and Munich have jointly tried to re-evaluate the earlier excavations, and to record and number the various passages, as well as to excavate in a few selected spots. Many parts of the galleries were surveyed for the first time; others are still not explored because of partly collapsed ceilings and side walls, which makes access sometimes dangerous or completely impossible. Not only time, but also the ancient quarry workers themselves are responsible for the ruinous state of these galleries. The workers honeycombed and thus destabilized the sidewalls of the galleries with large niches, thus rendering the walls extremely fragile. In addition to the man-made destabilization, the rock in which the galleries are carved is unstable. Thus, the workers had to find solutions to bypass the fragile rock formations and galleries that sometimes filled with sand intruding from the desert surface.

The ibis catacombs of Tuna form a fantastic subterranean region, four to five meters beneath the ground. Long main passages were hewn into the fossiliferous (and therefore fragile) limestone rock, the chambers illuminated only by the dim light of smoking oil lamps placed into small niches carved into the side walls. The galleries have, for the most part, a trapezoidal cross-section. They are 2.5 m in breadth, at the bottom, and between three and four meters in height. Sometimes they are enlarged into wide, high halls. Only a few areas are illuminated by daylight, either from natural recent breaks in the surface of the rock caused by earthquakes, or by ancient apertures, which once facilitated the transport of the debris to the surface when the galleries were being cut. The main passages that, in former times, were much more accessible than today, are now largely filled in with debris of fallen rock, collapsed walls, and heaps of pottery that have been smashed into pieces by robbers and visitors, intermingled with the dusty remains of torn bandages and disarticulated animal mummies. To the sides, going off the large main galleries, chambers of varying sizes are carved out of the rock. These were used for the internment of baboons and other larger animals. Other long passages, totally filled with pottery jars containing mummies of different species, also branch off from the main galleries. Once full, these were sealed with mud-brick walls. Only a very few intact passages have escaped human interference and promise rich scientific results in the future. Other intact strata are still hidden under thick layers of dust and debris.

Fig. 6.5 A gallery (B–A) littered with pots. Courtesy of Dieter Kessler.

The Development of the Early Ibiotapheion at Tuna

The ibiotapheion of Tuna al-Gebel offers the chance to evaluate and understand the evolution of an animal cemetery in Egypt over more than 700 years. The gallery of the early Saite Period had been cut into the fragile rock to the west, in the shadow of the steep limestone cliff that lies behind. The passage is oriented (and was filled with animal bundles in pottery jars) from north to south; its small entrance lies to the north. Two narrow mud-brick walls protect the entrance that was orientated to the west. The steps and the entrance building were formed of thick limestone slabs. A small staircase leads into the gallery. Air holes to the north of the entrance and in the south of the gallery allowed the transport of the subterranean debris to the surface. The ancient workers simply heaped up the debris on the desert surface behind the entrance. The sand transported by the heavy winds across the desert plain collected at the foot of the debris hill, soon covering the entrance. Even in antiquity, the access to these galleries had to be constantly kept free from sand.

Rock-cut side chambers, measuring about 10 to 20 m in length, flanked the main subterranean passage of the Saite Period. The wide mouthed jars dating from this period were closed with plastered linen, and contained linen bundles consisting of the bones of macerated ibises and other sacred animals. The jars were placed one upon the other, forming a high wall of pottery. In between and near to the walls of the side passages stood large wooden chests for the burials of anonymous sacred baboons, probably those of the sacred Hermopolitan baboon group.

Fig. 6.6 A view of a side branch of gallery C–D showing pre-Ptolemaic ibis pots and scattered wooden boxes that contained baboon burials. Courtesy of Dieter Kessler.

The side walls of the early part of the main passage were kept free of burial niches. Inside the jars originating from the side galleries, Gabra, who first excavated the area, discovered three wooden chests containing a quantity of bronzes, as well as jars containing papyri, faïence amulets, and other small objects. These jars were probably placed there by the people responsible for depositing the animal bundles that were delivered to Tuna and put in the locally produced pottery jars. Some jars contained sealed documents naming members of the king's administration. In the middle of the ibis jars lay the untouched burial of Ankhhor, a Hermopolitan high priest of Thoth. He was buried in a rock pit deepened in the rock of a side passage (G–D–D–10). After bringing in his heavy stone sarcophagus, the ceiling of the burial chamber was constructed using large limestone slabs.

In the Persian Period the number of ibis bundles brought from all over Egypt to Tuna al-Gebel necessitated an enlargement of the galleries to the east (Gallery part C–D). A beautifully decorated wooden ibis chest inscribed with the name of the Persian king Darius, and papyri of the same time, date this passage. Aramaic papyri found in a jar prove the presence of foreign merchants and mercenaries passing through Tuna and participating in the Egyptian feasts.

The bedrock of this area sloped gradually to the east. Therefore, in order to enlarge the galleries and to reach the deeper rock layers, a small staircase was constructed. At this point, where daylight enters from above, illuminating this spot, the Egyptians made reference to the Hermopolitan theology by placing two rows of eight rounded lime-stone coffins with ibis-headed lids.

The last indigenous dynasty (Dynasty 30) decided to follow the harder rock formations and continued the ibis burials by turning to the north (southern part of G–C–D and crossing gallery C–D and C–C). This alteration might have been made under Pharaoh Nectanebo II (360–342 B.C.), who seems to have initiated more local ibis breeding places (ibiotropheia) throughout Egypt. At first the baboons were still interred in side niches, then (C–C–10ff.) along the main passage. Unfortunately, this section lacks inscriptions. One of the few chronological hints is a painted pre-Ptolemaic inscription on a reused amphora from the Phoenician coast mentioning "oil, (belonging) to the king of Tyre" (from C–C–35).

Fig. 6.7 Gallery B–C showing the niches that were used for ibis burials. Courtesy of Dieter Kessler.

The Ptolemaic Galleries: New Baboon Gods
and En Masse Burials of Ibises

In the Ptolemaic Period, ibises were buried en masse in local necropoleis, rather than being transferred to major centers from all over Egypt. In fact, during this period, all the sacred species in any area were deified and buried locally. This reduced the transportation costs for local ibis organizations. Their task was instead limited to the transfer of very special ritual and festival animals, whose colorful wrappings became increasingly refined over time, to Tuna. The absence of inscriptions on pre-Ptolemaic Period jars found at Tuna, however, make it difficult to trace these changes precisely. From the reign of Ptolemy I (304–284 B.C.) the jars, still closed with plastered linen, begin to contain for the first time what can be described as real ibis mummies, i.e., actual corpses of birds. The birds had been left with their wings and feathers, and treated with a kind of turpentine oil and wrapped as a whole in linen bandages. Chemical analyses are underway.

During this time, the burial of all sacred ibises and falcons in Egypt was systematically reorganized. Ptolemy I seems to have established new rules, and to have forced villagers to work and to pay for the new cult associations. In the area of Hermopolis alone nearly a dozen ibis breeding places (ibiotropheia) are known. Each is an independent institution with associated fields, providing cereals for feeding the ibis colony, and for the maintenance of the gods in the form of animal statues. Although situated in the toparchy of the Upper City Area (Peri polin ano), the sacred territory of Tuna-South, known as "Hermopolis-the-protection," seems to have had some independence from the local nome administration in Hermopolis. It is commonly believed that the new mass burials of ibises and the increased installations of breeding places all over Egypt were due to the impact of pilgrims wanting to offer a personal ibis mummy on their own behalf. However, the Tuna galleries and their objects do not support this theory. The now standard single animal mummy, with feathers and wings preserved, seems to be the result of a simple change in embalming technique rather than in religious practice. The installations of new cult statues in the area may also have provided a certain economic advantage for the state treasury.

Ptolemy I created new posts for priestly families by introducing the cult of the special Osiris-Baboon gods. Every sacred baboon of

Hermopolis bore an individual name. Upon the death of the baboon, a priest was assigned to it within the subterranean baboon chamber, which contained a niche for its burial and daily worship. This priest was responsible not only for the baboon's daily worship, but also the weekly oracle praxis. The deceased god was served as Osiris-Baboon-NN-the-justified. The Ptolemaic administration sold numerous new oracle places, in Tuna and elsewhere, to Egyptian families with the simple intention of gaining money for the national treasury. In Thebes the costs for such a cult place at an ibiotapheion amounted to 210 Greek drachmae: the priest—his wife could be the priestess for subterranean goddesses for 70 drachmae—could divide and sell these cult positions again for profit (*UPZ* II, 153–155).

Hieroglyphic inscriptions on the inner side of the wooden lids of the pre-Ptolemaic baboon chests contain excerpts from religious spells taken from the more than two-thousand-year-old Pyramid Texts. Most common is especially the spell of the sky goddess Nut who protected the god Osiris-Baboon. Individual names of baboons begin to appear regularly only from the time of Ptolemy I onward (in galleries C and B). They are included in hieroglyphic formulae, describing the nocturnal and diurnal travels of the new god in the sky boat as companions of the sun god Ra. These inscriptions are written on limestone slabs that once covered the burial places of the baboons. As one might expect, the names are religious ones, 'Thoth-has-come,' 'Thoth-is-found,' 'Thoth-his-flesh-may-live,' 'Thoth-has-given-him,' 'It-says-the-face-of-the-enduring-one,' etc., and are often shared by humans who are in the service of these gods. Only in one case is the name of the mother animal reported. The painted slabs show different forms of festival kiosks, scenes of the adoring king or a priest, or ibises and baboons squatting. The expenses for the early cult places in front of the subterranean places for the baboons must have been high. The floors of the rectangular rock chambers were carefully paved with limestone blocks, the lower zone of the walls often decorated with relief blocks, the upper zone painted, and both areas embellished with ritual scenes. The gods in the ritual scenes are primarily the family of Osiris, different forms of the moon god Thoth, and the deified individual Osiris-Baboon. References to rare divine forms, like the moon god Shepsi or Osiris, lord of the Osireion of the Hermopolitan necropolis, also appear. The ceilings show the goddess Nut swallowing the sun, or astronomical scenes of the northern and southern sky, the star constellations with their accompanying gods, the decan star list and their representations, as well as pictures of planets.

Priestly activity for the single baboon-gods was focused on the burial niches. In the early Ptolemaic Period, each niche was fronted by a staircase made of stone slabs, flanked by a pair of conical stone columns that acted as bases for flat bronze offering plates for burnt offerings. Between them lay a limestone offering-table for libations that were poured out of a bronze situla. Behind a limestone slab, the mummy of the baboon rested in a wooden coffin placed in a limestone sarcophagus. The wooden frame was decorated with blue inlaid faïence pieces and inlaid hieroglyphic characters. Faïence amulets, all in connection with the resurrection of the mummy god (scarabs, figures of Nut, Djed pillars, falcons, life signs, faïence beads, etc.) were inserted between the bandages of the mummy. The burial place of a baboon in Gallery C–C–4 yielded thirteen faïence figures of the birth god Bes in two different sizes, probably arranged in front of the limestone sarcophagus. Linen cloth, painted with designs similar to those found on the slabs, marked some of the baboon burials.

The long main baboon chamber near the entrance below the temple (C–C–2), an integral part of the new temple plan, served not only as cult place for two baboons, but also as a central assembly and oracle room in connection with the temple cult above. An altar-like construction in the midst of the room, and fragments of granite statues of a walking ibis and of a baboon, point to the religious transformations from Osiris-Baboon to the reborn god Thoth-Baboon, the city god of Hermopolis. Wine was an important part of the cultic ritual, as attested by the discovery of Greek wine lists and large Greek wine amphora. One ostracon shows a Greek alphabet. Stone seats for the assembly of priests were found in Gallery C–C; no doubt, the priests gathered here also to drink.

Different decorated baboon chambers (C–A–28 and C–A–31) dating to the reign of Ptolemy I are to be found in a large area of gallery C, to the south of the new Ptolemaic entrance in between the passage of the Thirtieth Dynasty (chamber C–C–34). From the beginning, the new gallery was generously proportioned. Smaller side passages in between contained either rows of the special delivered ibises in wall niches or were completely filled with ibis jars. The trapezoid small entrance was then sealed with mud bricks, and its outer face sometimes painted. The finds of bronze offering plates inside some chambers with small side niches for ibis sarcophagi makes it evident that all the mummy-gods of Osiris-ibis brought from distant Egyptian sites and placed in the chambers of the side passages, participated in the cult at least once a year, when priests entered the room carrying bronze offering stands.

During the reign of Ptolemy I, the production of ibis jars suddenly changed. The broad jars closed by plastered linen were replaced by smaller jars with a narrower body and shoulder. Their smaller openings were closed by a pottery lid, fixed with plaster. Another type of pottery container had a rounded or flat bottom. It contained only one or two mummies. Its lid was cut out of the body of the vessel during production, using a wire, then refixed with plaster.

Fig. 6.8 King Ptolemy I offers to Osiris-Ibis and other gods of the Osiris family. Courtesy of Dieter Kessler.

In the southern part of Gallery C, some baboon chambers dating to Ptolemy II's reign (284–246 B.C.) were built in between the older ones. The most important, a large chamber of a baboon named Thothefankh (C–B–2), was carved into the bedrock next to the entrance staircase. In front of the baboon chambers the floor of the main passage was carefully laid with stones, the ceiling decorated with stars, and the sidewalls with colored bands.

Far to the north, the ceiling of the main passage must have collapsed in the early Ptolemaic Period. The most northern parts of the galleries could be reached only through a new complicated bypass. Therefore the Hermopolitan administration of Ptolemy II decided to build a new entrance to the galleries to the north of the earlier one. A four-cornered altar for burnt offerings stood in front of a roofed, but undecorated limestone building. A broad staircase, going first to the north, then changing its direction to the east, was constructed. It led into a new subterranean area (Gallery B). The entry is marked by the huge piles of debris that were deposited as a result of the excavations that created the underground galleries. As usual, the access was soon covered by aeolian sand.

The entrance to Gallery B was built some 50 m away from the old main axis, and developed in two main directions: two branches went south to meet the former main axis of Gallery C, while another passage, beginning at the foot of the staircase, ran straight to the north. Opposite the staircase is a small rectangular rock chamber. An isolated rectangular niche, suitable for an ibis sarcophagus, was cut into the rear wall. The painted decoration of the side walls indicate the cult of the god Osiris-Teephibis-the justified, the name meaning "The Osiris, It says the face of the ibis." The image depicts an ibis sitting on a pedestal, with the feather of the goddess Maat in front, adored by Pharaoh Ptolemy II. The ibis burial niche at the back implies that a single living sacred ibis was kept and revered in addition to the statue of the already established oracle god Teephibis.

The northernmost parts of gallery B are dated to the later Ptolemaic Period. At this time the larger rock chambers for baboons become rarer. Instead, the earlier Ptolemaic chambers were reused for new baboon burials. In chamber G–C–C–34, dated to the Ptolemaic Period, the painted relief scenes and the ceiling of Ptolemy I were painted over, and the cartouches of the pharaoh left blank. In G–C–B–6 the once accessible passage, to be dated into the time of Ptolemy II, was refilled with heaps of pottery jars, and the former cult in front of the baboon burials deserted. Priests continued to celebrate the cult in some of the older baboon chambers, but apparently the installation of cult areas for new baboons decreased and finally stopped. Sacred baboons were once again interred in simple wooden baboon chests. The number of ibis mummies originating from the ibiotropheia must have been still high, but signs of careless treatment of the mummies are noticeable. The limestone sarcophagi all but disappear. Single mummies are buried now in layers of resin in cheaper wooden cases, nearly all of which bear a demotic inscription similar to those found on the limestone sarcophagi. An untouched section in the northern part of gallery B still yielded the special wooden ibis coffins for a deified animal. However, these were placed on the top of the heaps of the pottery jars, filled with the common ibises. A few of these wooden coffins are wonderfully painted, showing different forms of the god Osiris-Ibis as a mummy or a crouching ibis, the inscriptions for the same ibis form changing from Osiris-Ibis to Thoth. Special larger ibis mummies, 60 to 80 cm long, wrapped in multicolored bandages, with a gilded wooden beak or wooden crowns, were also found on top of the piles of pots. These special mummies might originate from one of the more prominent feasts like that of the moon god. The large amphorae containing ibis eggs changed their form, and become smaller, usually with a ridged body and a narrow mouth.

The northern part of Gallery B was extended into geologically unstable rock layers. Large parts may have been collapsed already in ancient times, maybe due to the same earthquake, which led to the destruction of many sections of the early Ptolemaic Gallery C–A. This may also be the reason why in later Ptolemaic times another entrance far to the north had to be built (Gallery A). Only the staircase to the ground is left today. The latest Gallery A, nearly totally cleared by Gabra, is partly unfinished. Broad and high halls without burials were prepared for further use. To judge from Roman oil lamps and the pottery, especially the amphora types, the last phase of ibis burials here belongs to the earlier Roman Period. Unfortunately datable inscriptions are unavailable.

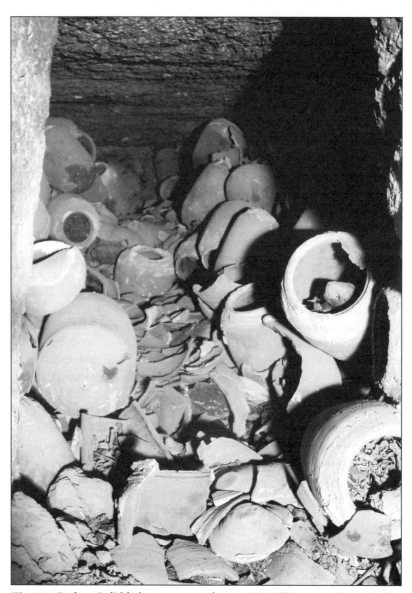

Fig. 6.9 Ptolemaic lidded pottery vessels containing ibis mummies.
Courtesy of Dieter Kessler.

The End of the Ibiotapheion at Tuna

From the Great Temple to the north, passing in front of the temple of
Osiris-Baboon, stretches a mud-brick track in the direction of Gallery
A. It is 261.5 m long and 3.6 m wide and, due to wind erosion, is today
between one and fourteen layers of bricks high. Judging from its orientation, it must have been built after the entrance of gallery A. It was
first seen as a gigantic wall, showing the typical undulating mud-brick
construction, which hid the western Osiris regions that lay behind. It
was later also used as a raised mud-brick way, used by groups of priests
to reach the sacred way (dromos) of the Osiris-Baboon temple and the
northern galleries. The track starts at the foot of the southern end of the
debris hill, to the south of the Osiris-baboon temple. On flat ground
no traces of bricks remain. Thus the priests, acting as pastophors, and
mounting the raised track, did not have to walk through the deeply
sanded areas at the foot of the debris hills. Limestone chips directly in
front of the temple of Osiris-Baboon, to the west of the mud-brick passage, indicate a former paved floor. The mud-brick passage wall
remained unfinished like gallery A.

The sudden cessation of ibis burials originating from the local
ibiotropheia, and that of other sacred animals, probably including
those sent from other parts of Egypt, is not intelligible without sup-
posing a firm decision of the Roman administration to stop the
financial and personal support of the extended animal cult. This does
not mean that the cult of the Ptolemaic baboon gods ceased entirely,
although currently we have only a rough idea about when the practice
ceased. Greek graffiti on the walls of the baboon chamber decorated in
Gallery A (A–31) do not date beyond the first half of the first century
A.D. Maybe the delivery of animals to the ibiotapheion was stopped
much earlier than the cult of the Osiris-Baboon temple and its oracular
practice. Furthermore, the nearby priest's house contains no pottery
belonging definitely to the second century A.D., thus supporting the
idea that the cultic activity at the Osiris-baboon temple ended at about
this time. Christian tomb inscriptions of the fifth/sixth centuries A.D.,
found inside the galleries and perhaps originating from tombs above,
are the latest ancient traces known until the time of the modern travelers and robbers who entered and plundered the site continuously
from the seventeenth century A.D. until today. The whole desert area

to the east of the temple was afterwards used extensively as a human burial ground in Late Roman times.

Recent excavations (2002–2003) to the east of the animal cemetery revealed huge mud-brick buildings of Ptolemaic times. These are situated along a desert track leading for 700 m from the settlement area at the desert edge to the Osiris-baboon temple in the west. The compound C to the south of the Taha Hussein house had numerous administrative rooms, rows of vaulted granaries, ovens in open courtyards, and rows of small chambers filled with special large storage jars, painted around their shoulders with a floral design. To the north lay a cult room with a limestone staircase, probably erected in front of a wooden naos, as is known already from the baboon burials inside the galleries and from room V of the priest's house. It was followed to the north by an assembly room, used for drinking and gambling, as revealed by the find of numerous game stones, dices, and drinking cups. All buildings seem to have been chronologically closely connected with the installation of numerous new cult places for priests in and outside the galleries during the reigns of Ptolemy I and II. They would have provided residences for the families of the new cult personal. Even here, the administrative buildings seem to have been temporarily out of function at the beginning of the Roman Period. The rooms of compound C were reused for some time as a production center at least during the second century A.D.

Common People and Insiders, or Who Entered the Ibis Galleries?

Texts found inside the galleries mention generals, administrators, scribes, and other priestly persons, all of whom had the right to enter the galleries on the occasion of the processions from Hermopolis to the necropolis. The second group of people who had access to the sacred subterranean spaces consisted of the cult servants responsible for the administrative organization: cult priests, who brought in personal objects and petitions given to them by villagers; and the 'bearers' of animal mummies. All these people also participated in the cyclic renewal ceremonies, a process performed during the feast days. Thoth as a High God gave life to his juvenile son gods. His manifestation was in the shape of a protective ibis-god, such as was found at every Egyptian temple site. The social stratum of people who could enter the galleries is recognizable by typical inscriptions on votive bronzes dedicated here (Naguib 1943):

1. Bronze from the Saite gallery D–2: Thoth, twice-great, lord of Hermopolis, he may give life, prosperity and sanity and the lifetime of Ra and a high and beautiful age for the general Petosiris, son of the general Nakht-ef, born of the lady of the house (. . .).

2. Bronze showing the walking ibis in front of the goddess Maat, from the Saite gallery (numbered by Gabra 1134): Words spoken by Thoth, the very great, lord of Hermopolis, lord of the words of god, first of the House-of-the-Net, being over all Pat (?) and Rechit. May he give life, prosperity, and sanity, a high lifetime and a high and beautiful age to the Prophet of Horus-Re (?) lord of the Dju-ef region Iset-juf-ankh, son of the Great Leader of the Ma Takelothis.

3. Bronze from an unknown Saite gallery (numbered 1104): Thoth, twice great, lord of Hermopolis, given life (to the) servant of Thoth Amenirdis, son of Peftjau-khent-Neith.

The diversity of the pre-Ptolemaic bronze groups is impressive compared to the more uniform shape of the Osiris- and ibis bronzes found in Ptolemaic times. One early wooden chest contained 123 bronzes. Photos of Gabra show that most bronzes originating from the earlier branches of the subterranean galleries were wrapped in linen, comparable to the common ritual of covering statues with linen in the days of the Osiris feast. Outnumbering all others, are bronzes of the god Osiris (in a standing and sitting position, fixed on a wooden base, sometimes inscribed in demotic). These were followed by images of Isis and Harpokrates in all sizes, and then, finally, figures of the ibis in two forms: as a squatting and walking animal, representing forms of the gods Osiris-Ibis and Thoth and their transformations. Images of other divinities that participated in the major festivals were also recovered from the galleries: Ptah, Maat, Amun, Sekhmet-Bastet, Hathor, Khnum, Bes, The Horus-Falcon, as well as bronze and clay figures of animals, such as baboons, dogs, cats, bulls, and rams. Other finds include a bronze aegis plate, the Menat counterweight, and different staves, some surmounted by animal figures. Sometimes the bronzes form complex theological groups of Egyptian gods. Statues and statuettes of private persons (men and women), can be attributed to the group of acting and adoring priests.

Bronzes found inside pottery jars were certainly dedicated by local people who placed the animal bundles into the locally produced pottery jars. Bronze deposits from people who participated in the feast days above ground have yet to be discovered. The scarcity of bronze finds above ground are a clear indication that visits to the Osiris-Baboon sanctuary were transitory; the temple must have been the aim of religious activities mainly during the great processions.

Animals Buried in the Ibiotapheion of Tuna al-Gebel

Every Egyptian animal cemetery contains a variety of different animal species. The following list of sacred animals represents the results of the survey of mummies or animal bundles from the Tuna catacombs carried out between 1983 and 2002. Further excavations of certain selected spots will definitely add new species to the list. The identification of the animals is mostly due to the continuing research of the Institute for Palaeoanatomy, Animal Domestication and History of Veterinary Medicine at the University of Munich (J. Boessneck (+), A. von den Driesch, J. Peters).

Mammalia Mammals

Wild Mammals

Crocidura olivieri	Greater Musk Shrew
Papio hamadryas	Hamadryas Baboon
Papio cynocephalus anubis	Olive Baboon
Cercopithecus aethiops	Green Monkey, Grivet
Erythrocebus patas	Red Guenon
Macaca sylvanus	Barbary Ape
Herpestes ichneumon	Egyptian Mongoose
Sus scrofa	Wild Boar
Gazella dorcas	Dorcas Gazelle
Arvicanthis niloticus	African Grass Rat

Domestic mammals

Canis lupus f. familiaris	Dog
Felis silvestris f. catus	Cat
Sus scrofa f. domestica	Pig
Ovis orientalis f. aries	Sheep
Capra aegagrus f. hircus	Goat
Bos primigenius f. taurus	Cattle

Aves Birds

Wild birds

Pelecanus onocrotalus	White Pelican
Podiceps cristatus	Great Crested Grebe
Phalacrocorax africanus	Shag
Anhinga melanogaster	Darter
Phalacrocorax carbo	Common Cormorant
Casmerodius albus/Ardea cinerea	Great White Egret/Grey Heron
Egretta garzetta	Little Egret
Bubulcus ibis	Cattle Egret
Nycticorax nycticorax	Night Heron
Platalea leucorodia	Spoonbill
Plegadis falcinellus	Glossy Ibis
Threskiornis aethiopicus	Sacred Ibis
Ciconia ciconia	White Stork
Anastomus lamelligerus	African Open-bill Stork
Anas clypeata	Northern Shoveler
Haliaeetus albicilla	White-tailed Eagle
Milvus migrans migrans	Black Kite
Milvus migrans aegyptius	Black Kite
Elanus caeruleus	Black-winged Kite
Circaetus gallicus	European Snake Eagle
Accipiter nisus	Sparrowhawk
Accipiter brevipes	Levant Sparrowhawk
Micronisus gabar	Gabar Goshawk
Accipiter gentilis	Goshawk
Buteo buteo rufinus	Buzzard
Buteo lagopus	Rough-legged Buzzard

Buteo rufinus rufinus	Long-legged Buzzard
Buteo rufinus cirtensis	Long-legged Buzzard
Aquila heliaca	Imperial Eagle
Aquila pomarina	Lesser-Spotted Eagle
Torgos tracheliotus	Lapped-faced Vulture
Gyps fulvus	Griffon Vulture
Neophron percnopterus	Egyptian Vulture
Circus aeruginosus	Marsh Harrier
Circus macrourus	Pallid Harrier
Circus pygargos	Montagu's Harrier
Falco cherruq	Saker Falcon
Falco biarmicus	Lanner Falcon
Falco peregrinus peregrinoides	Peregrine Falcon
Falco subbuteo	Hobby
Falco naumanni	Lesser Kestrel
Falco tinnunculus	Kestrel
Fulica atra	Coot
Gallinula chloropus	Common Moorhen
Grus grus	Common Crane
Hoplopterus spinosus	Spur-winged Plover
Pterocles sp.	Sandgrouse
Tyto alba	Barn Owl
Bubo bubo ascalaphus	Eagle Owl
Asio flammeus	Short-eared Owl
Athene noctua	Little Owl
Caprimulgus europaeus	Nightjar
Caprimulgus aegyptius	Egyptian Nightjar
Coracias garrulus	European Roller
Upupa epops	Hoopoe
Galerida cristata	Crested Lark
Motacilla alba	White Wagtail
Corvus corone sardonius	Carrion Crow

Domestic birds

| *Anser anser f. domestica* | Domestic goose |

Pl. 5.1   Cat's head
(part of coffin?)
in stuccoed wood.
Photograph by
P. Chapuis/MAFB.
© Hypogées.

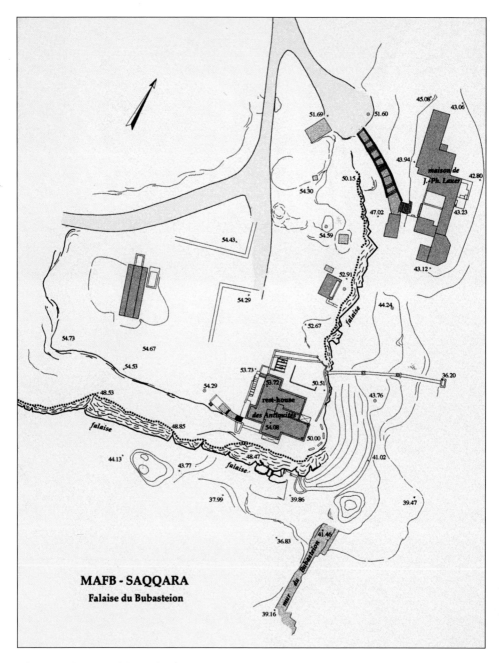

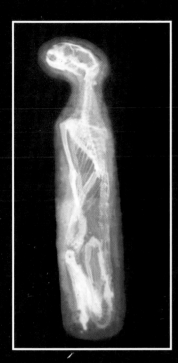

Pl. 5.3 Intact cat mummy (ref. 501)
found in its limestone sarcophagus
during the excavation of the chapel of
the timb of 'Aper-El, and an X-ray
showing the cat in the typical position
of cat mummies, on its haunches.
Photograph by R. Lichtenberg/MAFB
© Hypogées.

Pl. 5.4 Limestone sarcophagus containing a cat mummy, discovered in the chapel of Maïa's tomb. Photograph by P. Chapuis/MAFB. © Hypogées.

Pl. 5.5 Table showing the causes of death in cats according to age. Photograph by R. Lichtenberg/MAFB. © Hypogées.

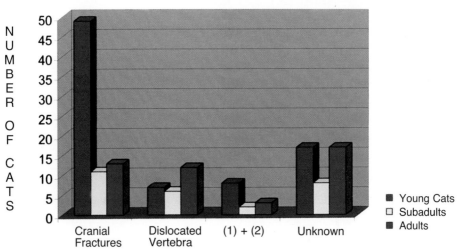

Cats: Natural Causes of Death and Age Relationships

Reptilia **Reptiles**
Crocodilus niloticus   Nile Crocodile
Naja haje   Egyptian Cobra
Malpolon sp.   Snake
Gen. et sp. indet.   Lizard

Pisces **Fish**
Mugil sp.   Mullet
Mormyridae   Mormyrid spec.
Clarias sp.   Catfish
Bagrus spec.   Bagrus spec.
Synodontis schall   Gray catfish
Lates niloticus   Nile Perch
Barbus bynni   Barb
Tedraodon fahaka   Nile puffer

It appears that all mummies of sacred animals and even all parts and remains of sacred animals found inside the bundles and mummies of the ibiotapheion, were ritually made into gods. The buried animals consist of two groups. One are the selected sacred animals who were ritually needed for processions and offerings, acting in the role of a god, even those who often got killed cruelly, strangled, burnt, martyred, and decapitated. However, after they had served their purpose, their body or what was left of it, was deified and carried to their final resting place as gods. They were always distinct from the second group of their sacred companion by their coloration and marking, who lived and died near or within the sacred feeding enclosures. The distinction may be reflected in how they were wrapped, and in the choice of a more solid and expensive burial container.

The vast majority—hundreds of thousands, if not millions—of animals buried at Tuna were ibises. It is difficult to give exact numbers because the pre-Ptolemaic bundles sent from all over Egypt to Tuna mainly contain parts of ibises and other birds, rather than single intact creatures. Considering the time factor, the Ptolemaic era probably yielded a reasonable number of sometimes more or less one thousand annual mummies from each of the numerous Hermopolitan breeding places. So we may assume that altogether about fifteen thousand ibis mummies a year were brought to the galleries from ten to fifteen local ibiotropheia. Many Ptolemaic mummies are also often made of parts of sacred ibises: of single bones, feathers, or simply of dried grass from a bird's nest. Many scholars explain these away as deliberate fakes, provided by priests to gullible pilgrims, or alternatively suggest that these were made when there was a supply problem to fulfill a heavy demand for 'medium' gods. On the contrary, these dummy mummies are evidence for the careful collection of all animal remains, even fragments, from the site of the sacred local ibis colonies. Some of the mummies in the shape of a falcon may contain bones of falcons or not, demonstrating also the close institutional and religious connection between the ibis and falcon organization. It is not surprising to find ibis bones within baboon mummies.

A Ptolemaic ibis jar normally contains three to four large ibis mummies. Pre-Ptolemaic–Period jars are sometimes filled with a varying but higher number of bundles. Several smaller bundles are wrapped together within an outer bundle and fixed with different kinds of string. Many of these bundles contain feathers, reeds, grass, or parts of wings only. It appears, that in many instances, birds were interred to macerate the flesh and to skeletonize it. When mummy bundles were prepared, the embalmers felt no need to collect and wrap a whole bird again, or to add the feathers to the bones; they simply dug out what remained of the skeletonized bones of a bird, and mixed them with single bones belonging to other sacred animals from the local breeding place. Then they formed a bigger bundle to send to Tuna. The combination of animal parts inside a bundle varies from one sample to the other. For example, we discovered the complete skeleton of a fish, together with two isolated ibis heads, all glued together. Another bundle contained parts of three cats, small parts of fishes, a bone of the glossy ibis, the skull of an ichneumon, and birds of prey. A human rib in between animal remains may be due to the proximity of a human embalmer's workshop to that of the animal embalmers.

From the inception of the tradition of depositing animals inside an ibiotapheion, all remains of sacred animals kept around the local ibis breeding area that was connected to a temple institution were collected and sent to Tuna regardless of their species. The combinations of parts

Fig. 6.10 A gallery (B–E) showing niches for ibis burials and emptied pots thrown into the main passage. Courtesy of Dieter Kessler.

of cats, fishes, birds, snakes, crocodiles, mongooses, shrews, pigs, etc., continue until Ptolemaic times. However, starting in Persian times the embalming technique changes. From this period onward, a kind of turpentine was spread over the bones in order to shorten the process of maceration. No doubt the sweet smell of the liquid hid the terrible smell of rotting flesh. Due to the intensive use of turpentine and/or bitumen, an oxidation process started which burned the bones from inside, leaving sometimes jars filled with the crumbling dust of the bundles. Through cultic reorganization in Ptolemaic times, certain groups like the institutions of 'Cats and Dogs,' supported by new lands given to them, seem to have acted locally in an increasingly independent manner. Finally, at the end of the reign of Ptolemy I, again through the support of the state that guaranteed the costly regular delivery of turpentine and linen, the complete ibis mummy appears totally immersed in turpentine or bitumen. Unfortunately, in most cases these mummies

Fig. 6.11 An early Ptolemaic baboon chapel (C–C–34) reused and decorated with ritual scenes by a later Ptolemaic king. Courtesy of Dieter Kessler.

were totally burnt and then wrapped. Mummies that are apparently well wrapped, at least externally, might have been used during special feast ceremonies for an unknown purpose. Occasionally, some of the earlier Ptolemaic wrapped mummies are adorned with painted appliqués, representing Thoth on a throne, the fetish of Abydos, and even a figure of Ptah.

From the Saite Period onward, eggs from ibises and other sacred birds (falcons, pelicans) were collected at Egypt's breeding places and sent to Tuna together with the wrapped bundles. The fertility of the egg was apparently irrelevant to the egg collectors. Sometimes eggs were kept in lesser numbers in small wooden chests and baskets, but in most cases the eggs are intermingled with animal bundles inside the typical large jars. In the Ptolemaic Period ibis eggs were sometimes kept in large Greek wine amphorae. A smaller early Roman amphora contained more than sixty ibis eggs. Perhaps the amphora had been filled with water to stop the eggs from cracking. Single eggs were sometimes embedded in a clay mantle. We have no proof that the eggs came from an artificial breeding apparatus as it is sometimes claimed by some scholars (Meeks 1997: 134). It seems sufficient to assume that cult servants of the ibis organization collected many deserted ibis eggs directly near the lake of the breeding place. The ibis egg itself, like other eggs, had a certain cosmogonical significance.

Many ibis bundles contain the remains of the glossy ibis, which has a red or brownish shining plummage. It may be that this red color had a certain negative connotation, corresponding to that of other red animals, which were often used for offerings (due to their identification with the god Seth). Falcon-shaped mummies often contain different kinds of falcons, or fragments thereof, sometimes mixed with portions of ibises. Until now the origin of these falcons is unknown. Maybe they were caught and then kept in special cages? Herons, belonging to the animals of the sacred lake area, were deposited in the galleries prior to the Ptolemaic Period. Instead of ibises, single herons were found in a series of about twelve small jars, each with a special rectangular opening. All these were inscribed with the same demotic inscription of a certain Thothirdis, son of Harsiese, apparently the scribe responsible for the ibis organization at Tuna. It may be that the heron had been an animal somehow connected to the extinct ibis comata and the Phoenixbird. Vultures, kept in special pottery containers, together with other birds of prey were deposited in groups, but there is still no exact archaeological evidence for their original position in the galleries.

Surprisingly, in some parts of the Ptolemaic branches of the galleries, a certain percentage of the ibis jars did not contain the usual blackened ibis mummies, but rather a mixture of body parts of various animals, birds, shrews, etc., including a few human bones. One jar contained more than seven thousand single bones wrapped into a linen cloth. Ninety percent of these belonged to ibises, while the other isolated bones came from other birds, shrews, and other smaller animals. The swallow and the nightjar were found among them. These birds were diurnal, and, like the group of owls, they apparently belonged to their own theologically well-defined animal group.

Baboons were interred in Tuna from the beginning. More than two hundred baboon skulls have been examined until now, perhaps about only one tenth of all buried baboons, to judge from the niches found along the walls of the main passages or in special chambers. Most of them are Olive baboons *(Papio cynocephalus anubis)*, simply placed in a wooden box. The first intact Hamadryas baboon burial was found in gallery C–D–4 (Thirtieth Dynasty), its niche sealed with mud bricks. The wrapped body of the baboon was protected under a heap of gypsum-like powder. Surprisingly, the neighboring baboon niches in C–D–4 were used only for the deposit of the embalming vessels: two to three oil vessels and two to four small bowls, used probably during the Opening-of-the-Mouth ceremony. The earlier baboon mummies—the bones were held together by thick layers of bandages only—had no or only a few amulets between the linen strips: strings of faïence beads or single faïence scarabs. Flower garlands sometimes covered the wooden boxes. Later on their wrapped body was often embedded in thick layers of resin. The more expensive outer limestone coffins for baboons, typical of the earlier Ptolemaic Period, contained inner wooden boxes decorated with an Uraeus frieze, with more amulets adorning and protecting the mummy.

Many of the baboons died very young, which might reflect the harsh conditions of their captivity. Deformations of baboon bones (arthrosis) are common, hinting at rachitis, insufficient nutrition and lack of space. Tuberculosis seems to have been frequent. Their teeth are generally in a deplorable condition. Continuous stress led to a permanent hormonal overproduction of the parathyroid glands, which heavily affected the consistency of the bones. On the other hand, ibises with broken bones, or a baboon with a heavy deformation of the jawbone could not have survived without special human aid and additional feeding. Some baboons found in Tuna might have been born in Egypt like those in Saqqara (see Nicholson, this volume), while monkeys like the Green monkeys and the Barbary apes, would have been imported from abroad.

Parts of two mighty crocodiles, one more than five meters long, were found dispersed in the galleries B and C. Together with the fish, they belong to the theologically important group of the 'animals of the water,' the animals of the primeval landscape, which could also be dangerous. The gods Sobek and Seth could transform themselves into crocodiles. The sacred crocodiles must have been kept near a temple lake (perhaps in Hermopolis), served by the members of a small association of the god Sobek (Suchos) with a sanctuary (Suchieion) nearby. Parts of fishes were also often found in pre-Ptolemaic galleries, perhaps in close connections with cat burials. Cat and fish are both found on standards pictured in New Kingdom tombs.

Dogs and cats are both found from the beginning of burial animal cults, but rarely as complete skeletons. They are generally represented only by a few bones. It seems that in Saite times the bulk of sacred cats and dogs of the Egyptian temple rites may have been brought to and buried centrally in special main burial places of Egypt like Kynopolis or Bubastis (not in Saqqara which does not show cat or dog burials until later, to the author's knowledge), leaving only a few cats and dogs of the local breeding places to be combined with the ibises. Demotic texts, dating to before the Ptolemaic Period, mention fields of the dog and cat organization that were used for the maintenance of the cult. Their local religious cult buildings, always closely connected to one another, the Anubieion and the Bubasteion, must have been located somewhere near the Great Temple of Tuna.

Concentrated burials of bovids, mostly cows and oxen, were also found in the pre-Ptolemaic part of the galleries (C–C–D). It is probable that these animals were members of the sacred bovine herd of Thoth. Thoth transformed himself into the form of a bull, in a manner parallel to the god Ptah who was manifested as the Apis-bull, and Re's incarnation as the Mnevis bull. The common Hermopolitan name 'The one, whom the Gem-calf-has given' hints at a cult image of the young Thoth-bull in the court area of the Great temple in Tuna-South. The bovids must have been buried in large wall niches on the ground. Other bones were discovered in the early Ptolemaic part (G–C–A–6) and in a middle Ptolemaic section before (G–B–E–14). In some cases all the bones are burnt except their forepart. It seems that most of the bones of their skeleton were laid in layers, the wrapping giving only a rough outline. A single gazelle mummy was found lying on top of ibis pottery jars in an untouched side chamber in Gallery A.

The discovery of pig bones in certain jars was surprising. They first came to light in the middle Ptolemaic Gallery B, in a Saite context, associated with the bones of other animals. Pigs are normally excluded from Egyptian temples, because they were associated with the class of the abominable animals of the god Seth. However, one may assume that they too lived on the primeval hill. Perhaps in the Late Period sacred pigs were related to the feast of Isis, who transferred herself into a sow. The pig bones were often burnt, and consisted only of small pieces. Until now we may offer only preliminary considerations, indicating that these animals which were burnt in offerings as dangerous animals also had to be transferred into the status of immortal gods.

The class of sacred 'animals of the earth,' i.e., worms, rats, small snakes, beetles, rats, lizards, and the shrew are found already in linen bundles dating to the Saite Period. In Ptolemaic times they were sometimes wrapped in rounded bundles, which were intermingled with mummies of ibises and falcons. All these small animals were deified. The contents of the bundles vary. For instance, one bundle contained ten small snakes and the complete bones of one shrew. The simple theological idea behind their combinations seems to be that antagonistic animal species could destroy each other. This would be dangerous for gods in the form of another special animal, and thus also for the transformation of the Horus-king. This could be especially true when Seth/Apophis, the opponent of Horus, took the shape of such dangerous animals. During the fight on the primeval hill, Seth could use the power of dangerous snakes, while the ibises fought against them. Because all kinds of snakes and also worms belonged to the terrestial animal category, headed by the snake god, the ibis was ultimately (but incorrectly), classified as a snake killer. In fact, the ibis seems to devour only small worms or small fishes. The Egyptians knew that falcons devour mice or rats, that a snake kills a shrew, an ichneumon attacks a snake, that a cat eats a fish, a crocodile kills a ram, and so on. But as deified gods the antagonistic animals could not be eliminated. Therefore their bones wrapped together have nothing to do with buried animals getting their proper food as is sometimes claimed. The protective aspects of the snake was visibly associated with the sacred ibis standard; statues of rams and crocodiles stood near each other in Egyptian temples; cats and fish were found on the same standard. Cat and fish acted together, e.g., during the New Year festivals, especially in the town of Bubastis, where the male cat (as the visible power of the sun god Ra) and the catfish (as a power of the hidden god Atum) were the protecting city gods.

Fig. 6.12 Baboon chapel C–C–34 with later Ptolemaic ritual scenes. Courtesy of Dieter Kessler.

Similarly, the nocturnal shrew and the diurnal falcon were forms of the hidden and the visible solar falcon god. Haroeris (the old Horus) and the young Horus both transformed themselves into a shrew and a falcon, respectively. The mongoose was considered as both snake killer and an animal of the solar god. He was an opponent of the animals of the earth, i.e., of the shrew. Wooden sarcophagi surmounted by the figure of a shrew do not always contain shrews, but can also include Nile rats. The precise contents of the numerous other small wooden or stone sarcophagi of the scarab-beetle or of the wooden obelisk-like containers (of the goddess Sekhmet) need further study, but here also can often be observed a certain distinction between the animal form of the high god and the kind, color, or species of the buried sacred animal.

7

The Cult and Necropolis of the Sacred Ram at Mendes

—— *Susan Redford and Donald B. Redford** ——

Since the dawn of Egyptian history the roster of numina worshiped in the territory of the sixteenth township of Lower Egypt has always featured ram and fish at the head (Helck 1974: 191–194; Zibelius 1978: 278–279; Gomaà 1987: 246–250; Edwards 1960: L6, vs. 63–65; Naville 1888: pl. 5, register 2). Together the two animals indicate the probable subsistence base of the human community in this part of Egypt from prehistoric times. The fish (*schilby*, rather than dolphin)[1] became the symbol and emblem of the township; but the ram dominated the city as "Lord of the Abiding Place *(Ḏdt)*." Textual sources attest to a thriving cult during the entire third millennium B.C. (de Meulenaere and MacKay 1976; de Meulenaere 1982: 209–216; Redford 1988: 49–51), which can now, somewhat gratifyingly, be confirmed archaeologically.[2] Excavations undertaken by the present writers in 1996 and 1998–2001 penetrated beneath the thick foundational sand of the New Kingdom temple to reveal a substantial podium of mud brick, c. 40 m wide (east–west) and c. 3 m high, dating from the later Old Kingdom (Redford 1996, 1999). Whatever had once stood upon the podium had been swept away in a destructive conflagration either at the close of the Sixth Dynasty or early in the

---

* The authors wish to acknowledge the following technical staff of the Mendes Expedition for their contributions to the documentation of the area of the ram sarcophagi: Keith Meikle, architect; Rupert Nesbitt, artist; Alexander Nesbitt and David George, photographers; and Lawrence Pawlish, geophysicist. The site plan and architectural reconstruction was done by Keith Meikle; drawings of the vaulted ceiling and the sarcophagi and lids are the work of Rupert Nesbitt.

First Intermediate Period; but one presumes that the podium had once supported an early shrine of the ram.

The 'Theology' of the Ram, Lord of Mendes

While Mendes is seldom mentioned in the P(yramid) T(exts), the C(offin) T(exts) contain some theologically significant references to the town and its god. A prominent theme depends upon the homophony of *ba/b3*, "ram," and *bai/b3j*, "hypostatic projection of identity and power."[3] Possibly through the mediacy of Andjety, "the shepherd"[4] and his association with Osiris, the latter was brought to Mendes, where he is said to be "pure," (CT VII: 38) and commands the respect of the "lords of 'Anpet" (CT VI, 404).[5] The concept of vital coalescence of active and latent power (Re and Osiris) finds one of its earliest expressions in a Mendesian context: ". . . when he (Osiris) entered Mendes and found the *b3j* of Re there, whereupon they embraced each other." (CT IV, 278) [cf. BD 17a 14; Kees 1956: 165; Altenmuller 1975: 45; Spiegel 1975: 144–146; Hornung 1982: 93; Herbin 1994: 122; *Dendara* X: 280, 12]. Osiris was to remain "the Mendesian *b3i*, the precious deity"[6] "rejuvenated as the ram" (*Dendara* X, 288: 12) and Banebdjed to become, through Osiris, "the living *bai* of the gods." (Gutbub 1973: 468–469; Kessler 1989: 12–16).

As these passages make plain, the Ram of Mendes also enjoyed a close solar association. He was the "*bai* of Re" as he was that of Osiris, "the living one of Re," (*Edfou* I: 334; Brugsch 1883–1891: 815; Faulkner 1933: 23, 25; Wild 1960: 59–65; Zivie 1975: 53b; de Meulenaere and Mackay 1976: pl. 23 [55]), "who is in heaven, lord of heaven" (Mysliewic 1979: 201); and as a common aspect of the sun in the night, the ram-form makes an appearance in certain underworld books (Piankoff 1964: pl. 71, 76, 90, 105). In the beatification text on the only inscribed ram-sarcophagus lid yet to be found at Mendes, Banebdjed as Osiris is described in a distinctly solarized form (de Meulenaere and Mackay 1976: 213(163), pl. 38; Kakosy 1970: 114). "Hail Osiris, the living *bai*! May thy mother embrace thee as thou liest in her womb and art born like Re every day! Mayest thou enjoy youthfulness on the horizon of heaven, and transform thyself into the living *bai*. Mayest thou traverse heaven as a 'Heliopolitan'. . . . No eye will ever fail to see thee! May thy mother protect thee like thy father Re, may she conceal thee as

Khopry, her arms extended over thee, so that no creeping thing shall go into the cavern in which thou art. The 'Mistress' has made thy protection like Re, she has put fear of thee in their hearts!"

Two other attributes of Banebdjed, the ram of Mendes, came to prominence no later than the New Kingdom and Third Intermediate Period respectively. The first can arguably be derived from the ancient mythological theme of the royal pedigree whereby the king, through the totality of the cosmic elements, lays claim to the universal legitimacy of the creator (Barta 1973: 195 n. 1). This concept issues as the quadruple manifestation of the god, as four individual rams (Hornung 1999: 77 fig. 41, 109 fig. 60; *M. Habu*: pl. 420; Quaegebeur 1991: 253–268), or as four ram-heads on a single animal (Borghouts 1978: 9 (Chester Beatty VIII); Kees 1956: 438; de Wit 1957: 25ff; Wessetsky 1981: 493–494; Sauneron 1962: 208; *Edfou* III: 258: –7; Kurth 1983: 154.19; Cauville 1987: 4–5). The quadripartite deity represents the totality of the cosmos in the form of the four elements: sun, air, earth, water (for the hypostatic demands of the cult identified as Re, Shu, Geb, and Osiris [Wild 1960: 43–68; Woodhouse 1997: 139]). The second attribute of the ram of Mendes is its alleged ability to enunciate oracles, a characteristic which may be traced to the homophony of *sr*, "ram," and *sr*, "to announce (in advance), to foretell." Oracular clairvoyance is already a hallmark of the god in the New Kingdom, when "the united *bai*," i.e., Re and Osiris combined in the Mendesian ram, is said to make daily pronouncements: "The Majesty of Thoth stands before you copying down what comes out of your mouth; as for anything you say with one voice, they are my (the king's) directives for the daily schedule" (*KRI* VI, 22:16–23:2). During the Twenty-second Dynasty the ram-oracle was resorted to in order to bolster political succession at Mendes; and in folklore predictions of dire events to come were assigned *post eventum* to the animal (Kakosy 1981b: 139–154; Griffiths 1970: 550; Assmann 1996: 422–424).[7]

While the ram Banebdjed thus became the center of a rather high-flown speculation on theological imponderables, there was no denying the fact that, in the minds of people at large, the beast remained a crass manifestation of earthy, sexual activity. He is described as "the coupling ram that mounts the beauties," (*Urk.* II, 31: 13; Zivie 1977: 52; Sauneron 1963: 46; de Meulenaere and MacKay 1976: pl. 23 (55); P.

Louvre I 3079 iii.95–96; Kurth 1983: 154 (17)) and belief that the latter were to be construed as human lent an air of debauchery to the town (de Meulenaere and MacKay 1976: 1–3).[8] Banebdjed's reputation for prowess in the procreative act, and his link with Re, insinuated him into the royal pedigree: under the guise of the Mendesian ram Ptah comes to earth to cohabit with the queen to produce the heir (K*RI* II, 263: 5–11; Sandman-Holmberg 1946: 176–177; *Urk.* IV: 224.17; Kessler 1989: 119–120).

The Temple of the Ram and its Priesthood

The temple of Banebdjed that occupied the site in the Middle Kingdom had been levelled during the New Kingdom, but the building, which arose to replace it can still be traced, at least in plan (Redford 1999) (See fig. 7.1). It was oriented to (local) north and constructed of limestone with some fixtures and columns of black granite. An inner core, possibly erected during the early Eighteenth Dynasty, had later been fronted by a pylon and forecourt under Ramesses II. Sundry internal adjustments were probably carried out during the Third Intermediate Period, but the building never exceeded the final dimensions of c. 170 x 40 m reached under the Ramessides. Amasis (569–526 B.C.) replaced an early cella with a naos court, 40 x 35 m, at the southern end of the complex, to accommodate four granite naoi, each c. 10 m tall, containing cult images of the four avatars of the ram (Arnold 1999: 81–82). The structure is called variously "the temple *(ḥwt-nṯr)*," (Daressy 1913, 126; Soghor 1967: 25, 30 fig. 10; de Meulenaere and MacKay 1976: pl. 21(d), 25 [63]), "house" *(pr)* (*Urk.* II, 32: 2, 38: 5) of Banebdjed; but can also be referred to by one of its component elements, *pars pro toto*: "residence (or seat) of the august ram" (*Urk.* II, 38: 10–13; 50: 9), "the great seat" (*Urk.* II, 46: 13), "the shrine/cella" (Daressy 1913: 125; *Urk.* II, 49: 10), "birth-place" (Daressy 1913: 126). Although difficult to identify in the excavations, the temple undoubtedly contained an ambulatory *(smmt)* in which statues were displayed.

Apart from the naos court, which has a curious layout, nothing in the plan of Banebdjed's temple would suggest a cult any different from that accommodated in the usual processional temple.[9] And the list of priestly and lay titles associated with the cult bears this out:[10] First Prophet (Vandier 1968: 93; Daressy 1913: 125) or "the shorn one" (de

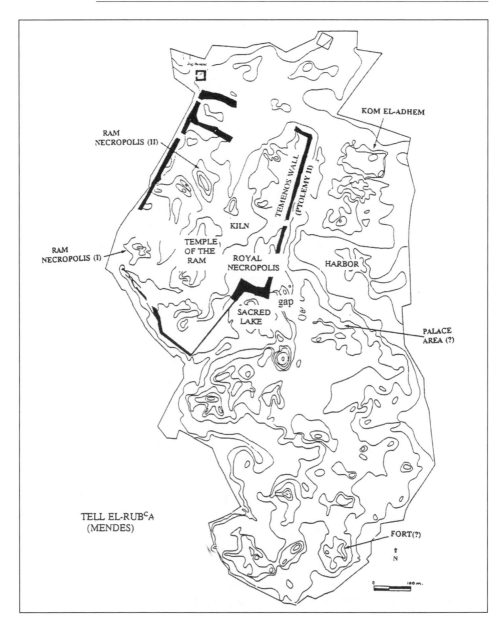

Fig. 7.1 Plan of Mendes. Courtesy Mendes Excavation.

Meulenaere and Mackay 1976: pl. 25 [3]); Second Prophet or 'comman-der of the host' (Daressy 1917: 21; de Meulenaere and MacKay 1976: pl. 24 (61); Chevereau 1985: no. 266; Redford 1991–1992: 8); Chief Celebrant or 'He-whose-decay-is-hidden' (*Edfou* I: 334; Griffith 1889: pl. XI (24); Dendara X: 24: 2); Chief Priestess or 'She-who-soothes-his-*b3i*' (*Edfou* I: 334; Griffith 1889: pl. XI.24); "*Episkopos*" (*jmy-r ḥmw-ntr* [Soghor 1967: 25; Chevereau 1985: 61–63; Davies and MacAdam 1957: 378; Mendes 5M30 (unpublished statue inscription)]); Prophets (Begelsbacher-Fischer 1981: 223; Maspero 1914: CB 29303; *PM*III: 810 [IM.4.42]; Posener 1936: 96 n.*h*.; de Meulenaere and MacKay 1976: pl. 23 (58); Montet 1946: 48); W*ʿb*-priests (de Meulenaere and MacKay 1976: pl. 25 (63); Wild 1960: pl. I; Bierbrier 1982: 98 no. 312); *lesonis*-priest (Chevereau 1985: no. 253); *jmy-ḥnt* priest or 'he-who-separates-the divine pair' (Wild 1960: 50f; de Meulenaere and MacKay 1976: pl. 183–183 (nos. 46, 47, 48, 58, 101, 103, 104); Donadoni 1969: 103; *PM*III: 800, 814; Mendes 5M30;[11] shrine-opener (de Meulenaere and MacKay 1976: pl. 25 (63)); 'scribe of the god's-book of Ba-neb-djed' (de Meulenaere and MacKay 1976: pl. 25 (63); Mendes 5M30; Schott 1990: no. 1427a);[12] flautists (Kitchen 1969–70: fig. 1); singers (Bierbrier 1982: pl. 98 [312]).

There is every reason to believe that, from an early period,[13] one specific member of the species was selected and identified as the earthly manifestation of the god. The ancients in the first millennium B.C. entertained some uncertainty as to whether the beast was a sheep or a goat,[14] but there is little doubt today that the Mendesian animal was a sheep *(Ovis aries longipes)*.[15] As was the case in most animal cults, the criterion of selection was color: the ram of Mendes was pure white.[16] Some of the building names listed above suggest that he resided in the temple proper; but to date no accommodations for a ram have been identified archaeologically. Texts during the Late Period allude to a special structure associated with the ram called "the Mound of the Shearing"; but the references support the interpretation of a sort of holding shrine, where the new ram might be kept during initiation (de Meulenaere and MacKay 1976: pl. 15 (36), 25 (63); Daressy 1917: 22; *Urk.* II, 48.7). Classical authors assert that in some animal cults sacred pens lay adjacent to the temple proper (Diodorus 1.84.5; Clement *Paed ii 4.2–4.4*, Hodjash and Berlev 1982: 214 no. 147, line 2); but no such enclosures have been unearthed as yet at Mendes. The description of the sumptuous lifestyle of the sacred animal avatars, vouchsafed by classical writers, applies also without doubt to the ram (Diodorus 1.84.4–1.84.8; de Meulenaere and MacKay 1976: pl. 25 [63]).

The Ram Necropolis: the "Mansion of the Rams"

We are now much better informed as to how the rams were treated and housed in death. The Mendes stela of Ptolemy II tells how the king on his tour of the ruined city "paid a visit *(ph.r)* to the Mansion of the Rams" (*Urk.* II, 38: 4, 46: 9; Duemichen 1865–1868 III, 49 [Philae]); and in an early Twenty-ninth Dynasty text this structure is alluded to in the phrase "the entombed rams who are in the Mansion of the Rams" (de Meulenaere and MacKay 1976: pl. 23 (58)). This structure we believe has now been unearthed.[17] (pl. 1)

Fig. 7.2 Aerial view of the area. Courtesy Mendes Excavation.

Massive granite sarcophagi, made for the interment of the sacred rams, are a notable feature of the present terrain of the Tell al-Rub'a. They are distributed, broadly speaking, in two groups across the site. The first, the northern group (Holz 1980: pl. 31 c–d), which a visitor encounters entering the tell from the north lies immediately to the west of the central axial approach to the temple mound (see fig. 7.1: Ram Necropolis II). The line of tumbled and battered ram-sarcophagi here marks the southwest boundary of a low-lying area approximately 20 x 40 m in extent. The field is possessed of a gravelly surface, notably bare except for symmetrically-placed oval patches covered with coarse grass. These oval patches were in every case slightly larger than the extant sarcophagi. The excavation of one such patch proved that they are pits, c. 1 m in depth, sunk in a thick layer of fine building sand over 2 m thick. It is very tempting to conclude that the oval pits represent the original positions of the sarcophagi. Further excavation of other parts of the site to a depth of 3.5 m revealed a layer of smashed stone of various kinds—limestone, granite, quartzite—along with some huge architectural blocks of granite. The carefully worked surfaces, gave them the appearance of pier blocks and architraves. Below this destruction lay a two-meter bed of clean sand, clearly the *soubassement* for some massive stone construction, which was perhaps partly subterranean. The perimeter of this now destroyed structure is distinctly delineated as a rectangle by the outlining growth of vegetation.

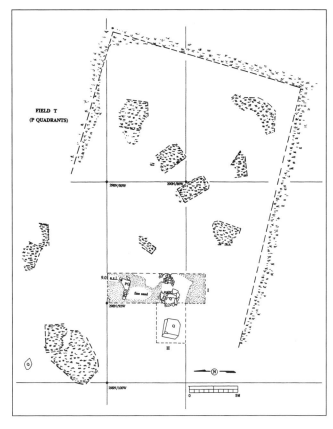

Fig. 7.3 Plan of Field T. Courtesy Mendes Excavation.

Situated within the southwest corner of the Ptolemaic temenos wall that encloses the temple environs, some 220 m west of the temple mound, is a second burial ground [the southern group] (de Meulenaere

Fig. 7.4 A view
of the excavations
with sarcophagi
in the foreground.
Courtesy Mendes
Excavation.

and MacKay 1976: pl. 1b). (see fig. 7.1: Ram Necropolis I). Here thirteen sarcophagi and their lids lie strewn within a sandy, rectangular
depression measuring c. 33 x 13.5 m. The area encompassing this con-
centration of overturned and desecrated sarcophagi became the initial
excavation unit for archaeological investigation of this part of the tell.
The field was sectioned into sixteen two-meter trenches laid out from
east to west in order to proceed with a controlled clearance and map-
ping of the sarcophagi and lids. As with the northern group, it was also
hoped that some architectural patterns would emerge to indicate the
original positions of the sarcophagi and the type of edifice that stood to
protect and house them. For the most part, nothing remained within
the unit but a layer of clean, fine building sand running along the north
and south perimeters. At the northeast and southeast corners the sand
was over a meter in depth. This substantial foundation of pure sand-fill
in itself indicates that a monumental stone structure once occupied the
site. In the interior of the unit there were irregular plots of fine building
sand and thin but expansive patches of pulverized limestone, one of
which transected the unit in half. This feature together with occasional
pieces of slightly larger limestone chips suggests that the superstructure
was built of limestone and suffered the same fate as the Great Temple
of the Ram wherein the wall blocks were removed and burned in lime

furnaces during Roman times. The two easternmost trenches were cleared completely of the sand fill and surprisingly revealed that the foundations of the structure rested upon domestic occupation of late Old Kingdom date.

Later investigation of this area of Tell al-Rub'a, which was designated the R(am) S(arcophagus) area, expanded on the original excavation unit to include the surrounding terrain. Efforts primarily concentrated on the area adjacent to the northern perimeter of the sandy depression where the ground gradually rises to a substantial height for a distance of over thirty-five meters. Removal of a thin, top layer of silty overburden revealed a large expanse of a huge mud-brick edifice with thick, sturdy walls. The broad massif of mud brick was punctuated by slightly off-line intervals by small, rectangular chambers. A similar irregularity of the layout can be seen in the ram cemetery at Elephantine (Kessler 1989: Abb. 16). In one of these chambers a sarcophagus of Aswan granite was found in situ nearly filling the entire cubicle, and thus elucidating one aspect of this enigmatic structure. The east and west walls of the mud-brick building were aligned exactly with the eastern and western perimeters of the sand-filled rectangle and abutted the sandy depression all along its northern edge indicating that the mud-brick section was integrated with the stone structure which once stood on the sand foundation (see Fig. 7.6).

Fig. 7.5 A ram sarcophagus as it is being uncovered. Courtesy Mendes Excavation.

Fig. 7.6 Plan of the
Ram Sarcophagus
area. Courtesy
Mendes Excavation.

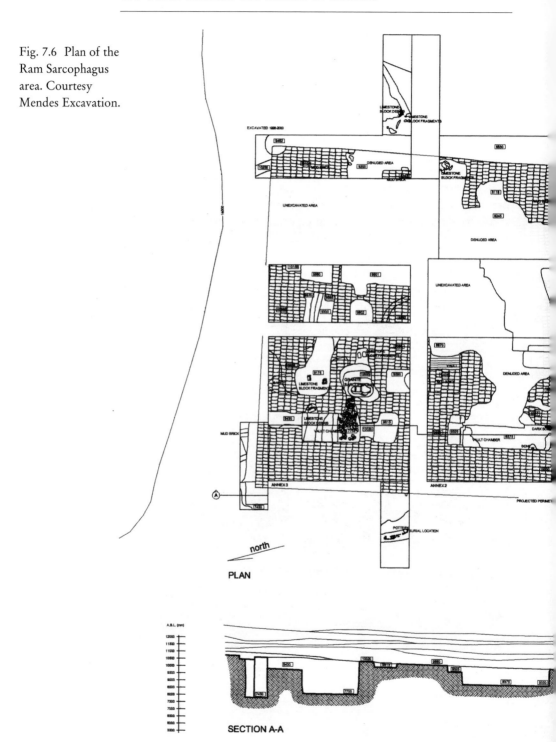

PLAN

SECTION A-A

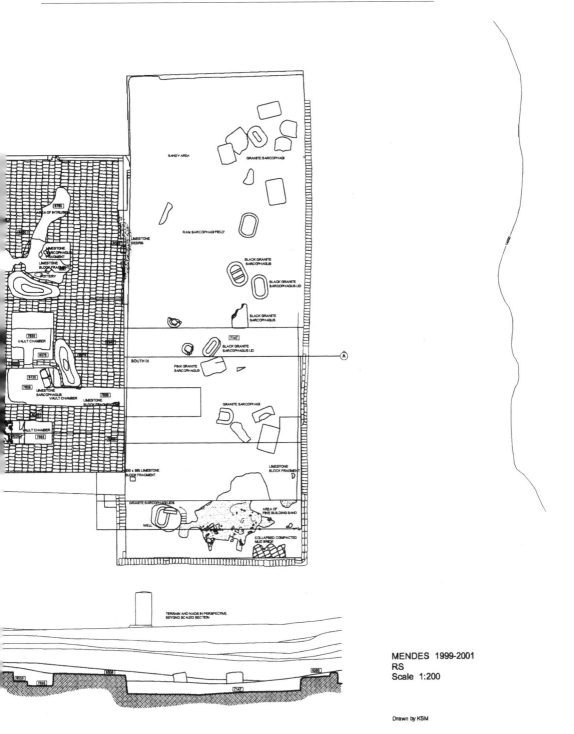

SANDY AREA

GRANITE SARCOPHAGI

AREA OF INTRUSION

RAM SARCOPHAGI 'FIELD'

LIMESTONE
DEBRIS

LIMESTONE
SARCOPHAGUS
FRAGMENT
LIMESTONE
BLOCK FRAGMENT
POTTERY

BLACK GRANITE
SARCOPHAGUS

BLACK GRANITE
SARCOPHAGUS LID

BLACK GRANITE
SARCOPHAGUS

VAULT CHAMBER

BLACK GRANITE
SARCOPHAGUS LID

SOUTH IX

PINK GRANITE
SARCOPHAGUS

LIMESTONE
SARCOPHAGUS
VAULT CHAMBER

LIMESTONE
BLOCK FRAGMENT

GRANITE SARCOPHAGI

VAULT CHAMBER

LIMESTONE
BLOCK FRAGMENT

450 x 350 LIMESTONE
BLOCK FRAGMENT

GRANITE SARCOPHAGUS LIDS

AREA OF
FINE BUILDING SAND

WELL

COLLAPSED COMPACTED
MUD BRICK

TERRAIN AND NAOS IN PERSPECTIVE
BEYOND SCALED SECTION

MENDES 1999-2001
RS
Scale 1:200

Drawn by KSM

As the excavation progressed more architectural features became apparent (see fig. 7.2). The northern half of the edifice rises sharply in height giving the impression of an upper tier. In this, the best-preserved area, it was discovered that the cubicles were vaulted. A partially intact vaulted ceiling over one chamber connected with the chamber that held the in situ sarcophagus by a doorway. In the southern half, a long, narrow corridor running north–south was uncovered, which opened onto the sandy depression and joined with two of the chambers. In one of these chambers, badly broken and resting on its side, was a roughly hewn sarcophagus, but unlike those that litter the surface, this one was of limestone. The doorway entries in both the north and south sections of the building had been barricaded with limestone destruction that included large pieces of limestone sarcophagi and their lids. (See fig. 7.5) In addition, fractured lintel blocks, some with delicate relief, were recovered at the base of one of the doorways as well as fragments of bronze door bolts. The use of limestone on the interior was complemented by a stone veneer on the exterior of the building as evidenced by patches of pulverized limestone detected over sections of the mud-brick surface.

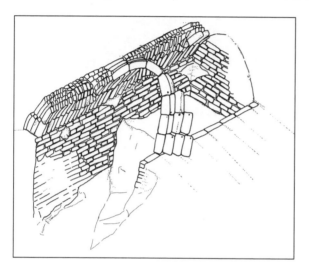

Fig. 7.7 The vaulted chambers. Courtesy Mendes Excavation.

The eastern mid-section of the mud-brick remains has fared badly in terms of preservation. It appears as a long, 'scooped out' denudation running east–west flanked by mud-brick walls. Although one cannot be certain, as no distinct edge or architectural pattern can be discerned, there is a vague impression of yet another corridor.

Most of the entire expanse of the east and west external walls of the mud-brick building was laid bare delineating a space with a width of 23 m. Both the northeast and northwest corners were exposed, the latter to its

Fig. 7.8
A limestone
sarcophagus.
Courtesy Mendes
Excavation.

full depth of twenty-two pan-bedded courses. Abutting the southern line of the sandy depression, a mud-brick retaining wall of single-course width marked the southern boundary and provided the full dimensions of the installation. At two intervals along the wall, the mud-brick course dropped to a lower depth for a stretch of about two meters, possibly indicating the placement of side-entry doors. Overall the "Mansion of the Sacred Rams" measured 52 m in length (north–south); the main entry to the complex however was not immediately apparent.

It was initially assumed that the approach and expected monumental entry to the ram hypogeum would face east toward the Great Temple of the Ram, but surprisingly no physical evidence could be found. In fact there is every indication that the installation was oriented in the opposite direction. The east wall of the mud-brick edifice shows no interruption in the line of bricks, nor in the adjacent straight-sided trench line that demarcates the sandy depression. Immediately outside the perimeter, domestic occupation of late Old Kingdom date is encountered at surface; and it is into this layer of occupation that the installation of the hypogeum has been cut. We then hypothesized that entry might be on the south, connected to an ancient waterway that linked the Mendesian branch of the Nile with the city. The later erection of a temenos wall in Ptolemaic times would have effectively sealed off the entry to the precinct if one existed on that side.

It should be noted that cultic operations may have ceased with the Persian destruction in 343 B.C. Sondages were made within the ten-meter wide area between southern boundary of the hypogeum and the temenos wall, but no evidence of an entry was uncovered. Instead, the remains of an Old Kingdom enclosure wall oriented true north was discovered and revealed to have been cut through by the emplacement of the ram compound.

As the north side is fronted by the remains of a substantial mud-brick building that has yet to be investigated, there remained only the west side to consider. From the western line of the temenos wall the tell drops off within 50 m to cultivated farmland. In ancient times, however the town site continued to the banks of the Mendesian branch of the Nile, for a distance of about 0.5 km. While the mud-brick section of the hypogeum showed no access through its west wall, the western boundary of the sand-filled depression manifested some curious features. For one thing, the mud-brick retaining wall that edges the southern line of the structure's foundations turns and continues along the west line of the depression. The pure sand-fill that at the east end was free of rubble, was here heavily laden with limestone destruction.

Fig. 7.9 Evidence of the continuing foundations. Courtesy Mendes Excavation.

The substantial limestone debris, situated adjacent to the western retaining wall at center, formed a telling pattern reminiscent of the outline of a portal. At the inside edge of this outline, two fragments of a royal statue were uncovered. Carved slightly smaller than life-size, the black granite fragments show a striding figure wearing a royal kilt and lappet wig. Several fragments of limestone door sockets recovered from the debris confirmed suspicions of a gated entry. Moreover, in line with the putative gate at approximately 42 m due west

Fig. 7.10
Fragment of a
granite statue
of a king.
Courtesy
Mendes
Excavation.

lies another sarcophagus of Aswan granite, turned on its side, apparently hauled from the compound through this entry.

To our amazement, we discovered a well of Roman date sunk immediately beside the area of the portal. The excavation of this well over 5 m in depth proved extremely fruitful: massive limestone blocks were packed in layers up to the surface and the well capped by two granite sarcophagus lids.

Approximately 270 blocks have been recovered to date, with dimensions varying from 53 x 46 x 40 cm to 35 x 17 x 15 cm. Many show gypsum plaster on drafted faces; one or two have worked, curving edges. One takes the form of a roughly worked torus roll, and another a fragment of a stylobate. About forty bear traces of masons' marks in red ochre, non-

Fig. 7.11 Sarcophagi and stone fragments appearing during excavation.
Courtesy Mendes Excavation.

Fig. 7.12
A fragmentary
inscription
featuring the Ram
of Mendes.
Courtesy Mendes
Excavation.

decipherable. The total cubic meterage represented by these blocks can be calculated at approximately 435 m—i.e., approximately 15 percent of the total masonry used in the walls of the monumental hall.

A few of the blocks carved in delicate low relief represent all that remains of the decorated walls of the hypogeum. Among these the following are to be noted:

1. SF317 (RS XV/XVI loc. 1003; well)
—upper: foot of figure moving right in a line(?) of figures (adjacent figure in evidence on right). Remains of text *[. . . ʿnḥ] dt,* "may he live forever."
—lower: part of horizontal text read from the right *b3 ʿnḥ ṇd [nṯrw(?) . . .],* "the living Ram, protector [of the gods(?). . . .]."[18]

2. SF327 (RS XIV/XV loc. 1000; gate area)
—limestone fragment with star border in relief (4 x 4 x 2 cm).

3. SF323 (RS XV/XVI loc. 1003; well)
—limestone fragment showing feathers of vulture in low relief (20 x 6 x 8 cm)

4. SF303 (RS XV loc. 1006; well)
—limestone fragment in relief with cartouche over *nbw* sign flanked by uraeus. (8 x 5 cm).

5. SF309 (RS XV/XVI loc. 1003; well)
—limestone fragment in relief: arm of a god (?) holding staff facing left (15 x 9 x 9.5 cm).

6. SF308 (RS XV/XVI loc.1003; well)
—limestone fragment of relief: god's head and shoulder, facing left.; perhaps from one Ennead grouping (8.5 x 8 x 5 cm).

7. SF319 (RS XV/XVI loc. 1003; well)
—fragment of fine limestone relief; *dd*-pillar; (30 x 20 x 19 cm). If part of a vertical column with the expected formula, *B3-nb-Ddt,* the whole would have occupied slightly in excess of 60 cm of vertical space.

8. SF314 (RS XV/XVI loc. 1003; well)
—fragment of fine limestone relief; unidentified configuration on left, column of text on right, probably to be restored *[B3 n]dt[y] n [jt.f/nṯrw (?) . . .],* "[The Ram pr]otect[or] of [his father/the gods(?) . . .]."

9. SF320 (RS XV/XVI loc. 1003; well)
—fragment of limestone relief, with leg of individual facing left and before him column of text: *[. . . sh ṛw ḥ ft] yw.k m pt t3 rʿ nb],* "[. . .] your [enemi]es [are overthrown] in heaven and earth da[ily]" (46 x 26 x 21 cm).

Fig. 7.13
A possible
restoration of the
temple and vaulted
areas. Courtesy
Mendes Excavation.

One of the most interesting objects recovered from the well was a miniature mock-up of the *pr-nsr* carved in limestone. In the light of this discovery one wonders whether the shape of the individual cubicles was architecturally modeled after this type of vaulted edifice.

Although the site is in a relatively poor state of preservation, the archaeological investigations of the area have gleaned enough information to attempt an architectural reconstruction of the complex. The superstructure of the "Mansion of the Sacred Rams" consisted of a monumental hall, possibly a columned hypostyle, a little over 33 m long by 13.5 m wide, with limestone walls. An interior cross-wall divided the hall in half, and a single doorway in the hall's north wall gave access to an adjoining building of mud-brick construction. This part of the complex employed vaulted construction, with support vaults packed with earth. Partly subterranean, a second tier was added which gave the outward appearance of a terraced structure. Small cubicles with vaulted ceilings honeycombed the building and provided for the emplacement of stone sarcophagi. These cubicles, averaging roughly 2-2.5 m x 1.5-2 m in size, were connected by narrow passages of varying lengths. Doorways to at least some of the cubicles had decorated limestone lintels and were sealed with door bolts made of bronze. The exterior mud-brick walls were veneered in limestone and the vaulted ceilings covered by an external flat roof. The complex was oriented west toward the Nile and perhaps had a short *dromos* leading up to a screen-walled façade of the monumental hall.

The Sarcophagi

The northern group of sarcophagi is distinct from the southern group in several aspects. Those at the northern site were made only of black diorite and were all of one shape, indistinguishable from each other. Of a simple ovoid form, straight sided with rounded ends, the diorite sarcophagi were left roughly cut and unfinished on the exterior. This is an indication that the sides were not meant to be seen and further confirmation of their placement in the subterranean pits revealed by the excavations. They measure approximately 1.80 x 1.30 m with an exterior depth of 86 cm. The lids were flat-topped and similarly shaped to the sarcophagi, but slightly larger at 1.95 x 1.40 m.

Unlike this northern group, there were noticeable differences among those found at the southern area. Although general categories based on stone material and form can be established, no two sarcophagi were exactly alike: each showed some slight variation in form (for the types, see figs. 7.14 a–c). Three types of stone were utilized throughout the period of cultic operations: black granite, mottled rose-colored quartz, and limestone. Several varieties of design and overall finish were exhibited, but none confined to a particular type of stone. The majority is of black granite numbering eleven and understandably the best preserved. Both the black granite and rose quartz (of which there are four) were roughly the same in size, measuring on average 1.70 m long by 1 to 1.25 m wide and about 1 m in height. These two types also shared similar forms: one, an exterior ovoid shape but the interior with sharply notched sides; and the other, an ovoid with flaring bulbous sides at one end. There were, however, other designs in black granite that included the simple ovoid form similar to those of the northern group, but unlike those, polished and well-finished on the exterior. And there was another design which was similarly carved on the exterior but with an interior rim that had been hollowed out at one end in a peculiar bulbous shape. The two bulbous-carved designs are the most distinctive in terms of specific function: the rounded flanges that distort the ovoid shape along the straight edges of the sides were obviously made to accept the splaying spiral horns of the ram. Common to both stone types and all designs were raised slats carved on the bottom of the sarcophagus and probably intended to imitate wooden boards.

The lids of the black granite and rose quartz sarcophagi were domed but also showed some variety of design (see fig. 7.14 c). Most of the black granite lids were low and gently rounded domes with a flat-banded base. A high, flat-topped dome lid of mottled rose quartz material unearthed on site is similar to a finely-decorated lid of black granite now housed in the Cairo Museum, which had been removed from the site early in the last century (see below). Thus far, no other lid discovered on site has been found to be inscribed. In the ram cemetery at Elephantine, only one sarcophagus lid decorated with the image of a ram was found by Charles Clermont-Ganneau in 1907–1908.

The few sarcophagi and lids made of limestone prompted some interesting speculation. One was found partially intact, and numerous fragments recovered in the excavation indicate the presence of at least

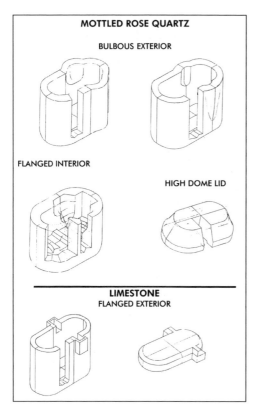

MOTTLED ROSE QUARTZ

BULBOUS EXTERIOR

FLANGED INTERIOR

HIGH DOME LID

LIMESTONE
FLANGED EXTERIOR

Fig. 7.14 a Different types of ram sarcophagi.
Courtesy Mendes Excavation.

three more, including one that was restored along with its lid.[19] The two were quite dissimilar in that the intact sarcophagus was of simple ovoid shape but the one that had been restored possessed unique features. While it was roughly ovoid in shape on both the interior and exterior, well-carved, squared flanges jutted out from each side. A thick, flattened lid matched the shape of the sarcophagus rim exactly. The overall measurements of the two sarcophagi proved to be somewhat smaller both in width and length (approximately 90 x 150 cm) when compared with their granite and rose quartz counterparts. This gave rise to an interesting consideration. One could not help but notice that the outwardly splaying flanges of the limestone sarcophagi appear to fit inside the similarly notched interior rim of the rose quartz sarcophagus found within the cubicle. This may possibly suggest that limestone was utilized as a sort of 'inner liner.' It is equally possible, however, that the resort to limestone indicates a period when hard stone from Aswan and the Wady Hammamat was unavailable. Clearly more evidence is needed to resolve this issue.

Considering the thoroughness with which the entire site of Mendes was raped of limestone, it is of no wonder that so little evidence of limestone sarcophagi remains. Certainly, it was a much easier process to break up massive blocks of limestone than of granite; however, the hard stone sarcophagi still present on the site also show attempts at destruction. According to Lawrence Pawlish, who participated on the excavation at Mendes (June 1999), physical evidence of the use of fire to break apart the stone has been detected. For the most part, these attempts were unsuccessful or at least required too much effort to continue.

Pl. 6.1 Wooden coffin for an ibis showing the king offering before an image of the god. Courtesy of Dieter Kessler.

Pl. 6.2 A statue of a baboon in a niche. Remnants of the oils poured as libations are visible as black smudges. Courtesy of Dieter Kessler.

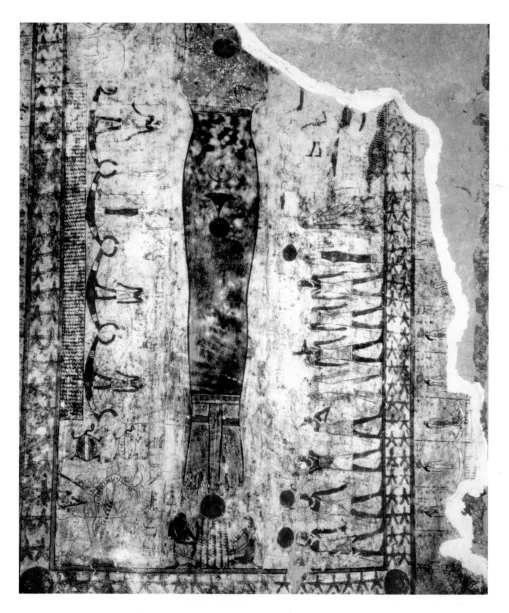

Pl. 6.3 Nut, the sky goddess, stretched over the length of a chamber, protecting the baboons and overseeing cult practices. Courtesy of Dieter Kessler.

Pl. 7.1   A metal
ba-bird. Courtesy
Mendes Excavation.

Pl. 7.2 A miniature column capital. Courtesy Mendes Excavation.

Pl. 7.3 A model limestone *pr-nsr*. Courtesy Mendes Excavation.

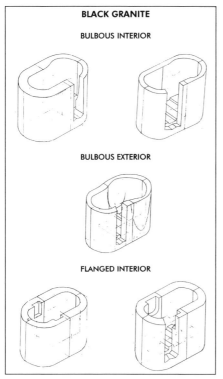

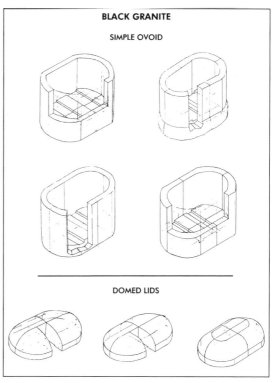

Fig. 7.14 b   Fig. 7.14 c

Cultic Objects

Apart from a single bronze coin found in the destruction fill of the northern burial ground (see below), objects recovered by the excavations were exclusively from the southern area. A substantial quantity of faïence beads from necklaces that once adorned the bodies of the sacred rams was found throughout the complex and complemented the otherwise meager collection of cultic objects.[20] Among the latter we may note the following:

1) finial in the shape of a human-headed *bai*-bird exquisitely detailed in bronze and overlaid with gold lead

2) ram's horn made of bronze over 12 cm in length
3) miniature papyri-form column capital in limestone with incised detailing
4) two sets of bronze door bolts and latches
5) an uninscribed scarab
6) an amulet of lapis in the shape of a djed-pillar
7) miniature *pr-nsr* in limestone of cubic shape, 20 x 13 x 13 cm

In the fine building sand of the northeast corner of the 'hall,' items turned up that appear to be from a disturbed foundation deposit. These are:
1) an uninscribed faïence plaque
2) a miniature cup made of faïence

Fig. 7.15 Metal door bolts and latches. Courtesy Mendes Excavation.

The structure just described was founded and in use during the first millennium B.C. Analysis of the ceramics supports an optimum date of the sixth through the fourth century B.C. with squatter occupation in late Roman times. As pointed out above, its foundations were sunk into domestic strata (partly re-used for human burials in the First Intermediate Period) dating to the last quarter of the third millennium B.C. No Middle or New Kingdom occupation is in evidence anywhere in the vicinity.

A statue inscription, originally coming from Mendes, and containing references to 'great rams' and 'Banebdjed' (de Meulenaere and MacKay 1976: pl. 21 (52); Perdu 1990: 38–49), provides information consonant with the archaeological data, and may indicate the founder of our necropolis. The statue belongs to Nessuhor, son of Efraw, known from four other inscriptions of Delta provenience, with the "good" name of Psamtek-menekh-ib (de Meulenaere 1966: 14 no. 42; Chevereaux 1985: Doc. 118; Perdu 1990: 39). In the Louvre statue A 90 he is the raconteur and central figure of the incident involving the attempted desertion of the foreign mercenaries at Elephantine under Apries (Schaeffer 1904: 152ff, Taf. 1–2; Lloyd 1976: 129–132 (Herod. ii.30); 180 (Herod. ii.163)). The back-pillar of the Mendes statue reads as follows:

"(*I*) *Hereditary prince, count, seal-bearer of the King of Lower Egypt, unique friend, general*[21] *of the army on the day of battle, stout-hearted on the day of rebellion (sb), one who assuaged hearts that had been enraged; recipient of praise for every assignment, colonel of elite troops [. . .]*

(*II*) *for my lord, the King of Upper and Lower Egypt, Haa-ib-re, son of Re Apries, may he live for ever! I was (so greatly) thanked that those who come into being (in the future) shall hear (of it).*[22] *I laid out(?) the sarcophagi of the great rams, for never had [the like] been done (before)*

(*III*) *[. . .] Horus W3h-ib; my favours came from the Lord of the Two Lands in exchange for these things. H.M. allowed me the things which I had produced with my own hands: grain(?) [. . .]*

(*IV*) *fine wine of the southern oasis, a vessel(?) of various incense(?) [. . .]*

(*V*) *a stela of a block of greywacke (Bhn, Lucas and Harris 1962/1989: 419–420; Aufrère 1991: 701–702; Christensen 1983: 7–24)—it was set up in the temple— [. . . that(?) I might abide]*

(*VI*) *in the following of Harpokrates, the great god, who resides in Mendes [. . .]*"

The use of the plural, "great rams," usually points to an unspecified number, not to the single, "quadripartite" entity with "four faces" residing in the main temple. The latter is usually acknowledged, when the elemental make-up is under discussion, by an explicit reference to his being "four." The great naoi of Amasis in fact did not contain ram images but anthropomorphic representations of the elemental gods (Bothmer 1988: 205–209). The Mansion of the Rams (plural) is a structure separate from the main temple, and its mortuary purpose is made plain by the phrase "the entombed rams who are in the Mansion of the Rams" (see above).

The word rendered "sarcophagi" in column II is written with an ideogram, thus: ⌒ While a similar shape is rarely used to determine "naos," the present form we submit is reflective of reality, and not generic. All naoi that have come to light so far at Mendes, including the large ones in the naos court, have pyramidal roofs, canted at various angles: none have the rounded top of the present sign.[23] Moreover, naoi would presumably be represented with a stepped approach, but the sign shows a shallow, asymmetrical (?) base. Finally, the word for naos, *k3ry*, is not accommodated by the feminine indirect genitive of the text, which militates strongly in favor of reading *db3t*, "sarcophagus." In fact the sign resembles most closely the granite boxes with their *curved* lids in which the sacred rams were buried.

If the hypogeum, which we have excavated, was designed by Nessuhor, it will have dated from the reign of Apries,[24] or approximately 575 B.C., after the episode at Elephantine, which appears to be referred to in col. I. In the text of Louvre A 90 Nessuhor is fulsome in his praise of Khnum and his divine associates for having saved him in a difficult situation, and records how, at royal command, he refurbished the divine income and the temples at Elephantine. Clearly his gratitude extended thereafter to another ram deity with whom in the Late Period Khnum was becoming increasingly identified.

From an early period the ancients discerned a shared essence among the principal ram gods of Egypt. The nature and character of Banebdjed suggested identifications with Arsaphes of Herakleopolis (Smither 1939: pl XX; Mokhtar 1983: 168; Vernus 1976: 297; Moret 1988: 139 (P. Berlin 3055 xx.6–8)), Amunre (Davies 1953: pl. 33, cols. 26ff; Yoyotte 1982–1983: 129–136), and especially Khnum (Kees 1956: 438; Sauneron 1962: 208; Sauneron 1963: 45–46; Griffiths 1970: 351).[25] His association with the last, coupled with long-standing links to Ptah-Tatenen (Sandman-Holmberg 1946: 176–177; Cairo 48831: 16–17, K*RI* VI, 23: 12–13; Herbin 1994: 122) and the solar group (see above), led to his being considered creator of all the gods (*Urk.* VI: 74.9; Sauneron 1963: 46 *passim*).

Now the link between Banebdjed and Khnum may indirectly shed light on the *end* of the (southern) Ram Hypogeum at Mendes. The decade of rebellion between 411 and 400 B.C. witnessed the successful liberation of Egypt under the leadership of Sais and Mendes (Briant 1996: 653–654). Under the leadership of the short-lived Neferites I (399–393 B.C.) who unseated his Saite colleague and erstwhile free-dom-fighter, and founded the Mendesian Twenty-ninth Dynasty (Traunecker 1979: 395–436), all trace of Persian authority ceases, and the garrison in Persian employ at Elephantine disappears.[26] It has plau-sibly been suggested that Neferites singled out the Elephantine garri-son for annihilation largely because of the close spiritual bond between the god of his home-town and Khnum, with whom the foreigners had always been at odds (Kraeling 1953: 113). For the popularity of Khnum among members of the Twenty-ninth Dynasty, one has but to examine their prenomina and epithets (Traunecker 1979). This act of violent nationalism, coupled with the fact that he had been one of the chief leaders in the rebellion against them, kept alive a hatred of Neferites' memory among the Persians, so that when, fifty years after his death Persia reconquered Egypt, Mendes became a target for revenge.

There is now abundant proof that the Persian invasion and recon-quest of Egypt in 343 B.C. resulted in the destruction of the city of Mendes (Redford, 2004). Our excavations have demonstrated that, sometime after the middle of the fourth century B.C. but before the onset of the Ptolemaic, Neferites' tomb was dismantled, smashed and desecrated, the city wall erected by Nektanebo torn down (Diodorus records the destruction of city-walls by the Persians during 343–342 B.C., XVI.51.2), and store-chambers lining the inner harbor were burned and left in ruins. It would make eminent sense historically and archaeologically if the destructive activity of the conquerors on this occasion extended also to the ram hypogeum.[27] The absence of significant amounts of Hellenistic pottery except in the overburden, would militate in favor of a date before Alexander for the ruination and abandonment of the area: even as late as Ptolemy II the site still lay in ruins. Mendes Stelae, line 9 states: "Then H.M. paid a visit to the Mansion of the Rams and he found the House of the Ram still under construction, as H.M. had ordered, to remove the destruction the rebellious foreigners had wrought in it."

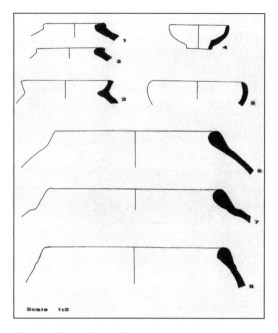

Scale   1:2

Fig. 7.16 Examples of jar types. Courtesy
Mendes Excavation.

The postulate of two and one quarter centuries of occupation (c. 570 B.C. to 343 B.C.) for the southern cemetery would suit the archaeological evidence admirably. If the sixteen odd sarcophagi unearthed represents the total number of interments, and if a pampered ram averages approximately fourteen to sixteen years of life, as confirmed by farmers in central Pennsylvania, the 225 years could be nicely accounted for. The ceramic contents of the period of (initial) occupation are consonant with a span of time from the sixth through mid-fourth century B.C.: the repertoire shows Saite jars, hole-mouth storage jars, Phoenician 'torpedo'-amphorae, Persian Period mortaria, and East Greek wine jars. Only a surface scatter of Hellenistic wares is present. (In Late Roman times [compare Fig. 7.17 and Fig. 7.18] the ruins were reoccupied by squatters who broke up some of the limestone sarcophagi to block up unwanted apertures (See fig. 7.4).

The date parameters of the northern ram cemetery are more difficult to ascertain, in part because our work there is still in progress; but the following items of evidence are clearly significant:

1. The northern hypogeum seems to be related to a broad area of limestone and quartzite construction, cleared (and destroyed) by Naville. The Ptolemaic Hathor capital now in Cairo may come from this area (de Meulenaere and MacKay 1976: pl. 13 (25)). In our surface survey this area shows Ptolemaic pottery.

2. Two massive mud-brick walls excavated by our expedition in 1995 appear to provide an approach to this site from the dromos of the Banebdjed temple. Here again ceramic evidence militates in favor of a Ptolemaic date.

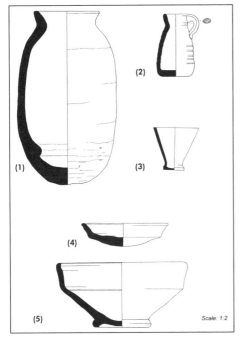

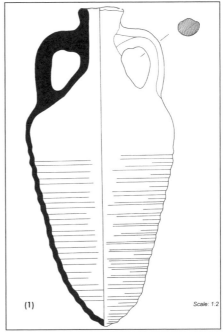

Fig. 7.17 Different pottery types.
Courtesy Mendes Excavation.

Fig. 7.18 An amphora. Courtesy
Mendes Excavation.

3. In the excavations of the gravelly rectangle west of the dromos, wherein the emplacements for the sarcophagi were found (see above), the meager ceramic content yielded Roman diagnostics. In addition, a coin of the Judaean revolt was recovered (c. 68 A.D.). It is curious that, on his march with his army from Alexandria to the seige of Jerusalem in 68 A.D., Titus passed by Thmuis/Mendes: Josephus *Bellum* IV.11.5. Presumably the same legions retraced their steps at the end of the war.

In the light of these considerations, it is tempting to construe the northern ram cemetery as the burying ground for the sacred animals during the Ptolemaic Period. It will have been built as part of the restoration of Ptolemy Philadelphos (c. 270 B.C.) who, for some reason, abandoned the older location; and will have passed out of use sometime during the first or (early) second century A.D. The final destruction of this part of the site might be put down to Christian fanaticism during the fourth century A.D., when it is now evident the temple was converted to a church.

Ram and Fish: The Veneration of Species

In general comments on animal worship in Egypt, classical authors stress the sanctity in which the sheep (sic—see above) was held by the Mendesians (Herodotus II.42; Strabo XVII.1.19; Lloyd 1976: 295). Members of the species were not considered appropriate victims for sacrificial ritual (Herodotus II.42), an assertion that seems to be born out by Brewer's observation on the lack of sheep remains from the excavations (see below). Moreover, Egyptians refused to consume the milk of sheep (Van der Horst 1984: 37–38; Chaeremon Frag. 23D). This reverence for the entire species may well have encompassed the burial of its members in necropoleis at Mendes set aside for the purpose, as was the case elsewhere with other species (Ray 2001: 346–348). No such intact burying ground has so far been uncovered at Mendes, as has been surmised to have existed at a few other sites, such as at Saqqara, location of a "branch"-cult of the "Mendesian, the Ram of Anpet" (Davies and Smith 1997: 118), where osteological evidence has been interpreted of the possible indication of the presence of an animal catacomb.[28] However, one is struck by the enormous quantity of bone material amassed in Roman times at Kom al-Adhem, perhaps for industrial purposes. Could these have been taken from some hitherto undetected animal necropolis (Kessler 1989: 42, n. 33; Lovell 1994: 20–36)?

The only mass burials of animals thus far unearthed at Mendes are those of the *schilby*-fish. In 1995, in the excavations of the royal necropolis in Field AL, it was discovered that the foundations of the mastaba tomb of Neferites I had been sunk in an area which, in New Kingdom times, had been the eastern slope of the tell, descending into a watery tract. During the Twentieth Dynasty the slope had been reserved for the deposit of cups and jars, many (if not all) containing the remains of immature *schilby*-fish (Mumford 1997: 1–3; Brewer 2001: 535). In the vicinity had once stood a number of votive stelae—twenty-four were recovered, with additional fragments—which were later 'recycled' in the walls of Neferites' tomb: half of a hieratic stelae of Ramesses VI, a personal memorial of a Saite priest Nessubanebdjed, and twenty-two anepigraphic representations of the *schilby*. The basic pattern in this latter group shows a large fish toward the top of the stelae, sometimes under a single ram, with a vast array of smaller fish ranged in two or three columns under the 'mother'-fish above. It is interesting to note that a strange reference in Aelian xvi.35 alludes to the feeding of fish to goats!

The fish cemetery at Mendes is one of the earlier examples of a practice that became ubiquitous only in the first millennium B.C. While animal burials in numbers can be attested for the Predynastic and Archaic Periods,[29] we cannot be at all certain that the motivation for such interments was the same as it was 2,500 years later. In fact, in both periods the Egyptian rationale is difficult to elicit. While in the case of the single cult animal, one can invoke the concept of an individual god's "power-manifestation," the *b3j* or avatar (Kessler 1986: 572), why during the second quarter of the first millennium B.C. should the Egyptians change their focus? Was the *entire* species now revered as a collective manifestation of the divine?

Fig. 7.19 A stela showing a fish being revered. Courtesy Mendes Excavation.

Fig. 7.20 Limestone stela with both fish and rams. Courtesy Mendes Excavation.

Here lexical choices in texts bearing upon animal cults may be of assistance. The "sacred animals" (Gk. ιερα ζώια), the objects of reverence in life and the occupants of the vast necropoleis in death, may be called *nṯr* in Demotic (Ray 1976: 74; Preisigke and Spiegelberg 1914: 24/25; Daressy 1919f: 145); or θεος in Greek (Strabo XVII.1.31). Consequently, they must, to Egyptians, have partaken of the divine in some way. One passage in a text of the first century A.D. is more explicit. In a sworn affidavit (P.S.I. 901) Fayum fishermen declare that they have never fished for "the likenesses of the oxyrhynchos or lepodotus gods" (ίδωλα θεων εξυρύνχων καί λεπιδωτῶν) (Hunt and Edgar 1977: 374, no. 329). The single animal avatar of a god could also be called "likeness," but in that case it is the likeness of the *bꜣj* of the deity.[30] This use of ειδωλον, "likeness, image," suggests that the Egyptians conceived the relationship between earthly species manifestation and the god as one of representation: the animal species was the terrestrial "replication" of the divine *archetype* in the realm of the gods. It is tempting to identify the Egyptian term underlying the Greek as *wḥ.m*, 'replication,' the word used of Apis's conceptual relationship to Ptah (Otto 1938/1964: 25).

Notes

1 There has been some discussion as to the identity of this creature. For discussions and literature concerning this debate, see Meeks 1973: 209–216; Gamer-Wallert 1970: 43–45; Brewer and Friedman 1989.

2 Mendes has suffered a rather checkered history of archaeological investigation. On the main excavations to date see the following: Daninos Pasha 1887: 19; Naville 1892–1893: 1–5; Naville 1894: 15–21. For the New York University's excavations of the 1960s and 1970s, see de Meulenaere and MacKay 1976; Hansen 1965: 31–37; Hansen 1967: 5–16; Wilson 1982. For the joint expedition of Washington, Illinois, and Pennsylvania State Universities (the latter replacing the University of Toronto), see Wenke and Brewer 1994: 265–285; Redford 1988: 49–79; Redford 1991–1992: 1–12; Redford 2001 (campaigns of 1993 through 1995). The work on the temple area will be the burden of vol. II in this series.

3 CT I, 249 "living *bꜣi* which is in Mendes"; VI, 289 "the Mendesian *bꜣi*"; cf. VI, 75; VI, 74 "Mine is my *bꜣi*! I ejaculate through him! I am a Mendesian! What I say is what they do!" (cf. BD 17a S4); Altenmuller 1975: 44.

4 On the etymology, see Redford 1994: 205.

5 See P. Louvre 3079 iii: 95–96 "the lord of *Anpet* hears thy *bai*, you are Banebdjed . . . ," and Goyon 1967: 136 n. 234.

6 See Boeser 1910: pl. IV, 13. The expression *nṯr pn špsy*, though it might have application to the processional image, has much broader reference (*pace* Kruchten: 1989: 253 n. 4).

7 The prophecy of the lamb is usually tied in to Khnum or Arsaphes (see Thissen 1998: 1046–1047), but Banebdjed might also be a candidate. The use of *hyb*, "lamb," in place of *sr*, "ram," might seem odd. One wonders if it is occasioned by a word play: the animal's prophecy is one of woe (Copt.; cf. "lamb").

8 For the practice of exposing female genitals before the god to ensure pregnancy, see Stricker 1971: 37.

9 In fact, carrying the god in procession is implied: cf. Donadoni 1969: pl. 16; cf. *Urk.* II, 37: 15 (the barque-block).

10 Only titles specifically connected with the cult of Banebdjed have been included.

11 Cf. Thoth's epithet (Hermopolis Parva): *wp rḥwy*, "he who separates the two disputants."

12 Cf. CT IV, 95 for a "festival-book of Ba-neb-djed."

13 Cf. the PN *Sdšr.f–B3*, Kaplony 1963: 98: 406; *B3 'npt*, "the Ram of Mendes," Petrie 1910: pl. XXI; ". . . the Ram of the 16th township," *LD* II, Bl. 6.

14 See the discussion in Griffiths 1970: 547; Lloyd 1976: 191–192.

15 Douglas Brewer's report to be published in the next interim report.

16 Cf. P. Jumilhac iv.20, Vandier 1953: n. 900; Vos 1998: 709–718.

17 For other sacred ram cemeteries, see Kessler 1989: 18 (9) (Elephantine), 23 (41) (Hermopolis), 24 (52), (Herakleopolis), 26 (84) (Saqqara).

18 A possible restoration: cf. *Edfou* I: 183, 220, 435: 7 *Nḏty (ḥr) jt.f* is of course another possibility.

19 Credit is due to Rupert Nesbitt, staff artist of the Mendes Expedition, for the identification of the fragments and physical restoration of one of the limestone sarcophagi and its lid on site.

20 The Elephantine rams were found to have faïence and metal amulets and beads scattered through their wrappings. See Ikram Chapter 9, this volume.

21 Confusion between the Saite cursive forms of *mw* (Erichsen 1954: 154) and *mr* (Erichsen 1954: 165).

22 Locution attested in the Middle Kingdom: Gardiner 1979, Third edition, sec. 429: 2.

23 cf. Perdu 1990: 3, pl. 2A: Our excavations have brought to light roof fragments—all pyramidal—of three additional naoi, one in Aswan granite, a second in quartzite and the third in diorite. Only the second has an inscription but the king's name is missing.

24 For Apries was still honored in Mendesian toponymy 600 years after his death, see Verreth 1998: 468.

25 The real explanation of Banebdjed's appearance at this point in the *Contendings of Horus and Seth* is to be found in his common epithet at Mendes, "he who separates the Two Gods," i.e., Horus and Seth. (This is precisely what Atum requests that he do). For the popularity of the same "Ram-names" in the onomastikon of Mendes and Elephantine, see Verreth 1998: 472 n. 59.

26 The last acknowledgment of the reign of Artaxerxes II is in 398 B.C., as mentioned in Lemaire 1991: 199–201.

27 Cf. the tradition in Aelian concerning Artaxerxes III's treatment of the Mendesian ram, which can be found in de Meulenaere and MacKay 1976: 3, and *Varia Historica* iv.8; vi.8.

28 For a listing of the osteological and other evidence, see Kessler 1989: 17ff. Banebdjed enjoyed other "branch"-cults, e.g., at Per-Sopdu (Giveon 1975: 19–21), and perhaps Naukratis (but see Yoyotte 1982–1983: 129–136); but no mass ram interments have been reported from those sites.

29 For a fish cemetery at Gurob (of Nineteenth Dynasty Date), see Kessler 1989: 39 n. 17 (53); for one at Helwan (but certainly not predynastic), see Gamer-Wallert 1970: 107 n. 223; in general on predynastic animal burials, see Flores 1999. I am grateful to D. Flores for directing my attention to several bodies of evidence, and for discussing aspects of this topic with me.

30 For the *bai* of a god manifest in an animal, see the list in Zabkar 1968: 13–15; Griffiths 1970: 359B, where Apis is said to be the εἴδωλον τῆς ψυχῆς of Ptah; Banebdjed is the *b3j* of Amunre: Griffiths 1970: 364.

8

Sobek,
Lord of the Land of the Lake

*Edda Bresciani**

The primeval power of Sobek is already acknowledged in a hymn from the Pyramid Texts (PT 317), where the dead pharaoh identifies himself with the god, who here appears as son of the Great Neith-Meher-Weret, the celestial cow of the inundation: *"Sobek, green of feathers, alert-looking, broad-chested, sparkling, coming out from the legs and the tail of the Great One, who is in splendour."*[1] This very ancient description of the divine reptile, who in the same Pyramid Texts bears also the epithet of Shedite ("that of Shedet," the capital town of the swampy region of the Fayum lake), incorporates his basic characteristics, which we also find in later descriptions: the green feathers on the head which additionally might be interpreted as a tuft of aquatic plants, the muzzle with pointed teeth and shrewd look, the breadth of the scaled chest that emerges from the water, the large body that, while moving, raises waves of foam. A god who has, and will always have, the character of an animal, an aggressive and powerful animal, who only from the Middle Kingdom onwards accepted the solar association with Horus and Ra, and who only from the Middle Kingdom onwards was represented also with a feline head set on a human body.

The epithets that often describe his physical features are very revealing: "pointed of teeth," "who is standing still on his paws," as are those that refer to his avid and rapacious nature ("who loves robbing," "who lives on robbery"). He is a male animated by sexual appetites that are violent (he is called "lord of the semen," PT 510) and unrestrained ("who eats also while he mates," "who impregnates females," Coffin Texts (CT) IV,

---

* Translation by C. Rossi.

1–2). After all, is it not true that the etymology of the name *Sbk* is traced back by scholars (as an alternative to a possible form *s3q/sbq*, "he who unites" Osiris' limbs) to a causative form *S-b3k*, "he who impregnates" (Murray 1963: 107)?

The deification and the cult of the crocodile belong to the religious phenomenon of the ancient Egyptian animal cult. Created by the demiurge together with the human beings, animals were living hypostases of divine powers (Roveri et al. 2000); in order to manifest themselves on earth, ancient Egyptian gods could take the form of an animal but also of many animals (Amun had the ram and the goose as his hypostases, and the god Thoth a baboon and the ibis bird). Deities could be represented totally zoomorphically, or as a combination: a human with an animal head.

The animal specimen which embodied the god was always unique, as a new one took the place of the dead one, who was mummified and buried with special and solemn rituals; the animals of the sacred species could be, and in fact were, numerous, and in the Late Period one encounters the impressive habit of mummifying and burying in the local necropoleis animals of the sacred species in the thousands.[2] One must consider this practice essentially as an economical issue, since animals were reared and fed in order to be killed, and, once mummified, then sold as were ex votos to pilgrims.

I do not know of any mythological tales from the pharaonic period where the crocodile has a role, a family, or feelings. However, he can absorb reflected characters, thanks to the assimilation of Sobek with the solar demiurge deity, to the Nile and Osiris. Such an example is found in the Late Period hymn engraved on the wall of a corridor in the Kom Ombo temple, dedicated to Sobek and to Hor-Haroeris (Horus the Elder):

> *Great god from whose eyes came out the two starts (the*
> *   sun and the moon),*
> *his right eye that shines during the day, and his left eye*
> *   during the night,*
> *he, whose two venerable Udjat-eyes illuminate the darkness.*
> *The wind comes out from his mouth, and the northern*
> *   wind from his nose.*

The Nile flows as his living sweat and impregnates the fields.
He acts with his phallus to inundate the Two Lands with
*   what he created.*
Scares the evil ones with his appearance
in his name of Sobek-Ra that is in his lake.
His mightiness is strong as the one of His Majesty Ra
when he exterminates his enemy with his strength.
He is the noble divine of Maat,
who judged the right of the two gods (Horus and Seth) in
*   front of Geb,*
the old one who takes care of his children, who causes the
*   aridity [to vanish],*
the mighty god who protects the weak.
How sweet it is to pray to him,
he who listens and comes to the one who calls him,
perfect of sight, reach of ears, who exists in the words of the
*   one who needs him, strong, winner, to whom nobody is*
*   similar.*
He is the most prestigious god for his strength, Sobek-Ra
*   lord of Kom Ombo,*
who loves clemency after rage.

Not far from the Ptolemaic temple of Per-Sobek, "the precinct of Sobek" of Kom Ombo, lies the animal necropolis that yielded innumerable mummies of crocodiles of all periods (Lortet and Gaillard 1909: 295–299); necropoleis of crocodiles have been also found at Esna (Lortet and Gaillard 1903: 181–183), while the Samun caves at Maabad, dating to the Roman Period, yielded thousands of mummies stacked to a height of nine meters (de Gorostarzu 1901: 182–184).

But the region where the cult of Sobek was widespread, since the earliest periods, was the Fayum, the "Land of the Lake." Here, the presence of the great amphibious reptile—let us remember the amphibious state of the primeval beings, expressed by the crocodile—was favored by the nature of the landscape, terrestrial and aquatic, dominated by the Lake of Sobek, the modern Lake Qarun.

The geographic configuration of the Fayum region, the presence of the lake and of the great branch of the Nile (the Bahr Yusuf) with its canals and its swamps, must have strongly influenced the local religious beliefs, suggesting the identification of the large liquid surfaces with the mythical primeval ocean, the Nun, whence all the living beings originally came. In this landscape the crocodile, lord of the Fayum lake and denizen of the swamp, could acquire the identity and the veneration fit for a god of the primeval waters, the Nile, in his guise as the son of the great annual inundation.

The Greek writer Diodorus Siculus (I, 89) attributed the foundation of the crocodile cult at Shedet-Crocodilopolis in the Fayum to King Menes. The veneration of these creatures, hitherto known as "disgusting and men-eaters" was based on an act of gratitude toward the animal. The king had been chased by a pack of wild dogs to the edge of the lake. There, a crocodile rescued Menes by transporting the king on his own back to the other shore of the Lake Moeris.[3]

Sobek often is said to be "beautiful of face" (a little excessive, if not ironic!). Beauty is an attribute that is used to describe many manifestations of Sobek, and the epithet "the beautiful" (Pneferos) is borne by one of the various Sobeks who was endowed with a temple and a cult in the Fayum. Others variations in the names of the local crocodile deities who are attested in the Graeco–Roman Period include: Stotoes, Penebtunis, Petesuchos, Soknopaios, Soknebtunis, Soknobraisis, Soknobkonnis, Sokonopis, Sometis, Soknemunis, Soxis, and Sokonieus. In the Fayum village of Euhemeria, a pair of crocodiles called Psosnaus, "the two brothers," were venerated, while at Karanis the local pair consisted of Pneferos and Petesuchos.

At Medinet Madi (a village founded with the name of Dja by Amenemhat III of the XII Dynasty, see note 3), Sobek held a very stable position next to the titular of the Middle Kingdom temple, Renenut, the cobra-goddess mistress of the harvest. The new Ptolemaic temple that has been recently discovered at Medinet Madi by the mission of the University of Pisa was also dedicated to a pair of divine crocodiles, as yet unnamed.

The crocodile was worshipped throughout the Fayum, and reared—at least in the main temple of Crocodilopolis—in a special space provided with a large basin for water. After its death, the divine crocodile was mummified, displayed in the naos of the temple and carried in procession on an elongated carrying chair. Temples at Karanis & Qasr el Qarun shared this feature. Several priests had specific duties associated with Sobek, some of whose titles were "prophets of the crocodile-gods" and a "burier of the bodies of the crocodile-gods of the Land of the Lake."

Several crocodile necropoleis have been found in the Fayum, as well as in Upper Egypt (see above). These include the sites of Magdola, Kom al-Khamsin, Tell Maharaqa, Theadelphia, and Tebtynis. In many instances the buried animals were not the embodiment of the god, but rather were gathered up and buried either because they were regarded as worthy of reverence as they belonged to the same species as Sobek, or were votive offerings, or because they might have held other religious significance (see Chapter 1). The mummified and buried reptiles were of various ages, often newborns. Ancient fakes also were quite common as the trade in relics was very active.

Often eggs of crocodiles have been found in connection with the mummies. A particularly interesting deposit was found at al-Lahun (de Gorostarzu 1901: 182–184, fig. 1). There, in a hole, about one meter underground, crocodile eggshells were found arranged in a circle around the outline of the hole. Several mummies were also found. These included two adult crocodiles that were in two separate graves. One animal was surrounded by about fifty tiny crocodiles that had just left the egg (between 35 and 40 cm long, some still attached to the yolk). They were arranged as a little army marching towards the head of the mummy. In the other hole, which only contained a single mummy, the eggs were located inside a bag half a meter long and wide, with the majority of the shells broken.

Also at Hawara (Petrie 1889: 6, 10, pl. 25; Gaillard and Daressay 1905: 119) the necropolis of the sacred animals yielded eggs and crocodiles of all sizes. The necropolis of the sacred crocodiles at Tebtunis,[4] south of the temple, has been explored several times since 1899 by Grenfell and Hunt (Grenfell and Hunt 1900: 376–378; Grenfell and Hunt 1902). They discovered thousands of mummified crocodiles, approximately twenty of which were wrapped in papyri or had their bodies stuffed with papyri. The animals were buried in holes rarely deeper than one meter. Later, a few crocodiles were found in that necropolis by Otto Rubensohn (1902) and by Evaristo Breccia (1929–1930). Achille Vogliano (1934), who joined the Mission of Carlo Anti with whom G. Bagnani collaborated (1934: 3–13; 1952: 76–78, Turner

1982: 171, pl. 78),[5] found some carefully embalmed crocodiles wrapped in layers of papyri dating to the Ptolemaic Period in a hole in the necropolis. Two rolls of papyri bearing demotic inscriptions containing the statutes of the local religious association of Sobek (indicated by means of the profane name of *Meseh*, "Crocodile" [Bresciani 1994: 49–67]), who was buried in the local "place of rest," were found under the jaws of one of the crocodiles. Bagnani has estimated that during about six centuries approximately ten thousand crocodiles were buried there (1952: 76–78). The location of the hatchery for these crocodiles is unknown; perhaps it lay near the canal at al-Lahun, or, as Bagnani suggested, probably with some good reasons, at Kerkeosiris near the Gharaq depression. The 'sauretai' mentioned in the Magdola papyri might have been their guardians. The cemetery also included packages containing cats and kittens.

The recent discoveries at Medinet Madi (1995, 1998–1999) by the mission of Pisa University directed by the author (since a few years ago in collaboration with the chair of Papyrology of the University of Messina and the University of Trieste for the geo-radar investigation) revealed new details about the cult of the crocodile. Excavations showed that the eggs of the sacred reptiles were kept and allowed to hatch in a special building next to the temple. The newborn reptiles were reared in this area, named Temple C[6] of Medinet Madi by the University of Pisa's archaeologists. This new temple must be added to the Middle Kingdom temple (Temple A) and the Ptolemaic temple (Temple B), discovered by Achille Vogliano in the years 1934–1939 at this site.

The greatest novelty of this find concerns the history of the local religion. About ninety crocodile eggs, buried to be nursed under the sand, were found in two structures. Many contained foeti in different stages of development. The best-preserved egg hatchery or nursery had been organized in order to control the hatching of the eggs and to rear the little amphibians. The building was covered with a perfectly preserved vault, and located adjacent to the Temple C along the north side. Inside, a shallow square basin (30 cm) complete with two very low steps, was destined to receive the small Sobeks, who were prevented by a wall from freely circulating outside the sector that had been prepared for them. The newborn reptiles could spend some time in the water of the basin before being sacrificed, mummified, and sold to the pilgrims, who could then dedicate them in the chapel of the local necropolis of the sacred animals.

This practice of sacrificing votive offerings and maintaining sacred animals (Charron 1990: 209–213) is well-known in Egypt for all sorts of divine animals, cats, dogs, ibises, etc. However, the discovery of the hatchery at Medinet Madi casts a new light on these practices. Unfortunately so far the necropolis of Medinet Madi has not yet been located, let us hope that future discoveries will reveal the whereabouts of the sacred crocodile cemetery.

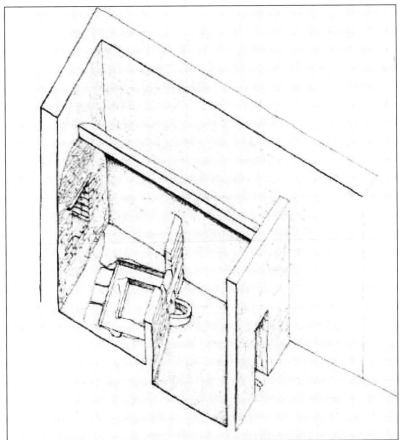

Fig. 8.1 Temple C, the area where the nursery for crocodile eggs was located. Drawing courtesy of Edda Bresciani.

Notes

1   All translations are by the author unless otherwise indicated.
2   For the identification of the Demotic title *tj n3 nṯrw Sbk* with the Greek title *theagos,* see Bresciani 1986: 50.
3   Diodorus conflates Menes, Egypt's first king, with Amenemhat III, who built the labyrinth at Hawara, leaving us confused as to which king established the cult. It is more likely Amenemhat III as he was very active in the area, far more so than Menes.
4   At Tebtunis there was also a cemetery of hawks and ibises linked to a chapel of Thoth.
5   Pictures of the mummified crocodiles found by Vogliano may be found in Gallazzi 2003: 195, fig. 9.
6   On the discoveries, beside the excavation reports annually published regularly in *Egitto e Vicino Oriente,* see Bresciani 2001: 51–54. The closest parallel to the new temple of Medinet Madi is the temple, also Ptolemaic, for the crocodile Pneferos at Theadelphia, discovered by Evaristo Breccia in 1912–1913, see Breccia 1926.

Pl. 8.1 Clutch of crocodile eggs with one egg partially hatched. Photograph by Edda Bresciani.

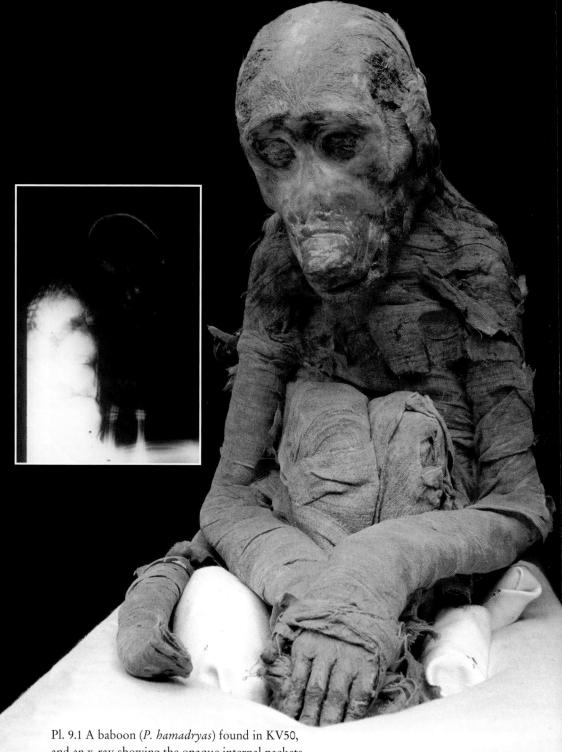

Pl. 9.1 A baboon (*P. hamadryas*) found in KV50, and an x-ray showing the opaque internal packets (CG 29837). Photograph by Anna-Marie Kellen.

Pl. 9.2 During the cleaning of this crocodile, some baby crocodiles were found inside its mouth. Photograph by Nicholas Warner

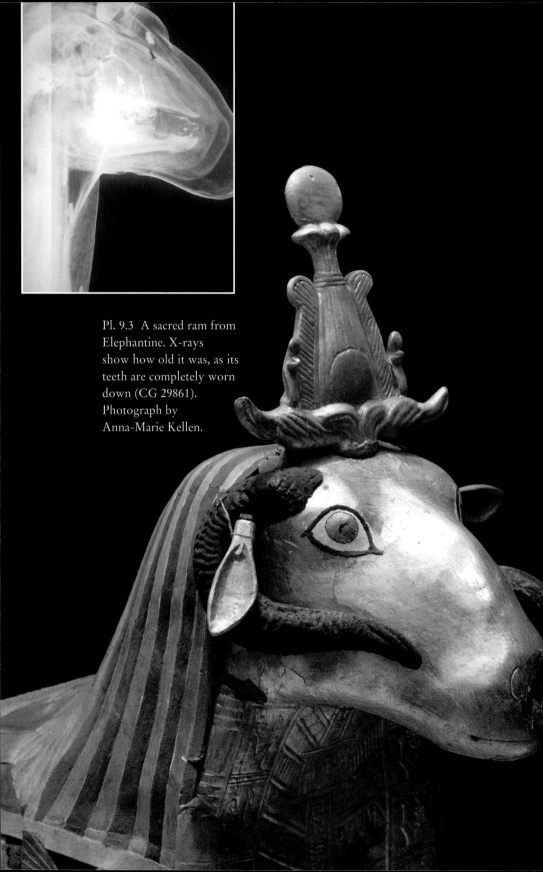

Pl. 9.3 A sacred ram from
Elephantine. X-rays
show how old it was, as its
teeth are completely worn
down (CG 29861).
Photograph by
Anna-Marie Kellen.

9

Protecting Pets
and Cleaning Crocodiles
The Animal Mummy Project

Salima Ikram

A lthough many museums in the world contain animal mummies, the Egyptian Museum in Cairo's collection is one of the largest. The collection, as we now know it, was started in the 1860s, containing only a few animal mummies, mainly ibises, crocodiles, and raptors, that were displayed as curiosities, as well as examples of intricate bandaging. A significant number were added between 1901 and 1904, thanks to the intervention of Charles Louis Lortet, grand doyen of the Faculty of Medicine at Lyon, who thought that through the study of these mummies, a greater understanding of the ancient fauna and environment could be gained.[1] In fact, the study of mummified animals provides information not only about the fauna of the country and, indirectly, its climate, but also about animal domestication, veterinary practices, human nutrition, mummification itself, and the religious practices of the ancient Egyptians.

These mummies were originally studied as representatives of the ancient fauna of Egypt, by Lortet as well as by his assistant Claude Gaillard, who, together with Georges Daressy, wrote the first *Catalogue Général* volume on mummified fauna, *La Faune Momifiée de l'Antique Egypte* (1905). These mummified animals were displayed in Room 53 of the Egyptian Museum in the room of 'Flora and Fauna.' This room was dedicated to the understanding and display of the ancient Egyptian environment.

The display of the animal mummy collection remained there, relatively intact, until the 1930s, when many of these mummies were moved to the new Agricultural Museum in Dokki. That museum took over much of the responsibility of describing the ancient Egyptian environment and the Egyptians' interaction with, and shaping of it. The removal of a large number of mummies from the Egyptian Museum to the Agricultural Museum left the collection in Room 53 much depleted. However, subsequent excavations throughout Egypt, most especially in the Sacred Animal Necropolis at Saqqara, as well as at other sites such as Tuna al-Gebel, have helped, once again, to increase the number of animal mummies housed in the Egyptian Museum. In May 1997, some animal mummies were moved to Luxor as part of the collection of the Mummification Museum, and in 2002 some more, coming from Abydos, were added to the collection.

It was not until 1998 that attention was once again focused on the 'Flora and Fauna' room, when, as a part of a larger survey of mummification, this author decided to study the animal mummy collection, and initiated the Animal Mummy Project (AMP), in cooperation with the Supreme Council of Antiquities and the Egyptian Museum, with Nasry Iskander being the designated collaborator from the latter institution. This project was one of the first modern, large-scale, non-destructive studies of animal mummies of all species undertaken anywhere in the world.[2]

The project's goals were manifold. This author's primary interest lay in studying the process of mummification when applied to animals, to see if chronological and geographical changes/particularities could be mapped, to understand the different categories of animal mummies, and to learn more about the ancient Egyptian environment. Furthermore, she hoped to establish a protocol for the non-destructive study of mummies, human or animal, in Egypt, as well as to (re)study the Egyptian Museum's holdings in order to identify the animals to genus and possibly species. The ultimate aim of the project, after the mummies had been examined, was to conserve them, to produce a new, updated *Catalogue Général* volume as the original one had been rendered obsolete, as well as to reinstall the mummies in a more sympathetic museum environment. All these goals have since been met, with some very rewarding results.[3]

The methodology used to study the mummies was non-destructive (visual and radiographic).[4] This method of study has been most satisfactory, as the identifications in the old *Catalogue Général* had come from unwrapping the mummies, a method of study that proved to contribute to their deterioration. Furthermore, several of the mummies that had not been unwrapped for the 1905 catalogue had been misidentified as the identifications had been based solely on the similarity of their shape and wrappings to unwrapped mummies. Thus many of the original inhabitants of the room were catalogued as, for example, "a wrapped animal mummy, probably a hawk/falcon/etc." The Animal Mummy Project's work has corrected many of these attributions and also discovered several ancient false and composite mummies (Ikram 2001: 18–25) in the process.

For the AMP, each specimen was provided with a data sheet on which several pieces of information were recorded, including the museum and display number(s), the date of examination, the supposed date of the item, the supposed identification of the item, its dimensions, a description of the wrappings, the state of conservation, the presence or absence of coffins, masks, etc. with accompanying descriptions and dimensions, the team members studying the mummy, any bibliography concerning the mummy, and general remarks. Each mummy was then photographed and x-rayed. The results of the x-rays were entered onto the data sheets, together with their museum number, and the mummy was then conserved, and rephotographed after conservation.

This study has yielded some important results for all the different types of mummies found in the collection: sacred, votive, victual, and pet. The number of ancient fake or partial mummies is surprisingly high, and raises interesting questions concerning the ancient Egyptians intentions vis-à-vis the mummies, particularly the votive offerings. Furthermore, for some of the votive mummies the AMP has been able to identify the method of death, and for many more, establish an age pattern at death. A select few of the more remarkable of these results will be presented here, as the scientific work on the bulk of the Egyptian Museum's corpus of animal mummies, together with their x-rays, has already been published (Ikram and Iskander 2002).

Pets[5]

Although there are many images of pets on tomb-reliefs, stelae, and coffins (e.g., JE 36445), few pet mummies have been found in undisturbed contexts, and only a small selection of these have made their way to the Egyptian Museum. The ones that have survived are quite remarkable, especially for the high quality of their mummification.

Fig. 9.1–3
Isitemkheb's pet
gazelle in its coffin,
and an x-ray of its
head (CG 29835).
Photograph by
Anna-Marie Kellen.

Obviously, for a pet to be mummified, it must have been extremely important to its owner, as the cost of mummification and the logistics involved were considerable. It is unfortunate that some of the sarcophagi (CG 5003, JE 30172), and perhaps even coffins, that must have been made for (or in the case of the coffins, shared by) such mummies are now empty.

One of the finest mummified pets is the Dorcas gazelle (*Gazella dorcas*, CG 29835) belonging to Isitemkheb D, or perhaps to another member of the Pinudjem family (Twenty-First Dynasty). It was a part of the royal cache found in tomb DB 320 in 1881. The visual and radiographic studies show that the animal was probably a female over four years old, and died naturally. It lies in a sycamore wood coffin that has been doweled together in the shape of the animal from several pieces of wood. The shaping of the coffin to the animal is a nice touch as it recalls the anthropomorphic shape of human coffins of this era. The coffin is entirely covered with a layer of white plaster, with the exterior further enhanced with black matte paint that also contains fragments of chaff.

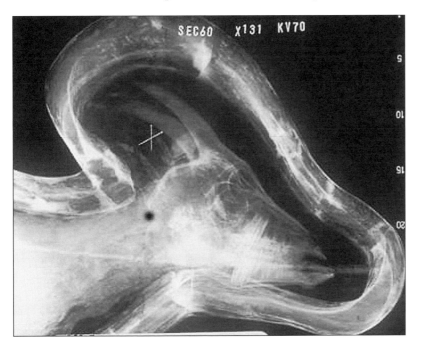

The animal is wrapped in several layers of linen, and at least one if not more larger garments. One of the bandages has a border decoration consisting of four lines of blue thread; more of this particular cloth is also found wrapped around some of the victual mummies found in the tomb, which would suggest either that the mummies were wrapped at the same time, or that this linen was commonly used in the household. Other blue-edged linen has been found from different Theban contexts, so this type of decorated border was not uncommon.

The mummification is extremely good: the animal's hoofs and fur are very well preserved. It is curious that the gazelle is missing the keratin-casing from the horns. The sheaths might have loosened and fallen off during mummification, but it is odd that they are not somewhere included in the mummy. They do not appear to have been used as handles for knives (as can be seen with camel drivers' knives today) or for anything else that was recovered from the tomb. The method of mummification used on the gazelle is very similar to that used on contemporary human mummies: evisceration, desiccation with natron, applications of oils and resins, the return of the vital organs to the body cavity, stuffing the body cavity to give it its original shape, and bandaging. Unlike the humans, the gazelle's evisceration cut was ventral rather than lateral, and the animal's brain remains within the cranial cavity. The embalmers used soils containing a high percentage of halite, a salty substance that doubtless contributed to the desiccation and preservation of the animal, as well as rolls of linen bandages to stuff the thoracic cavity and to give the gazelle the shape that it had enjoyed in life.

Other well-known pet mummies are a group of monkeys and a dog that were recovered from the Valley of the Kings (KV50 and KV51). Their identification as pet mummies is somewhat circumstantial as they were without human companions; there is a slight possibility that the monkeys were associated either with Re or possibly with Thoth, while the dog might have been associated with Anubis or Duamutef

The dog (CG 29836, JE 38640), *Canis lupis familiaris*, seems to have been related to the Saluki, and was probably used as a hunting dog (see Ikram, this volume: Fig.1.2). It was found in tomb KV50, and the robbers who had emptied it of its contents in antiquity appear to have arranged the dog so that it faced the mummy of a sad-looking young baboon, *Papio hamadryas* (CG 29837, JE 38747), who, was seated with its knees drawn up to its chest, and its tail curving around the right side of its body. The dog was ventrally eviscerated, desiccated using natron, and the body cavity partially stuffed with bandages, before being wrapped in bandages that were held in place with resin. These have long since fallen off, though one or two scraps are visible in the paw areas. According to its dentition and the epiphysial fusion of its bones, the dog was over six years old at the time of its death. The monkey appears to have been eviscerated through an enlarged cut in the anal area rather than evisceration through enema; radiographs show that a series of large packets that appear to contain soil were inserted into the animal's torso to help hold its original shape. Traces of resin, natron, and exterior bandages are still visible on the animal. The brain is unidentifiable in the radiographs; it probably has desiccated and shrunk, rather than being removed as there are no breaks in the bone. Theodore Davis, who excavated these creatures in 1906, speculated that they belonged to King Amenhotep II (c. 1427–1401 B.C.) who was buried nearby in KV35.[6] If one is using proximity to indicate possession, it is also possible that they belonged to King Horemheb (1319–1307 B.C.), buried in KV57. As both these kings were keen hunters, the dog could have belonged to either one, as could the monkey.

Four other baboons were found in KV51, two of which remain in the Egyptian Museum. This tomb also contained an ibis, three mummified ducks, and wrapped viscera covered by a mask that was dated to the Eighteenth Dynasty.[7] The entire deposit has been dated to this period by the excavators as there was no evidence to the contrary. Certainly there is evidence that all of these species, save the ibis, were kept as pets in ancient Egypt. If there is some other religious significance to this deposit, it has yet to be determined.

The two monkeys (*Papio* sp.; *P. hamadryas* or *P. anubis*) that remain in the Egyptian Museum (CG 29838, JE 38746; CG 29839, JE 38744) are both well prepared similarly to that of KV50. They might have been eviscerated per anum (but not with turpentine as parts of the windpipe are still visible in the radiographs), and then the hole slightly enlarged to introduce a few bandages into the lower abdomen. Both seem to have had the heart intact, although the latter's seems to have been slightly moved from its natural position. This baboon's lungs and windpipe were imperfectly removed as portions

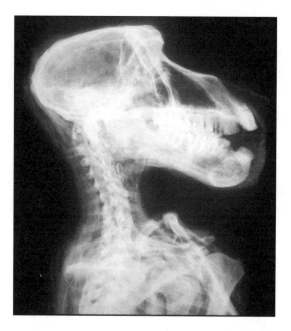

Fig. 9.4 An x-ray of a large male baboon showing how its canine teeth have been removed (CG 29839).

of the latter can be seen in the radiographs. The brain of CG 29838 has probably shrunk through desiccation. CG 29839 appears to have part, if not all of its brain in situ. Based on dentition and epiphysial fusion of the bones, CG 29838 was between three to six years old when it died, and CG 29839 well over five years in age. The canines of both animals have been extracted in order to lessen the seriousness of any bites or loving nips that they might have bestowed upon their owners or handlers. This operation would have been quite difficult and painful, and suggests advanced surgical knowledge. It also raises questions about anaesthetics (or the use of cloves and alcohol for numbing pain) in the ancient world.

Victual Mummies[8]

The Museum's collection of victual or food mummies is probably the largest in the world, numbering 46 (Ikram and Iskandar 2002). They date primarily from the New Kingdom, with some examples from the Twenty-first Dynasty coming from Isitemkheb D's burial. Such offerings clearly belong to royal as well as elite burials. The manner of preparation was fairly standard, and followed the procedure outlined in Chapter 2 of this volume. The cuts of meat that form these offerings are also standard and parallel the joints pictured on tomb walls. They can be used to reconstruct the funerary feast and to see how many creatures might have been given as offerings. Only a few of the more unusual types will be mentioned here.

Isitemkheb D (or some other member of the Pinudjem family, perhaps even Pinudjem II himself, who shared the tomb) had a few unusual cuts amongst her victual offerings (Ikram 2004b); some, like the animal's head, do appear in tomb decoration, but are not generally recovered from the food offerings, although they are a standard

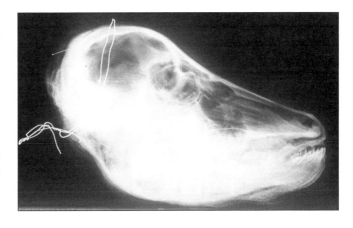

Fig. 9.5 X-rays reveal the calf's head (CG 29841).

part of offering deposits. It seems that almost an entire animal was jointed, prepared, and buried with her. The calf's head (*Bos taurus*, JE 46868, CG 29841), belonging to an animal that was aged between six and eight months at the time of its death, based on tooth eruption, formed part of the offerings. Presumably most of the remaining joints came from the same animal. The other unique offerings included a calf's tail (CG 29856, JE 46906), lungs, and windpipe (CG 29846, JE 46895). Are these just straightforward food mummies (all could be consumed in soups and stews), or do they have additional royal iconographic significance? The bull's tail was part of a king's regalia, and as this mummy was found as part of a semi-royal burial, it is possible that royal iconography was being alluded to with the inclusion of the tail. Similarly, the inclusion of the lungs and windpipe might allude to the *sema-tawy* symbol of unification that appears most commonly on the base of thrones, and could also refer to the royal nature of the burial. Although this is clearly speculation, these offerings are unique, and might have served a dual purpose in the funerary assemblage.

Tomb representations often show the sternum being cooked or carried away from the jointed beast. Although the sternum is poor in meat, it can be stewed to good effect, and is indeed sometimes consumed in this manner in contemporary Egypt. It is nice to see the reification of the tomb decoration with the inclusion of the sternum amongst the other victual mummies. Examples of this joint come not only from DB 320 (CG 29852), but also from the Eighteenth Dynasty tomb of Yuya and Thuiu, KV46 (CG 51101).

 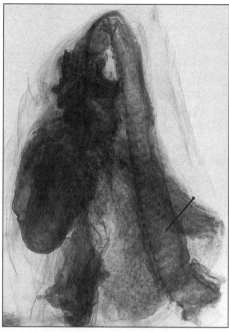

Fig. 9.6 This offering came from a collection associated with Isitemkheb and consists of a pair of lungs and a windpipe (CG 29846). Photograph by Anna-Marie Kellen.

Fig. 9.7 The *sema-tawy* or unification symbol carved on the base of a throne. Photograph by Salima Ikram.

Poultry also formed an important component of these offerings. Ducks, geese, and pigeons/doves were all prepared and buried as part of the funerary assemblage. A fine example of a goose, either *Anser albifrons* or *A. erythropus*, placed in its own wooden coffinette that was covered with plaster, black paint, and some oils, comes from KV46 (CG 51092). A well wrapped pigeon or dove (CG 51094, *Columba* sp. or *Streptopelia* sp.), whose internal cavity contained, like that of the larger water birds, the wrapped internal organs, also forms part of these offerings. It would seem that pigeons were a popular food in ancient Egypt, just as they are in modern Egypt.

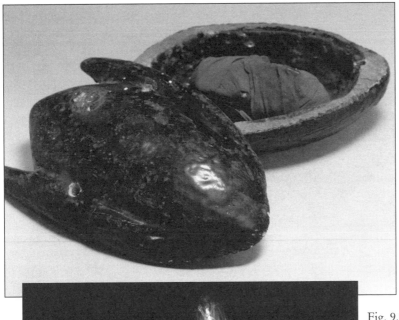

Fig. 9.8 A food offering of a dove of some sort (*Columba* sp. or *Streptopelia* sp.) (CG 51094). Photograph by Anna-Marie Kellen.

Sacred Animals

Only a limited number of positively identified sacred animal mummies form a part of the Museum's collection. The most impressive of these are two Nile crocodiles (CG 29628, CG 29630), measuring 5.20 m and 4.65 m in length, respectively. These massive creatures were manifestations of the god Sobek. They were mummified by ventral incisions of evisceration, desiccation by natron, and insertion of large quantities of resin and oils poured into the body cavities, much of which has spilled out. The resins have added considerably to the weight of the animals. Unfortunately there were no adequate facilities at the Museum for weighing these creatures; it did take nine strong men to lift the larger one.

Fig. 9.9 A massive crocodile, which was worshiped as an incarnation of the god Sobek at Kom Ombo (CG 29630). Photograph by Anna-Marie Kellen.

In the course of cleaning the larger of the sacred crocodiles, the author discovered that baby crocodiles had been placed within the animal's mouth. Most of these had deteriorated and were in pieces, but one was intact. The small crocodiles had also been desiccated and cursorily mummified. Crocodiles do transport their young in their mouths in order to ensure their safety.[9] Perhaps the insertion of babies in this manner was intended to emphasize the positive nurturing and caring aspect of this fearsome beast. A crocodile mummy in the British Museum has babies and eggs on its back, and another one just has babies.

Another possible sacred animal in the collection was the mummy of a White-tailed Eagle, *Haliaeetus albicilla*, or a Greater Spotted Eagle *Aquila clanga* (CG 29681). The bird had been covered by a resinous material and wrapped in coarse linen bandages, the outermost of which was arranged in a crossed pattern. The blackness of the linen suggests that the bird was immersed in resins or sacred oils. During conservation it was discovered that portions of the bird were gilded. Probably, the entire bird had originally been gilded, to underline its solar association with the god Re. In the second century A.D. human mummies often had their faces gilded after the skin was covered with a layer of resin so that the gilding would stick. The presence of gold on the mummy suggests that it might have been a sacred creature, rather than a mere votive mummy.

Radiographs of a sacred ram from Elephantine (CG 29861), a manifestation of Khnum, revealed the presence of several amulets. These are probably of faïence, although a few might be of metal. They comprised *wadjet* eyes, *tyt* amulets, and *djed* pillars strung around the neck, and distributed throughout the wrappings of the animal. The radiographs also showed a curious feature: the ram had no horns. It appears that the horn-cores of the animal had been sawn off! As holes are visible in the appropriate place in the x-ray it is clear that the creature originally did possess horns and was not a ewe (sacred by association, like the cows: the Mother of Apis or Buchis). Perhaps the horns were cut off and incorporated into royal or priestly headdresses; some rams seem to have their horns applied to the exterior headdresses, while a few have them on their heads. Clearly there are significant variations in the preparation of these sacred mummies. The x-rays also showed that the ram lived to a very old age as its teeth are extremely worn. It must have been fed on mashed food as it would have found difficulty in chewing.

Votive Offerings

As at any museum, the holdings of votive mummies in the Cairo Museum make up the bulk of the collection. The animals include scarabs (and even their accompanying dung balls), lizards, crocodiles, cats, dogs, shrews, serpents, ovicaprids, gazelles, cattle, raptors, ibises, and fish. Radiographs showed that several of these mummies were fakes—either due to economic/practical reasons, or because the pilgrims had been duped (see Chapter 1 for a discussion of this subject).

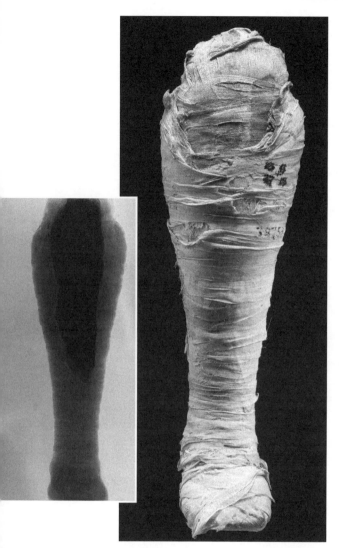

Fig. 9.10 This mummy (CG 29879) wrapped to look like a raptor originally had a mask. X-rays show that it is an ancient fake made of mud and linen. Photograph by Anna-Marie Kellen.

Proportionately, the largest number of faked mummies are of the raptors. Presumably this is because raptors are difficult to capture as they live deep in the desert, or nest in high, inaccessible places, and do not always breed successfully in captivity. One raptor mummy (CG 29685), however, lends credence to the idea that fakes were made when insufficient birds were available, and that in some cases a part of the animal could symbolize the whole. This example contains the body of what appears to be a small raptor, although the head is missing. The embalmers may have assuaged their guilt about the missing head—which could have been used to make up another mummy, not in this collection—by providing this mummy with a particularly fine cartonnage mask showing a lively looking hawk. Several ibis mummies in the collection are also ancient fakes that contain, like the hawks, mud, sand, and bandages. Some of the packages might have contained feathers, but they do not show themselves clearly in the x-rays. (for example, CG 29701, CG 29867, CG 29872, CG 29873, CG 29878, CG 29879). The collection and mummification (or burial in jars) of the detritus from

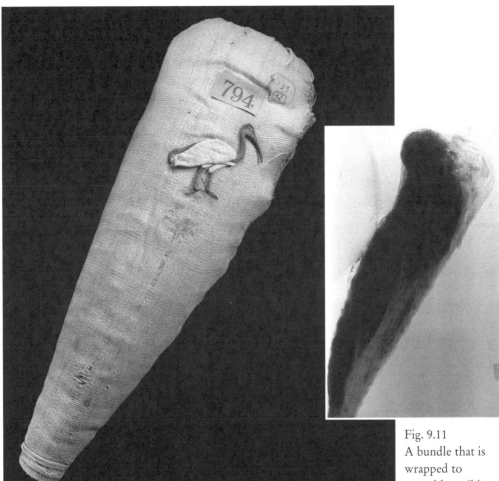

Fig. 9.11
A bundle that is
wrapped to
resemble an ibis
actually contains
loose sand and
mud (CG 29692).
Photograph by
Anna-Marie
Kellen.

these creatures was also a way of showing piety. Whether this was a
duty of the priests, or whether it was financed by pilgrims who did not
always dedicate whole mummies (a matter of economics, perhaps?), is
uncertain. However, portions of wrappings, feathers, and fragmented
bones were gathered together and fashioned into mummies, or (at Tuna
al-Gebel in particular) placed in large pottery vessels and sealed with a
pottery cover and/or a thick layer of plaster (for example, CG 29876).

A few of the cat mummies in the collection are also fakes. A particularly successful example that had been accepted as a real mummy by Lortet, Gaillard, and Daressy, had a well carved sycamore wood coffin that was painted white (CG 29775) and appeared to have been closed with a plug. The size of the aperture that the plug sealed suggested that the coffin contained a kitten; however, x-rays show that the sculpture is solid and not a coffin at all, and the plug was merely filling a broken part of the piece. Another cat mummy, in its small

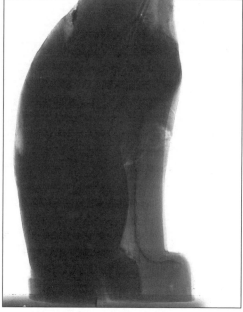

Fig. 9.12 A wooden image of a cat that was thought to contain a kitten mummy, but is actually solid (CG 29775). Photograph by Anna-Marie Kellen.

rectangular wooden coffin (CG 29783), consists of a few disarticulated bones wrapped to look like a complete mummy.

Although many of the mummies were carefully prepared so that they would not lose their fur, feathers, or fins, others were not so lucky, due to either accident or design. Some small animals, such as young crocodiles (e.g., CG 29816 *bis*) were desiccated and then covered with a thick layer of hot resin or pitch, which burned through the skin and 'cooked' the body, leaving it charred and the bones almost non-existent. Other methods seem to have involved defleshing the animal, either deliberately or through a preliminary burial where dermestid beetles and other natural forces managed to strip the bones of their flesh, so that they were collected later on, wrapped in linens, and then buried. A plastered and painted wooden image, dating to the Ptolemaic Period, in the form of an enthroned anthropomorphic Anubis figure (CG 29758) with its hands held in front of its chest, contains the disarticulated remains of a mature dog or jackal (the measurements of the bones are such that it is not possible to determine if it is a jackal; it is more probably a dog, *C. l. familiaris*). The bones have been gathered together, wrapped in a layer of linen, followed by a layer of papyrus, and a final layer of linen. Due to the disarticulated nature of the skeleton, it is impossible to tell whether or not the animal was deliberately killed.

A particularly attractive and large votive mummy belonged to a large wild cat (CG 29773, *Felis sylvestris tristrami* [?]), which was placed in a large, elegant, acacia wood coffin that was plastered and painted black. The workmanship and color of the coffin suggest an Eighteenth Dynasty date, but as the piece is unprovenienced, having come to the museum before 1903, this is difficult to determine. The coffin, carved in the shape of an enormous seated cat, more like a panther than a cat, is made in two vertical halves, and originally stood on a larger base to which it was attached by dowels. The cat's finely carved face was further enhanced with inlaid eyes, which are now lost. When it was made, the central seam between the two halves of the coffin would have been invisible, as it would have been disguised by a covering of plaster and paint. Radiographs show that the cat inside is eviscerated, with a small package reintroduced into the body cavity. All its limb bones are fused. The radiographs show an unidentified segmented object over the face and head of the cat that is very peculiar.

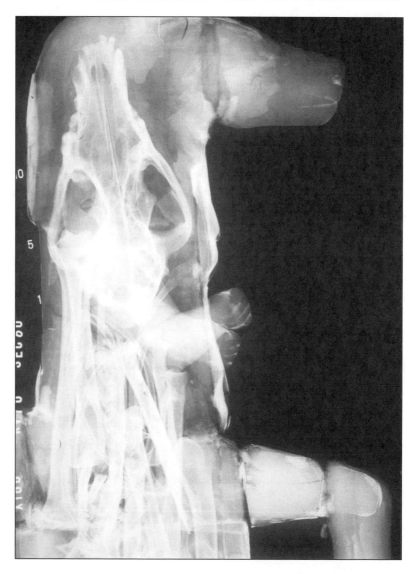

Fig. 9.13 A wooden image of Anubis (CG 29758) containing the disarticulated skeleton of a dog. It probably comes from Saqqara. It is probable
that the animal was defleshed before being wrapped and encoffined.

A curious type of votive mummy is the shrew mummy. These small creatures were sacred to the sun god as they were regarded as manifestations of his nocturnal aspect. Although some examples are mummified singly, in their own wooden or stone coffins (e.g., CG 29888, containing either a Dwarf shrew, *Crocidura nana*, or a Flower's shrew, *C. floweri*), many are mummified in large groups, some numbering over twenty (e.g., CG 29889, containing *Crocidura floweri*)!

One of the most unusual and delightful types of votive mummy is the crocodile egg. These were dedicated to Sobek, and were powerful symbols of rebirth and resurrection, as well as underlining the solar (circular) aspect of the god. These eggs were wrapped up in linen bandages and anointed with oils and resins. In general they were empty, the yolks and white long since having dried. However, one example in the Egyptian Museum, CG 29582, contains the remains of a fetal crocodile.

The most extraordinary type of votive mummy, that is not, in the strictest sense an animal mummy, is the dung ball. These were given, along with scarab beetles *(Scarebus sacer)*, as offerings to the sun god. The scarab

Fig. 9.14 An elaborately wrapped bundle containing over twenty-one shrew mummies (left), and a circular bundle containing snake mummies (CG 29889, CG 29724). Photograph by Anna-Marie Kellen.

beetle was associated with the sun god and the idea of creation and resurrection as it was thought that the young beetles sprung miraculously
from the circular ball that resembled the sun (magical creation), which
was pushed by the parent beetle across the ground in the same way as the
sun traversed the firmament. These dung balls were no doubt economical
gifts from devoted but poor pilgrims, and illustrate the extremes that
people went to in their devotions involving animal cults in the twilight of
Egyptian history.

These diverse types of animal mummies can be visited in a pair of
refurbished rooms (Gallery 53) on the Upper Floor of the Egyptian
Museum, Cairo.

Fig. 9.15 The Animal Mummy Room as it now looks. Photograph by Francis Dzikowski.

Notes

1   For a history of the animal mummy collections at the Egyptian Museum, Cairo, see Ikram and Helmi 2002: 563–568.
2   The staff of the project consisted of: A. Abd el Fatir, T. Abd el Alaa, A. Abd el Samea, K. Brush, F. Cole, F. Dzikowski, K. Fowkes, A. Helmy, R. Hoath, S. Ikram, N. Iskander, B. Jewell, A. Kellen, S. Olson, N. Warner, M. Wetherbee, and M. el Zeiny. The Animal Mummy Project would like to thank the SCA, particularly Drs. Z. Hawass, M. Chimmy, M. Eldamaty, M. el Helwagy, S. Abd el-Razik, I. Abd el Gawad, A. Mahmoud, S. el Sawy, and our donors, of whom only the most major are listed here: the Bioanthropology Foundation, the Institute for Bioarchaeology, the American University in Cairo, Proctor and Gamble, *KMT*, the Royal Netherlands Embassy, Mazda, B. Mertz, C. Boyer, and most of all R. Walker. Many other private individuals contributed to this project, and we are extremely grateful to all of them, but cannot list them here due to space constraints.
3   The Animal Mummy Room is now open to visitors in its reinstalled state, with fiber optic lighting, new labels, and new display cases. The *Catalogue Général of Non-Human Mummies* (Cairo: Supreme Council of Antiquities, 2002) has also been published.
4   A CT-scanner would have been most useful in this work; however, as none were available normal x-rays were taken.
5   Ikram and Iskander 2002.
6   Davis 1908: 4–5.
7   Davis 1908: 4–5, 17–18; Reeves and Wilkinson 1996.
8   Ikram and Iskander 2002: 1–3, 29–33, 48–52, 58.
9   The British Museum owns a crocodile mummy, excavated by W.M.F. Petrie at Hawara, that was mummified with several babies on its back.

Postscript to the 2015 Edition

Since *Divine Creatures* was written, the world of animal mummies has seen some major changes, perhaps in part due to the attention the subject garnered after the publication of this volume in 2005. From being a relatively obscure topic, it has moved more into the mainstream of Egyptology as well as scientific archaeology, with many more projects dedicated to it, studies carried out on assemblages, conferences on the subject (for example, the Egypt Exploration Society's *Ancient Animals: Mummies and Mysteries*), MAs and PhDs focused on different aspects of the subject, and television documentaries on different facets of the topic being devoted to it. Research is not limited to the mummies themselves, although they remain the major focus. In addition, scholars are intensifying their study of the texts, objects, and locations associated with the cult, dedication, mummification, and burial of these creatures (Meyrat 2010a, 2010b; Meyrat 2012a, 2012b; Charron and Farout 2008; Smith and Davies 2005; Smith et al. 2006; Smith et al. 2011; Davies 2007; Ray 2011; Ray 2013), as well as the economic impact of the whole institution of animal mummification (Ikram 2015a, 2015b)

Several new under the aegis of S. Porcier excavations of animal mummies have started, using traditional and innovative methodologies. The resulting publications elucidate the breeding and rearing of animals specifically for the temple cult, identify different breeds, and discuss the treatment of the animals by the keepers and handlers. These include the studies at Saqqara in the Necropolis of the Dogs associated with the

Anubeion (Ikram et al. 2013; Nicholson et al. 2015) and in the Teti cemetery (Hartley et al. 2011), the work on the dog burials at Asyut (Kahl and Kitagawa 2010; Kahl et al. 2009; 2011; 2012); the examination of the dog tombs in Kharga Oasis (Dunand and Lichtenberg 2005; Dunand et al. 2015; Ikram 2014); both human and canine interments in Baharia Oasis (Adam and Colin 2012; Ikram 2013) and Deir el-Banat in the Fayum (Ikram 2013); the analyses of the bird catacombs in Theban Tombs 11–12 (Ikram et al. in preparation), at Quesna (Rowland et al. 2013), Kom el-Ahmar/Sharuna, and Abydos (Bestock 2012; Ikram 2007). Material from old excavations related to animal cemeteries is also being published, using new technologies, such as the ram cemetery at Elephantine (Delange and Jaritz 2013; Ikram et al. 2013), and new approaches and technologies are being used to document and analyze animal cemeteries at sites, such as Abydos, which have been undergoing long-term excavation.

Some of these new excavations have yielded information that is leading us to a more nuanced understanding of the roles of different animal mummies within the tomb context. The work of Hartley et al. (2011) on a group of dogs found with humans in a tomb at the Teti Cemetery at Saqqara has led to a discussion of these animals being used as protective creatures, designated as amuletic mummies by their excavators. Although this definition is still being refined and debated (Ikram 2013), it indicates that animal mummies played a diverse role in the religious lives of the ancient Egyptians.

The vast reserves of animal mummies collected by Lortet and Gaillard in the Natural History museum at Lyon (now renamed the Musée des Confluences) that were the source of the seminal works on animal mummies (Lortet and Gaillard 1903–1909) are also being examined anew under the aegis of S. Porcier. The mummy bundles are being imaged, samples are being taken for DNA, the types of wrappings are being analysed, carbon 14 dating is being carried out on some of the mummies, and the embalming agents are also subject to analysis. Similar work is being carried out on the collection of animal mummies in the Egyptian Museum in Turin, and animal mummies in South African museum collections. In Manchester, the KNH Centre for Egyptology has established an ancient Egyptian animal bio bank where samples of mummified animals are to be kept (McKnight et al. 2011), and where imaging data from the mummies that they have examined are stored.

A host of exhibitions have sprung up with animal mummies as the driving force behind them. The Oriental Institute at Chicago hosted *Between Heaven and Earth: Birds of Ancient Egypt* (2012; LeSeur 2012), and the Brooklyn Museum has created a traveling exhibition *Soulful Creatures: Animal Mummies in Ancient Egypt* (2014; Bleiberg et al 2013) that is extremely well received wherever it has been shown. The Manchester Museum is planning an exhibition on animal mummies in 2015, there is one opening in Spain in 2015, there is a planned one for Italy in 2016, and the British Museum is carrying out imaging on its animal mummies, most notably a crocodile with its babies on its back, before putting them in a new display. Of course, special exhibitions on Egyptian mummies continue to feature animal mummies as well, such as the show in the Stuttgart Landesmuseum Württemberg *Ägyptische Mumien, Unsterblichkeit im Land der Pharaonen* (von Recklinghausen 2007; Ikram 2007), and the newly installed mummy galleries at the Smithsonian Institution (Ikram et al. In preparation).

The science that is used to study these mummies has also advanced considerably. In terms of imaging, both x-rays and CT-scans are being more commonly used to study mummies in museum collections, while x-ray imaging is fairly standard in the field. Increasingly, this imaging reveals curious features of mummification, including the provision of food for the afterlife for the mummified creature (Wade et al. 2012), as well as illustrating the health of the animals themselves. Creating three-dimensional models of animal mummies, extracted and printed from the imaging is also now possible (Slabbert et al. In press), providing one with a physical manifestation of the skeleton that lies within the wrappings. This can be used for a nuanced identification of species, as well as studies of disease and mummification methods.

Ancient DNA studies of animals are also taking place. Cat mummies have been studied to establish areas of domestication (Kurushima et al. 2012), crocodile mummies have been used to identify different species (Hekkala et al. 2011), and Sacred Ibis mummies are being studied to identify breeding populations (Spigelman et al. 2008; Lambert Group in Brisbane, Australia). Although Carbon 14 is well known as a dating tool, it is only recently that it has been used to compare the age of mummies with what is known from historical sources (Wasef et al. In preparation), thereby providing tighter dating for the tradition of animal mummification, as well as the phasing of construction of some of the catacombs that are anepigraphic.

Other technologies including Fourier transform infrared micro-spectroscopy, gaschromatography/mass spectrometry, pyrolysis/gas chromatography mass spectrometry techniques and enzyme-linked immunosorbent assay (ELISA), as well as electron microscopy/energy dispersive x-ray spectroscopy are being used to elucidate the materials used in the preparation of animal mummies (Buckley et al. 2004; Clark et al. 2013; Ikram 2013; Ikram 1995). The results from these studies show that expensive imported materials were being used to mummify animals, and not just for human. This work not only informs our understanding of the materials used in mummification, but also emphasizes the economic aspects of making mummies, involving masses of local as well as imported materials (natron, resins, beeswax, and oils) that impacted the Egyptian economy. Stable isotope analysis is being planned for mummies in the collection at Lyon as well as elsewhere. Such studies will yield information about diet and possibly the location of an animal prior to its demise—such a study, led by Nathaniel Dominy, is currently being used in order to establish the options for sources of the baboons brought to Egypt after the New Kingdom.

Clearly animal mummy studies are forging ahead, elucidating the role that these artefacts played in the lives of the ancient Egyptians. With each new piece of research informs our understanding of the way in which animals were bred for mummification, how they were treated during their life, how they died, the technologies used to produce mummies, the medical and technological expertise of the ancient Egyptians, the reasons for making mummies, the impact of the cults on the overall economy of Egypt, and the dates when animal cults flourished are increasing. Hopefully the increased interest in animal mummies will continue, allowing us to use these incredible objects to gain an insight into the life and culture of the ancient Egyptians and the animals that surrounded them.

Abbreviations

ASAE	*Annales du Service des Antiquités de l'Égypte* (Cairo)
BD	Book of the Dead
BES	*Bulletin of the Egyptological Seminar* (New York)
BIE	*Bulletin de l'Institut Egyptien/d'Egypte* (Cairo)
BIFAO	*Bulletin de l'Institut Français d'Archéologie Orientale du Caire* (Cairo)
BiOr	*Bibliotheca Orientalis* (Leiden)
BM	British Museum (London)
BMFA	*Bulletin of the Museum of Fine Arts* (Boston)
BMMA	*Bulletin of the Metropolitan Museum of Art* (New York)
BSAA	*Bulletin de la Société Archéologique d'Alexandrie* (Alexandria)
BSFE	*Bulletin de la Société Français d'Egyptologie* (Paris)
CdÉ	*Chronique d'Egypte* (Brussels)
CG	Catalogue Général des Antiquités Egyptiennes du Musée du Caire
CM	Egyptian Museum (Cairo)
CNRS	Centre National de la Recherche Scientifique
CT	Coffin Texts
DE	*Discussions in Egyptology* (Oxford)
Dendara	*Le Temple de Dendara*, vols. I–IV E. Chassinat, vols. VI–VIII E. Chassinat and F. Dumas, vol. IX F. Daumas and B. Lenthéric, vols. X–XI S. Cauville (Cairo: IFAO)
Edfou	*Le Temple d'Edfou*, vol. I Marquis de Rochemonteix, vols. II–III E. Chassinat and Marquis de Rochemonteix, vols.IV–XIV E. Chassinat. Cairo: IFAO/Paris: E. Leroux (early volumes)
EEF/S	Egypt Exploration Fund/Society
GM	*Göttinger Miszellen* (Göttingen)
IFAO	Institut Français d'Archéologie Orientale

JACF	*Journal of the Ancient Chronology Forum* (Redhill)
JARCE	*Journal of the American Research Center in Egypt* (New York)
JE	Journal d'Entrée (CM)
JEA	*Journal of Egyptian Archaeology* (London)
JNES	*Journal of Near Eastern Studies* (Chicago)
JSSEA	*Journal of the Society for the Study of Egyptian Antiquities* (Toronto)
KMT	*KMT: a Modern Journal of Ancient Egypt* (San Francisco/ Sebastopol)
KRI	*Ramesside Inscriptions: Historical and Biographical*, 1–6, K. Kitchen (1975-96) (Oxford: Blackwell)
LÄ	*Lexikon der Ägyptologie* I–VII, W. Helck and W. Westendorf (eds) (Wiesbaden: Otto Harrassowitz)
LD	Lepsius, K.R. *Denkmaeler aus Aegypten und Aethiopien* (Berlin)
MAFB	Mission Archéologique Française du Bubasteion
MDAIK	*Mitteilungen des Deutschen Archäologischen Instituts, Kairo* (Mainz)
M.Habu	*Medinet Habu* VI. (1930-1970) (Chicago: Oriental Institute)
MFA	Museum of Fine Arts (Boston)
MMA	Metropolitan Museum of Art (New York)
OMRO	*Oudheidkundige Mededeelingen uit het Rijksmuseum van Oudheden te Leiden* (Leiden)
P.	Papyrus
PT	Pyramid Texts
RdÉ	*Revue d'Égyptologie* (Leuven)
Rev. Ég.	*Revue Égyptologique* (Paris)
RT	*Receuil des Travaux* (Paris)
UPZ	*Urkunden der Ptolemaeerzeit*, U. Wilcken (1927/77) (Berlin-Leipzig: Walter de Gruyter and Co.)
Urk.	*Urkunden des ägyptischen Altertums* (Leipzig, Berlin)
Varia Historica	*Varia Historica, aangeboden aan Professor Doctor A.W. Byvanck ter gelegenheid van zijn zeventigste verjaardag.* (1954) (Assen: Van Gorcum)
ZÄS	*Zeitschrift für ägyptische Sprache und Altertumskunde* (Leipzig/Berlin)

Bibliography

Abd Allatif, A., and S. De Sacy, trans. 1814. "Extract from the Relation Respecting Egypt." In J. Pinkerton, ed., *A General Collection of the Best and Most Interesting Voyages and Travels in all Parts of the World*. London: Londman, Hurst, Rees, Orme, and Brown.

Abd el-Gelil, M., A. Saadani, and D. Raue. 1996. "Some Inscriptions and Reliefs from Matariya." *MDAIK* 52:143–56.

Abd el-Halim, N., and D. Kessler. 1996. "Das Priesterhaus am Ibiotapheion von Tuna el-Gebel." *MDAIK* 52:262–93.

Abdel Salam, A. 1938. "Rapport sur les fouilles du Service des Antiquités à Abou Yassin Charquieh." *ASAE* 38:609–22.

Abgrall, R. 1988. "La nature vue aux rayons x." *Le Manipulateur* 91:19–20.

Abou-Ghazi, G., ed. 1984. "In the City of Wisdom." In *Sami Gabra: From Tasa to Touna*. Cairo: Dar al-Ma'arif.

Adam, F., and F. Colin. 2012. "Inhumations d'enfants et de chiens à Qasr 'Allam, Bahariya, Égypte." In M.-D. Nenna, ed., *L'enfant et la mort dans l'Antiquité II: Types de tombes et traitement du corps des enfants dans l'antiquité gréco-romaine*, 315–30. Alexandria: Centre d'Etudes Alexandrines.

Aelian. 1958–59. *On the Characteristics of Animals*. Translated by A.F. Scholfield. Cambridge: Harvard University Press.

———. 1997. *Historical Miscellany X*. Translated by G. Wilson. Cambridge: Harvard University Press.

El-Alfi, M. 1972. "Recherches sur quelques scarabées de Ramsès II." *JEA* 58:176–78.

Alliot, M. 1949–54. "Le Culte d'Horus a Edfou au temps des Ptolémées." *Bi. Etud* 200:600–607.

Altenmuller, B. 1975. *Synkretismus in den Sargtexten*. Wiesbaden: Harrassowitz.

El Amir, M. 1958. "The Sekos of Apis at Memphis." *JEA* 34:183.

Ammianus Marcellinus. 1935–39. *Res Gestae.* Translated by J.C. Rolfe. Cambridge: Harvard University Library.

Armitage, P.L., and J. Clutton-Brock. 1980. "Egyptian Mummified Cats Held by the British Museum." *MASCA, Research Papers in Science and Archaeology* 1:185–88.

———. 1981. "A Radiological and Histological Investigation into the Mummification of Cats from Ancient Egypt." *Journal of Archaeological Science* 8:185–96.

Arnold, D. 1999. *Temples of the Last Pharaohs.* Oxford: Oxford University Press.

Assmann, J. 1996. *Aegypten. Ein Sinngeschichte.* Munich: Hanser.

Aston, D.A. 1989. "Takeloth II—A King of the 'Theban Twenty-third Dynasty'?" *JEA* 75:139–53.

Atherton, S.D., A.R. David, D.R. Brothwell, and L.M. McKnight. 2012. "A Healed Femoral Fracture of *Threskiornis aethiopicus* (Sacred Ibis) from the Animal Cemetery at Abydos, Egypt." *International Journal of Palaeopathology* 2:45–47.

Aubert, J.-F., and L. Aubert. 1974. *Statuettes Égyptiennes: Chaouabtis, Ouchebtis.* Paris: Maisonneuve.

Aufrere, S. 1991. *L'univers mineral dans la pensee egyptienne* I–II. Cairo: IFAO.

———. 1997. "Une Necropole ptolemaique de taureaux Apis visitee en 1716 par Paul Lucas et Claude Sicard?" In C. Berger and B. Mathieu, eds., *Etudes sur l'Ancien Empire et la nécropole de Saqqara dédiées à Jean-Philippe Lauer*, 55–68. Montpellier: Université Paul Valéry.

Ayrton, E., and W.L.S. Loat. 1911. *The Predynastic Cemetery at El Mahasna.* London: William Clowes.

Bacon, E. 1971. *Archaeology: Discoveries in the 1960s.* London: Cassell.

Al-Baghdadi, A. 1964. *The Eastern Key: Kitab al-ifadah wa'l-i'tibar of 'Abd al-Latif Al-Bahgdadi.* Translated by K.H. Zand, J.A Videan, and I.E. Videan. London: George Allen and Unwin.

Bagnani, G. 1934. "Gli scavi di Tebtunis." *Aegyptus* 19:3–13.

———. 1952. "The Great Egyptian Crocodile Mystery." *Archaeology* 5 (2): 76–78.

Bailleul-LeSeur R., ed. 2012. *Between Heaven and Earth: Birds of Ancient Egypt.* Chicago: Oriental Institute of the University of Chicago.

Barta, W. 1973. *Untersuchungen zum Götterkreise der Neunheit.* Munich: Deutscher Kunstverlag.

———. 1974. "Untersuchungen zum Götterkreis der Neunheit." *JARCE* 11:101–

104.

Batrawi, A. 1948. "Anatomical Reports 1948. A Small Mummy from the Pyramid of Dashur." *ASAE* 48:585–98.

Bauman, B. 1960. "The Botanical Aspects of Ancient Egyptian Embalming and Burial." *Economic Botany* 14:37–55.

Begelsbacher-Fischer, B. 1981. *Untersuchungen zur Götterwelt des alten Reiches.* Fribourg: Vandenhoeck & Ruprecht.

Bell, H.I. 1957. *Cults and Creeds in Graeco-Roman Egypt.* Liverpool: Liverpool University Press.

Bernand, E. 1990. "Le culte du lion en Basse-Egypte d'après les documents grecs." *Dialogues d'histoire ancienne* 16 (1): 63–65.

Bestock, L. 2013. "Brown University Abydos Project: Preliminary Report on the First Two Seasons." *JARCE* 48:35–79.

Beudels, M.-O., and G. Lenglet. 1989. *Les Chats des Pharaons: "4000 ans de devinité féline."* Brussels: Institut Royal des Sciences Naturelles de Belgique.

Bickel, S., and P. Tallet. 1997. "La nécropole saite d'Héliopolis: Étude préliminaire." *BIFAO* 97:67–90.

Bierbrier, M.L., ed. 1982. *Hieroglyphic Texts from Egyptian Stelae etc. Part 10.* London: British Museum Publications.

Bietak, M., and E. Reiser-Haslauer. 1982. *Das Grab des 'Anch-Hor II.* Vienna: Austrian Academy of Sciences Press.

Bisson de la Roque, F. 1924. *Abou-Roasch.* Cairo: IFAO.

Bleiberg, E., Y. Barbash, and L. Bruno. 2013. *Soulful Creatures: Animal Mummies in Ancient Egypt.* Brooklyn: Brooklyn Museum.

Boeser, P.A.A. 1910. *Beschreibung der aegyptischen Sammlung der Niederlaendischen Reichsmuseums,* III, *Stelen.* The Hague: Nijhoff.

Boessneck, J. ed. 1987. *Tuna el-Gebel I. Die Tierknochenfunde aus den Pavian- und Ibisgalerien von Tuna el-Gebel.* Hildesheim: Gerstenberg.

Boessneck, J., et al. 1987. *Die Münchner Ochsenmumie.* Hildesheim: Gerstenberg.

Bongrani Fanfoni, L. 1978. "Due elementi lignei di sarcofagi di babbuini." *Oriens Antiquus* 17:197–98.

Borghouts, J.F. 1978. *Ancient Egyptian Magical Texts.* Leiden: E.J. Brill.

Bothmer, B.V. 1949. "Statuettes of *W3d.t* as Ichneumon Coffins." *JNES* 8:121–23.

———. 1988. "The Great Naos at Mendes and Its Sculpture." In E. C. M. van den Brink ed., *The Archaeology of the Nile Delta Egypt: Problems and Priorities. Proceedings of the Seminar held in Cairo, 19–22 October 1986, on the Occasion of the Fifteenth Anniversary of the Netherlands Institute of*

Archaeology and Arabic Studies in Cairo, 205–20. Amsterdam: Netherlands Foundation for Archaeological Research in Egypt.

Brady, T.A. 1935. *The Reception of the Egyptian Cults by the Greeks 330–30 B.C.* Columbia: The University of Missouri Studies.

Brauenstein, E.M., et al. 1988. "Paleoradiologic Evaluation of the Egyptian Royal Mummies." *Skeletal Radiology* 17:348–52.

Breccia, E. 1926. *Le Rovine e i monumenti di Canopo, Teadelfia e il tempio di Pneferos*. Bergamo: n.p.

———. 1986. "Iconografia e culto di Premarres nel Fayum." *Egitto e Vicino Oriente* 9:50.

———. 1994a. "Dei Coccodrilli a Tebtynis P. Vogl. Demot. Inv. 77 e Inv. 78." *Egitto e Vicino Oriente* 17:49–67.

———. 1994b. "Nuovi statuti demotici di 'Confraternite' dalla necropoli dei Coccodrilli a Tebtynis." *Acta Demotica: Acts of Fifth International Conference for Demotists*, 49–67. Pisa: Giardini Editori E Stampatori.

———. 2001. "Archaeological Research Conducted by the University of Pisa from Aswan to Saqqara." In M. Casini and Istituto italiano di cultura per la R.A.U., Italy, *One Hundred Years in Egypt. Paths of Italian Archaelogy*, 51–54. Milan: Mondadori.

———. 2005. "Sobek, Lord of the Land of the Lake." In S. Ikram ed., *Divine Creatures: Animal Mummies from Ancient* Egypt, 199–206. Cairo: American University in Cairo Press.

Brewer, D. 2001. "Fish." In D.B. Redford ed., *The Encyclopaedia of Ancient Egypt*, vol. 1, 532–35. New York: Oxford University Press.

Brewer, D., and R. Friedman. 1989. *Fish and Fishing in Ancient Egypt*. Warminster: Aris and Phillips.

Briant, P. 1996. *Histoire de l'empire perse*. Paris: Fayard.

Brier, B., and M.V.L. Bennet. 1979. "Autopsies on Fish Mummies." *JEA* 65:128–33.

Brier, B., and R.S. Wade. 1996. "The Use of Natron in Human Mummification: A Modern Experiment." *ZÄS* 123:124, 89–100.

———. 1999. "Surgical Procedures During Ancient Egyptian Mummification." *ZÄS* 126:126, 89–98.

Brugsch, H. 1883–91. *Thesaurus inscritionum Aegypticarum*. Leipzig: J.C. Heinrichs.

———. 1884. "Der Apis-Kreis aus den Zeiten des Ptolemaer." *ZÄS* 22:110–36.

———. 1886. "Der Apis-Kreis aus den Zeiten des Ptolemaer." *ZÄS* 24:19–40.

Brunner-Traut, E. "Spitzmaus." *LÄ* 5:1160–61.

Brunton, G. 1930. *Qau and Badari III*. London: British School of Archeology in Egypt.

Bryan, B. 1991. *The Reign of Thutmose IV*. Baltimore: Johns Hopkins University Press.

Buckley, S.A., K.A. Clark, and R. Evershed. 2004. "Complex Organic Chemical Balms in Pharaonic Animal Mummies." *Nature* 413:837–41.

Callou, C., A. Samzun, and A. Zivie. 2004. "A Lion Found in the Egyptian Tomb of Maia." *Nature* 427:211–12.

Capart, J. 1927. "Rapport sur une fouille faite du 14 au 20 février 1927 dans la nécropole de Héou." *ASAE* 27:43-6.

Carter, H. 1932. "Notes on Meats in the Tomb of Tutankhamun." Unpublished paper. Griffith Institute, Oxford.

Cauville, S. 1987. *Essai sur la théologie du Temple d'Horus à Edfou*. Cairo: IFAO.

———. 1989. "Da Chapelle de Thot-Ibis à Dendera." *BIFAO* 89:43–66.

Cenival, F. de. 1977. "Deux papyrus inédits de Lille: avec une révision du P.dém. Lille 31." *Enchoria* 7:1–49.

Cerny, J. 1965. *Hieratic Inscriptions from the Tomb of Tutankhamun*. Oxford: Oxford University Press.

Chaaban, M. 1919. "Rapport sur la Découverte de la Tombe d'un Mnévis de Ramsès II." *ASAE* 18:193–95.

Charron, A. 1990. "Massacres d'animaux à la Basse Epoque." *RdÉ* 41:209–13.

———. 1996. "Les animaux et le sacré dans l'Egypte tardive: fonctions et signification." Ph.D. thesis. Thèse de doctorat Sci. relig. Ecole pratique des hautes etudes (E.P.H.E.), Paris.

———. 1997. "Des 'momies' de lions à Saqqarah." *Bulletin Société d'Égyptologie Genève* 21:5–10.

———. 2001. "Les Canidés sacrés dans l'Égypte de la Basse Époque." *Égypte, Afrique, et Orient* 23:7–22.

———. ed. 2002. *La mort n'est pas une fin, pratiques funéraires en Egpte d'Alexandre à Cleopâtre*, catalogue. Arles: Musée de l'Arles antique.

———. 2003. "Taxonomie des espèces animales dans l'Egpte gréco-romaine." *BIFAO* 156:7–19.

———. 2009. "Le Faucon d'Edfou." *Egypte, Afrique, & Orient* 53 (March–May): 49–58.

———. 2010a. "Les animaux momifiés d'Abou Rawash." *Archéologia* 481 (October): 51–53.

———. 2010b. "La nécropole du Ouadi Qaren." *Archéologia* 481 (October): 54–57.

———. 2011. "Les momies d'animaux: une classification des espèces dans l'Egypte ancienne." *Espèce* 1:58–65.

———. 2013. "De bien particulières momies animals." In G. Tallet and Chr. Zivie-Coche eds., *Le Myrte et la rose. Mélanges offerts à Françoise Dunand par ses élèves, collègues et amis*, 229–47. Montpellier: CENiM.

Charron, A., and D. Farout. 2008 "Le premier sarcophage en pierre du taureau Apis." *Egypte, Afrique et Orient* 48:39–50.

Chassinat, E. 1899. "Textes provenant du Sérapéum de Memphis." *RT* 21:56–73.

———. 1900. "Textes provenant du Sérapéum de Memphis." *RT* 22:9–26, 163–80.

———. 1901. "Textes provenant du Sérapéum de Memphis." *RT* 23:76–90.

———. 1903. "Textes provenant du Sérapéum de Memphis." *RT* 25:50–62.

———. 1916. "La mise a mort rituelle d'Apis." *RT* 38:33–60.

Chevereau, P.-M. 1985. *Prosopographie des cadres militaires égyptiens de la Basse Époque*. Paris: Cybèle.

Christensen, O. 1969. "Un examen radiologique des momies égyptiennnes des musées Danois." *La Semaine des Hôpitaux* 45:1990–98.

Christensen, T.F. 1983. "Comments on the Stea (ÆIN 1037 E 872; A 759), Ny Carlsberg Glyptotek, Copenhagen." *GM* 65:7–24.

Clark, K.A., S. Ikram, and R.P. Evershed. 2013. "Organic Chemistry of Balms Used in the Preparation of Pharaonic Meat Mummies." *Proceedings of the National Academy of Sciences Proceedings of the National Academy of Sciences* 110 (51): 20392–95.

Clarysse, W. 1988. "A Demotic Self-dedication to Anubis." *Enchoria* 16:7–10.

Clement of Alexandria. 2002. *Paedagogus*. M. Marcovich, ed. Leiden: Brill.

Clifford, W., and M. Wetherbee. 2004. "Piecing Together the Secrets of Mummification." *KMT* 15 (2): 64–65.

Clutton-Brock, J. 1988. *The British Museum Book of Cats*. London: British Museum Publications.

Curto, S. 1961. *L'Egitto antico nelle collezioni dell' Italia settentrionale, Museo Civico Bolgona, 31 Ottobre–3 Dicembre 1961*. Bologna: Museo Civico.

Dandamaev, M.A. 1989. A Political History of the Achaemenid Empire. Leiden: Brill.

Daninos Pasha. 1887. "Relatifs aux fouilles de San." *RT* 9:19.

Daressy, G. 1902. *Fouilles de la Vallée des Rois*. Cairo: IFAO.

———. 1908. "Construction d'un temple d'Apis par Nectanebo I." *ASAE* 9:154–57.

———. 1913. "Inscriptions historiques mendésiennes." *RT* 35:124–29.

———. 1917. "Statues de Mendes." *ASAE* 17:21–24.

———. 1919a. "Une Statue du Taureau Mnévis." *ASAE* 18:75–76.

———. 1919b. "La Gazelle d'Anoukit." *ASAE* 18:77.

———. 1919c. "La Tombe d'un Mnévis de Ramsès II." *ASAE* 18:196–210.

———. 1919d. "La Tombe du Mnévis de Ramsès VII." *ASAE* 18:211–17.

———. 1919e. "Samtaui-Tafnekht." *ASAE* 18:29–33.

———. 1919f. "Statue de Zedher le Saveur." *ASAE* 18:113–58.

Daressy, G., and C. Gaillard. 1905. *La Faune Momifiée de l'Antique Égypte.* Cairo: IFAO.

David, A. ed. 1979. *The Manchester Mummy Project.* Manchester: Manchester Museum.

David, R. ed. 1978. *Mysteries of the Mummies.* London: Book Club Associates.

Davies, N. de G. 1953. *The Temple of Hibis in El-Khargeh Oasis* III. New York: Metropolitan Museum of Art.

Davies, N. de G., and M.F. Laming MacAdam. 1957. *A Corpus of Inscribed Egyptian Funerary Cones.* Oxford: Oxford University Press.

Davies, S. 1998. "Uncharted Saqqara." *JEA* 84:50–51.

———. 2007. "Bronzes from the Sacred Animal Necropolis at North Saqqara." In M. Hill and D. Schorsch eds., *Gifts for the Gods: Images from Egyptian Temples*, 174–88. New York: Metropolitan Museum of Art.

Davies, S., and H. Smith. 1997. "Sacred Animal Temples at Saqqara." In S. Quirke ed., *The Temple in Ancient Egypt*, 112–31. London: British Museum.

Davis, S.M. 1980. "A Note on the Dental and Skeletal Ontogeny of *Gazella*." *Israel Journal of Zoology* 29:129–34.

Davis, T.M., et. al. 1908. *The Tomb of Siphtah, the Monkey Tomb and the Gold Tomb.* London: Constable.

Dawson, W.R. 1928. "References to Mummification by Greek and Latin Authors." *Aegyptus* 9:106–12.

Dawson, W.R., and P.H.K. Gray. 1968. *Catalogue of Egyptian Antiquities in the British Museum, I Mummies and Human Remains.* London: British Museum Publications.

Dawson, W.R., and E.P. Uphill. 1995. *Who Was Who in Egyptology*, 3rd ed., by M.L. Bierbrier. London: EES.

De Cenival, F. 1972. *Les Associations religieuses en Egypte, I.* Cairo: IFAO.

De Gorostarzu, M.X. 1901. "Lettre sur deux tombeaux de crocodiles découverts au Fayoum." *ASAE* 2:182–84.

De Meulenaere, H. 1966. *Le Surnom egyptien a la Basse Epoque*. Budapest: Musée hongrois des beaux-arts.

———. 1982. "Mendes." *LÄ* 4:209–16.

De Meulenaere, H., and P. Mackay. 1976. *Mendes, II*. Warminster: Aris and Phillips.

De Meyer, M., W. van Neer, C. Peeters, and H. Willems. 2005/2006. "The Role of Animals in the Funerary Rites at Dayr al-Barsha." *JARCE* 42:45–71.

De Morgan, J. 1897. *Carte de la nécropole Memphite, Dahchour; Sakkara, Abou-Sir*. Cairo: IFAO.

De Wit, C. 1951. *Le rôle et le sens du lion dans l'Egypte ancienne*. Leiden: Brill.

———. 1957. "Les Génies des Quatre Vents au temple d'Opet." *CdÉ* 32:25–39.

Debono, F. 1951. "Expedition Archéologique Royale au Desert Oriental Deft-Kosseir." *ASAE* 51:73–74.

Delange, E., and H. Jaritz eds. 2013. *Der Widderfriedhof des Chnumtempels, Mit Beiträgen zur Archäozoologie und zur Materialkunde*. Archäologische Veröffentlichungen des Deutschen Archäologischen Instituts 105. Elephantine 25. Wiesbaden: Harrassowitz.

Description de l'Egypte. 1826. Text Vol. 10. Paris: Pancoucke.

Devauchelle, D. 1994a. "Notes et documents pour servir à l'histoire du Sérapéum de Memphis." *RdÉ* 45:75–86.

———. 1994b. "Les stèles du Sérapéum de Memphis conservées au musée du Louvre." *Egitto e Vicino Oriente* 17:95–114.

———. 1995. "Le sentiment anti-perse chez les anciens Égyptiens." *Transeuphratène* 9:67–80.

Diener, L. 1973." A Human-masked and Doll-shaped Hawk-mummy." *CdÉ* 48/95:60–65.

Dimick, J. 1958. "The Embalming House of the Apis Bulls." *Archaeology* 11 (3): 183–89.

———. 1959. "The Embalming House of the Apis Bulls." In R. Anthes ed., *Mit Rahineh 1955*, 75–79. Philadelphia: University Museum.

Diodorus. 1985. *On Egypt*. Translated by E. Murphy. New York: McFarland.

Dodson, A.M. 1990. "Crown Prince Djhutmose and the Royal Sons of the Eighteenth Dynasty." *JEA* 76:87–90.

———. 1994. "Review of Bryan 1991." *JEA* 80:247–51.

———. 1995. "Of Bulls and Princes: the Early Years of the Serapeum at

Sakkara." *KMT* 6 (1): 18–32.

———. 1996. "An Unusual Canopic jar in the Royal Ontario Museum."
JEA 82:210–12.

———. 1999. "The Canopic Equipment from the Serapeum of Memphis." In A.
Leahy and W.J. Tait eds., *Studies on Ancient Egypt in Honour of H.S. Smith*,
59–75. London: EES.

———. 2000. "The Eighteenth Century Discovery of the Serapeum." *KMT* 11 (3):
48–53.

———. 2001. "Of Bulls, Pharaohs, Persians and Ptolemies: the Latter Years of
the Serapeum of Saqqara." *BES* 15:27–38.

———. In Preparation. "On the Serapeum in the later New Kingdom and Early
Third Intermediate Period."

Donadoni, S. 1969. "Un Frammento di Statua di Personagio Mendesio a Roma."
MDAIK 24:100–104.

Drew-Bear, M. 1979. *Le nome Hermopolite, Toponymes et Sites*. Ann Arbor:
University of Michigan.

Dreyer, G., et al. 1993. "Umm el-Qaab: Nachuntersuchungen im frühzeitlichen
Königsfriedhof, 7./8. Vorbericht." *MDAIK* 52:11–81.

Driesch A. von den, D. Kessler, F. Steinmann, V. Berteaux, and J. Peters. 2005.
"Mummified, Deified and Buried at Hermopolis Magna—The Sacred Birds
from Tuna El-Gebel, Middle Egypt." *Ägypten und Levante* 15:203–44.

Drioton, E. 1939. "Une stèle de donation de lan XIII d'Apriès." *ASAE* 39:121–25.

———. 1942. "Deux statues naophores consacrées à Apis." *ASAE* 41:21ff.

Du Quesne, T. 2002. "Documents on the Cult of the Jackal Deities at Asyut—
Seven more Ramesside Stelae from the Salakhana Trove." *Discussions in
Egyptology* 53:9–30.

Duemichen, J. 1865–68. *Geographische Inschriften altägyptischer Denkmäler an
Ort und Stelle* III, 49 Philae. Leipzig: J.C. Hinrichs.

Dunand, F., J-L. Heim and R. Lichtenberg. 2010. *El-Deir Nécropoles* I. *La nécropole Sud*. Paris: Cybèle.

Dunand, F., and R. Lichtenberg. 2005. "Des chiens momifiés à El-Deir. Oasis de
Kharga." *BIFAO* 105:75–88.

———. 2010. "Dix ans d'exploration des nécropoles d'El-Deir oasis de Kharga.
Un premier bilan." *CdÉ* 83:258–88.

Dunand, F., R. Lichtenberg, and C. Callou. 2015. "Dogs at el-Deir." In S. Ikram,
J. Kaiser, and R. Walker eds., *The Bioarchaeology of Ancient Egypt,
Conference Proceedings 2012*, 169–76. Amsterdam: Sidestone.

Dunand, F., R. Lichtenberg, and A. Charron. 2005. *Des animaux et des homes: une symbiose égyptienne*. Paris: Éditions du Rocher.

Dunand, F., and R. Lichtenberg, with the collaboration of A. Charron. 2005. *Des animaux et des homes: une symbiose égyptienne*. Monaco: Rocher.

Durisch, N. 1993. "Culte des Canidés à Assiout: Trois Noles Stèles Dédiés à Oupouaout." *BIFAO* 93:205–21.

Edwards, I.E.S. 1960. *Oracular Amuletic Decrees of the Late New Kingdom*. London: Trustees of the British Museum.

Emery, W.B. 1938. *The Royal Tombs of Ballana and Qustul*, I–II. Cairo: Government Press.

———. 1965. "Preliminary Report on the Excavations at North Saqqara, 1964–65." *JEA* 51:3–8.

———. 1966. "Preliminary Report at the Excavations at North Saqqara 1965–66." *JEA* 52:3–8.

———. 1967. "Preliminary Report at the Excavations at North Saqqara 1966–67." *JEA* 53:141–45.

———. 1969. "Preliminary Report at the Excavations at North Saqqara 1968." *JEA* 55:31–35.

———. 1970. "Preliminary Report at the Excavations at North Saqqara 1968–1969." *JEA* 56:5–11.

———. 1971. "Preliminary Report at the Excavations at North Saqqara 1969–1970." *JEA* 57:3–13.

Endreffy, K. 2010. "Reason for Despair: Notes on Some Demotic Letters to Thoth." in Basem El-Sharkaway ed., *The Horizon: Studies in Egyptology in Honour of M. A. Nur el-Din*, 241–51. SCA Press.

Englund, G. ed. 1989. *The Religion of the Ancient Egyptians: Cognitive Structures and Popular Expressions—Proceedings of Symposia in Uppsala and Bergen*. Uppsala: S. Academiae Ubsaliensis.

Erichsen, W. 1954. *Demotisches Glossar*. Copenhagen: E. Munksgaard.

Evans, E.A. 2001. "Did Cat Mummies Say 'Meow'?" *Research Notes, Frank H. McClung Museum* 20.

Falke, T.H.M. 1979–80. "An Egyptian Mummy in the Bijbels Museum, Amsterdam." *Jaarbericht van het vooraziat.-egyptisch Genootschap, Ex Oriente Lux* 26:35–38.

———. 1997. "Radiology of Ancient Egyptian Mummified Animals." In J. van Dijk, ed. *Essays on Ancient Egypt in Honour of Herman Te Velde*, 55–67. Groningen: Styx.

Falke, T.H.M. et al. 1987. "Computed Tomography of an Ancient Egyptian Cat." *Journal of Computer Assisted Tomography* 11:745–47.

Farid, A. 2000. "Sechs demotische Serapeumstelen in Louvre Paris und im Kunsthistorischen Musem Wien." *MDAIK* 56:181–201.

Faulkner, R.O. 1933. *The Papyrus Bremner-Rhind B.M. no. 10188.* Brussels: Fondation Egyptologique Reine Elisabeth.

Fleming, S., B. Fishman, and D. O'Connor, et al. 1980. "Mummification of Animals." *The Egyptian Mummy: Secrets and Science.* Philadelphia: University Museum.

Flores, D.V. 2003. *Funerary Sacrifice of Animals in the Egyptian Predynastic Period.* Oxford: BAR.

Fodor III, et al. 1983. "The Radiographic Investigation of Two Egyptian Mummies." *Radiological Technology* 54 (6): 443–48.

Foster, C. 2000. "The Zoology of Herodotus and his Greek Descendants." In J. Starkey and O. el Daly eds., *Desert Travellers from Herodotus to T. E. Lawrence*, 1–19. Durham: Astene.

Friedman, R. 2003. "Excavating an Elephant." *Nekhen News* 15:9–10.

Friedman, R. ed. 2012. *Nekhen News* 24.

Gabra, S. 1928. "Un sarcophage de Touna." *ASAE* 28:66–79.

———. 1935. "Touna el Gabal. Hermopolis Ouest, Terre d'Egypte." *Revue Egyptienne* 3 (3) (August): 17–18.

———. 1936. "Fouilles a Tounah el-Gabal." *CdÉ* 21:34–36.

———. 1939. "Fouilles de l'Université 'Fouad el Awal' a Touna el-Gebel Hermopolis Ouest." *ASAE* 39:483–527.

———. 1943. "Aspect du culte des animaux a Hermopolis Ouest." *BIE* 25:237–44.

———. 1947. "Tounah el-Gebel. Fouilles de l'Université Fouad." *CdÉ* 44:263–64.

———. 1971. *Chez les Derniers Adorateurs du Trismegiste.* Collection Bibliotheque arabe no. 119. Cairo: al-Hay'a al-Misriya al-'Amma li-l-ta'lif wa-l-Nashr.

Gabra, S. et al. 1945. "Rapport sur les fouilles d'Hermopollis Ouest Touna el-Gebel." *CdÉ* 10 (104): 237–44.

Gaillard, C. 1923. *Recherches sur les Poissons Represents dans Quelques Tombeaux Egyptiens de l'Ancien Empire.* Cairo: IFAO.

———. 1927. "Les animaux consacrés a la divinité de l'ancienne Lycopolis." *ASAE* 27:33–42.

Gaillard, C., and G. Daressy. 1905. *Catalgue Général des Antiquités Égyptiennes du Musée du Caire: La Faune Momifiée de l'Antique Égypte.* Cairo: IFAO.

Gallazzi, C. 2003. "La prima campagna di Vogliano in Egitto." In C. Gallazzi and L. Lehnus eds., *Achille Vogliano Cinquant'anni Dopo*, vol. 1, 131–95. Milan: Cisalpino.

Gamer-Wallert, I. 1970. *Fische und Fischekulte im Alten Agypten.* Wiesbaden: Harrassowitz.

Gardiner, A.H. 1932. "Notes on the Food Cases from the Tomb of Tutankhamun." Unpublished paper. Griffith Institute, Oxford.

———. 1937. *Late Egyptian Miscellanies.* Brussels: Fondation Egyptologique Reine Elisabeth.

———. 1979. *Egyptian Grammar.* Oxford: Griffith Institute.

Gautier, A., and S. Hendrickx. 1999. "Vultures and Other Animal Remains from a Tomb in the Elkab Necropolis, Upper Egypt: An Exercise in Salvage Archaeozoology." In C. Becker, H. Manhart, J. Peters, and J. Schibler eds., *Historia Animalium ex Ossibus. Beiträge zur Paläoanatomie, Archäologie, Ägyptologie, Ethnologie und Geschichte der Tiermedizin. Festschrift für Angela von den Driesch zum 65. Geburtstag*, 161–79. Rahden: Verlag Marie Leidorf.

Gessler-Löhr, B. 1991. "Weg zur Unsterblichkeit – Mumien und Mumifizierung im Alten Ägypten." *Antike Welt* 22 (1): 58–60.

Giddy, L. 1992. *The Anubieion at Saqqara.* Vol. 2: The Cemeteries. London: EES.

Ginsburg, L. 1999. "Les chats momifiés du Bubasteion de Saqqarah." *ASAE* 74:183–91.

Ginsburg, L., G. Delibrias, A. Minault-Gout, H. Valladas, and A. Zivie. 1991. "Sur l'origine égyptienne du chat domestique." *Bulletin du Muséum d'Histoire Naturelle*, series 4, no. 13: 107–13.

Girgis, V. 1965. "A New Strategos of the Hermopolite Nome." *MDAIK* 20:121.

Giveon, R. 1975. "A Late Egyptian Statue from the Eastern Delta." *JARCE* 12:19–21.

Goldbrunner, L. 2004. *Buch: Eine Untersuchung zur Theologie des heiligen Stieres in Theben zur griechisch-römischen Zeit.* Turnhout: Fondation Égyptologique Reine Élisabeth/Brepols.

Gomaa, F. 1973. *Chaemwese, Sohn Ramses' II und Hoherpriester von Memphis.* Weisbaden: Otto Harrassowitz.

———. 1987. *Die Besiedlung Aegyptens wahrend des Mittleren Reiches* II. Wiesbaden: Ludwig Reichert.

Goodman, S. 1987. "Victual Egyptian Bird Mummies from a Presumed Late 17th or Early 18th Dynasty Tomb." *JSSEA* 17 (3): 67–77.

Goodman, S., and P. Meininger eds.. 1989. *The Birds of Egypt*. Oxford: University Press.

Goudsmit, J., and D. Brandon-Jones. 2000. "Evidence from the Baboon Catacomb in North Saqqara for a West Mediterranean Monkey Trade Route to Ptolemaic Alexandria." *JEA* 86:111–19.

Goyon, J.-C. 1967. "La chaussée monumentale et le temple de la vallée de la pyramide de Khéops." *BIFAO* 67:49–69.

Granger, M. 1745. *Relation du Voyage fait en Egypte en 1730*. Paris: Bibliothèque de l'Institut de France.

Gray, P.H.K. 1966a. "Radiological Aspects of the Mummies of Ancient Egyptians in the Rijksmuseum van Oudheden, Leiden." *OMRO* 47:1–29.

———. 1966b. "Embalmers Restorations." *JEA* 52:138–40.

Gray, P.H.K., and D. Slow. 1968. "Egyptian Mummies in the City of Liverpool Museums." *Liverpool Museums Bulletin* 15:28–32.

Green, C.I. 1987. *The Temple Furniture from the Sacred Animal Necropolis at North Saqqara 1964–1976*. London: EES.

Greener, L. 1966. *The Discovery of Egypt*. London: Cassell.

Grenfell, B.P., and A. Hunt. 1900. *Fayum Towns and their Papyri*. London: EES.

———. 1902. *The Tebtunis Papyri*. New York: Oxford University Press.

———. 1903. *EEF Archaeological Report 1902–1903*. London: EEF.

Griffith, F.L. 1888. *The Antiquities of Tell el Yahûdiyeh and Miscellaneous Work in Lower Egypt during the year 1887–1888*. London: EEF.

———. 1889. *Two Hieroglyphic Papyri from Tanis*. London: EES.

———. 1910. "Apotheosis by Drowning." *ZÄS* 46:132.

———. 1970. *Plutarch's De Iside et Osiride*. Cardiff: University of Wales.

Guarnori, S. 1982. "Les vases canopes du Musée d'art et d'histoire." *BSEG* 6: 19ff.

Guilmot, M. 1962. "La Sarapieion de Memphis: etude topographique." *CdÉ* 37:359–81.

Gunn, B. 1926a. "Inscribed Sarcophagi in the Serapeum." *ASAE* 26:82–91.

———. 1926b. "Two Misunderstood Serapeum Inscriptions." *ASAE* 26:92–94.

———. 1926c. "Inscriptions from the Step Pyramid site." *ASAE* 26:177–96.

Gutbub, A. 1973. *Textes fondamontaux de la théologie de Kôm Ombo*. Cairo: IFAO.

Hansen, D. P. 1965. "Mendes 1964." *JARCE* 4:31–37.

———. P. 1967. "Excavations at Mendes 1965–1966." *JARCE* 6:5–16.

Hanzak, J. 1977. "Egyptian Mummies of Animals in Czechoslovak Collections." *ZÄS* 104:86–88.

Harris, J., and K. Weeks. 1973. *X-raying the Pharaohs*. New York: Charles Scribner's Sons.

Hartley, M., A. Buck, and S. Binder. 2011. "Canine Interments in the Teti Cemetery North at Saqqara during the Graeco-Roman Period." In F. Coppens, J. Krejsi eds., *Abusir and Saqqara in the Year 2010*, 17–29. Prague: Czech Institute of Egyptology.

Hartmann, R. 1864. "Versuch einer systematischen Aufzählung der von den alten Aegyptern bildlich dargestellten Thiere, mit Rücksicht auf die heutige Fauna des Nilgebietes." *ZÄS* 2:7–12, 19–28.

Hastings, E. 1997. *The Sculpture from the Sacred Animal Necropolis at North Saqqara, 1964–76*. London: EES.

Hastings, J. ed.. 1908–13. *The Encyclopedia of Religion and Ethics*. Vol. 4, 793; vol. 6, 397–400. Edinburgh: T. and T. Clark.

Hekkala, E., M.H. Shirley, G. Amato, J.D. Austin, S. Charter, J. Thorbjarnarson, K. A. Vliet, M.L. Houck, R. Desalle, and M.J. Blum. 2011. "An Ancient Icon Reveals New Mysteries: Mummy DNA Resurrects a Cryptic Species within the Nile Crocodile." *Molecular Ecology* 20 (20): 4199–215.

Helck, W. 1955. *Urkunden der 18. Dynastie*. Berlin: Akademie.

———. 1974. *Die altaegyptische Gaue*. Wiesbaden: Ludwig Reichert.

Herbin, F. 1994. *Le Livre de parcourir l'eternite*. Leuven: Peeters.

Herodotus. 1989. *The Histories* II, III. Translated by J. Gould. New York: St. Martin's Press.

Hery, F.-X, and T. Enel. 1993. *Animaux du Nil, Animaux de Dieu*. Provence: Édisud.

Hodjash, S., and O.D. Berlev. 1982. *The Egyptian Reliefs and Stelae in the Pushkin Museum of Fine Arts, Moscow*. Leningrad: n.p.

Hoffman, M.A. 1982. *The Predynastic of Hierakonpolis: An Interim report*. Cairo: Cairo University Press.

Holland, E. 1984. "Ohio's Mummies: Breaking Centuries of Silence." *Quest* 6 (4): 1, 11–14.

Holz, R.K., et al. 1980. *Mendes* I. Cairo: American Research Center in Egypt.

Hopfner, T. 1913. *Der Tierkult der alten Agypter nach den griechisch-römischen Berichten und den wichtigeren Denkmmälern*. Vienna: A. Hölder.

Hornung, E. 1982. *Conceptions of God in Ancient Egypt: The One and the Many*. Translated by J. Baines. Ithaca: Cornell University Press.

————. 1999. *The Ancient Egyptian Books of the Afterlife*. Translated by D. Lorton. Ithaca: Cornell University Press.

Houlihan, P. 1996. *The Animal World of the Pharaohs*. Cairo: American University in Cairo Press.

Houlihan, P., and S. Goodman. 1986. *The Birds of Ancient Egypt*. Cairo/Warminster: American University in Cairo Press/Aris and Phillips.

Hughes, G.R. 1969. "The Cruel Father: A Demotic Papyrus in the Library of G. Michaelides." In E.B. Hauser ed., *Studies in Honor of John A Wilson*, 43–54. Chicago: University of Chicago.

Hunt, A.S., and C.C. Edgar. 1932–41, 1977. *Select Papyri*, vols. 1–3. London: EES/Cambridge: Cambridge University Press.

Ibrahim, M., and D. Rohl. 1988. "Apis and the Serapeum." *Journal of the Ancient Chronology Forum* 2:6–26.

Ibrahim Aly, M. 1991. *Les Petits Souterrains du Serapeum de Memphis*. Lyon: Etude d'Archéologie, Religion et Historique, Textes inédits.

————. 1993. "Apropos du prince Khâemouas et sa mère Isetneferet. Nouveaux documents provenant du Sérapéum." *MDAIK* 49:97–106.

————. 1996. "Une stèle inédite du Sérapéum mentionnant le nom de Sheshonq Ier." *Bulletin Société d'Égyptologie Genève* 20:5–16.

Ibrahim Aly, M., R. Nageb, D. Devauchelle, and F.-R. Herbin. 1986. "Presentation des steles nouvellement découvertes au Sérapéum." *BSFE* 106:31–44.

Ikram, S. 1995a. *Choice Cuts: Meat Production in Ancient Egypt*. Leuven: Peeters.

————. 1995b. "Did the Ancient Egyptians Eat Biltong?" *Cambridge Journal of Archaeology* 5 (2): 283–89.

————. 2000a. "Animals for the Afterlife." *Egypt Revealed* 1 (1): 55–61.

————. 2000b. "Meat Production." In P. Nicholson and I. Shaw eds., *Ancient Egyptian Materials and Technologies*, 656–71. Cambridge: Cambridge University Press.

————. 2000c. "The Pet Gazelle of One of the Ladies of the Pinudjem Family." *KMT* 11 (2): 58–61.

————. 2001. "The Animal Mummy Project." *KMT* 12 (4): 18–25.

————. 2003a. "The Animal Mummy Project at the Egyptian Museum, Cairo." In Z. Hawass ed., *Egyptology at the Dawn of the Twenty-first Century*, 235–39. Cairo: American University in Cairo.

————. 2003b. *Death and Burial in Ancient Egypt*. London: Longman.

————. 2004a. *Beloved Beasts: Animal Mummies from Ancient Egypt*. Cairo:

Supreme Council of Antiquities.

———. 2004b. "Victual, Ritual, Or Both? Food Offerings From The Funerary Assemblage Of Isitemkheb." *Studi di Egittologia e di Papirologia* 1:87–92.

———. 2004c. *A Zoo For Eternity: Animal Mummies in the Cairo Museum*. Cairo: Supreme Council of Antiquities.

———., ed. 2005a. *Divine Creatures: Animal Mummies in Ancient Egypt*. Cairo: American University in Cairo Press.

———. 2005b. "The Loved Ones: Egyptian Animal Mummies as Cultural and Environmental Indicators." In H. Buitenhuis, A.M. Choyke, L. Martin, L. Bartosiewicz, and M. Mashkour, eds., *Archaeozoology of the Near East*, 240–48. Groningen: ARC.

———. 2005c. "Manufacturing Divinity: The Technology of Mummification." In S. Ikram ed., *Divine Creatures: Animal Mummies in Ancient Egypt*, 16–43. Cairo: American University in Cairo Press.

———. 2005d. "A Monument in Miniature: The Eternal Resting Place of a Shrew." In P. Janosi ed., *Structure and Significance*, 335–40. Vienna: Österreichischen Akademie der Wissenschaften.

———. 2006. "Portions of an Old Kingdom Offering List Reified." In M. Barta, ed., *Old Kingdom Art and Archaeology*, 167–74. Prague: Czech Institute of Egyptology.

———. 2007a. "Animals in a Ritual Context at Abydos, A Synopsis." In Z. Hawass and J. Richards eds., *The Archaeology and Art of Ancient Egypt: Essays in honor of David B. O'Connor*, 417–32. Cairo: Supreme Council of Antiquities.

———. 2007b. "Tiermumien im Alten Ägypten." In D. von Recklinghausen ed., *Ägyptische Mumien, Unsterblichkeit im Land der Pharaonen*, 292–310. Mainz am Rhein: Philipp von Zabern.

———. 2009a. "Embalmed Victual." In T.A. Bacs, Z.I. Fabian, G. Schreiber, and L. Török eds., *Hungarian Excavations in the Theban Necropolis: A Celebration of 102 Years of Fieldwork in Egypt*, 91. Budapest: Lorand University.

———. 2009b. "Funerary Food Offerings." In M. Barta ed., *Abusir XIII, Abusir South 2. Tomb Complex of the Vizier Qar, his Sons Qar Junior and Senedjemib, and Iykai*, 294–98. Prague: Dryada/Czech.

———. 2011. "The Forgotten Dead: Animal Burials in the Theban Necropolis." In Z. Hawass, T. A. Bacs, and G. Schreiber eds., *Proceedings of the Colloquium on Theban Archaeology at the Supreme Council of Antiquities, Nov.*

5, 2009, 73–75. Cairo: Supreme Council of Antiquities.

———. 2012a. "Animal Mummies." In R.S. Bagnall, K. Brodersen, C.B. Champion, A. Erskine, and S.R. Huebner eds., *The Encyclopedia of Ancient History*, 429–31. Oxford/New York: Wiley-Blackwell, print and web, http://dx.doi.org/10.1002/9781444338386.wbeah15033.

———. 2012b. "Animals, Egyptian Sacred." In R.S. Bagnall, K. Brodersen, C.B. Champion, A. Erskine, and S.R. Huebner eds., *The Encyclopedia of Ancient History*, 433–36. Oxford/New York: Wiley-Blackwell, print and web, http://dx.doi.org/10.1002/9781444338386.wbeah15036.

———. 2012c. "Animals, Non-domesticated Egypt." In R.S. Bagnall, K. Brodersen, C.B. Champion, A. Erskine, and S.R. Huebner eds., *The Encyclopedia of Ancient History*, 438–39. Oxford/New York: Wiley-Blackwell, print and web. http://dx.doi.org/10.1002/9781444338386.wbeah15035.

———. 2012d. "Creatures of the Gods: Animal Mummies from Ancient Egypt." *Anthro Notes* 31 (1): 1–5.

———. 2013a. "Canine Cults in Kharga Oasis: the Dogs of Dabashiya." In G.Tallet, Chr. Zivie-Coche eds., *Le Myrte et la rose. Mélanges offerts à Françoise Dunand par ses élèves, collègues et amis*, 349–55. Montpellier: CENiM.

———. 2013b. "A Curious Case of Canine Burials from Abydos." In M.C. Flossmann-Schütze, M. Goecke-Bauer, F. Hoffmann, A. Hutterer, K. Schlüter, A. Schütze, M. Ullmann, with the cooperation of P. Brose eds., *Kleine Götter-Grosse Götter:Festschrift für Dieter Kessler zum 65. Geburtstag*, 265–71. Vaterstetten: Patrick Brose.

———. 2013c. "Man's Best Friend for Eternity: Dog and Human Burials in Ancient Egypt." *Anthropozoologica* 48 (2): 299–307.

———. 2013d. "A Re-Analysis of Part of Prince Amenemhat Q's Eternal Menu." *JARCE* 48:119–35.

———. 2015a. "Experimental Archaeology: From Meadow to Em-baa-lming Table." In C. Graves-Brown, ed., *Experiment and Experience*, 53–74. Cardiff: University of Wales Press.

———. 2015b. "Speculations on the Role of Animal Cults in the Economy of Ancient Egypt." In M. Massiera, B. Mathieu, F. Rouffet eds., *Apprivoiser le sauvage—Taming the Wild: Glimpses on the Animal World in Ancient Egypt*. Montpellier: CENIM.

Ikram, S., C. Bosch, and M. Spitzer. In preparation. "Offerings to Thoth and Horus: the Avian Deposit of Theban Tomb 12, the Chapel of Hery." *JARCE*.

Ikram, S., C. Callou, and T. Borel. 2013. "The Sacred Ram Mummies of Khnum from Elephantine in Egypt." In E. Delange and H. Jaritz eds., *Der Widderfriedhof des Chnumtempels, Mit Beiträgen zur Archäozoologie und zur Materialkunde*, 214–22, pls. 75–81. Archäologische Veröffentlichungen des Deutschen Archäologischen Instituts 105. Elephantine 25. Wiesbaden: Harrassowitz.

Ikram, S., and A. Charron. 2008." Animal Mummies from Abu Rawash." *KMT* 19 (2): 34–41.

Ikram, S., and A. Dodson. 1998. *The Mummy in Ancient Egypt: Equipping the Dead for Eternity*. London/Cairo: Thames and Hudson, American University in Cairo.

Ikram, S., and A. Helmi. 2002. "The History of the Collection of the Animal Mummies at the Egyptian Museum, Cairo." In M. Eldamaty and M. Trad eds., *Egyptian Museum Collections*, 563–68. Cairo: Supreme Council of Antiquities.

Ikram, S., D. Hunt, M. Zeder. In Preparation. *The Animal Mummy Collection in the Smithsonian Institution's Natural History Museum*. Washington, D.C.: Smithsonian Institution.

Ikram, S., and N. Iskander. 2002. *Catalogue Général of the Egyptian Museum: Non-Human Remains*. Cairo: Supreme Council of Antiquities.

Ikram, S., P. Nicholson, L. Bertini, and D. Hurley. 2013." Killing Man's Best Friend?." *Archaeological Review from Cambridge* 28 (2): 48–66.

Irby, C.L., and J. Mangles. 1823. *Travels in Egypt and Nubia*. London: John Murray.

James, A.E., Jr. 1977. "Application of the Radiological Sciences to Advance Clinical and Fundamental Knowledge of the Animal Kingdom." *Radiology* 124:581–97.

James, T.G.H. 1982. "A Wooden Figure of Wadjet with Two Painted Representations of Amasis." *JEA* 68:156–65.

Jansen-Winkeln, K. 1987. "Thronname und Begräbnis Takeloths I." *Varia Aegiptiaca* 3:253–57.

Jasnow, R. 1997. "A Demotic Omen Text?' In J. van Dijk ed., *Essays on Ancient Egypt in Honour of Herman Te Velde*, 204–17. Groningen: Styx.

Jeffreys, D.G., and H.S. Smith, with a chapter by M. Jessop Price. 1988. *The Anubieion at Saqqara I: The Settlement and the Temple Precinct*. London: EES.

Jett, P., S. Sturman, and T.D. Weisser. 1985. "A Study of the Egyptian Bronze Falcon Figures in the Walters Art Gallery." *Studies in Conservation* 30:112–18.

Jones, M. 1990. "The Temple of the Apis in Memphis." *JEA* 76:14–47.

Jones, M., and A.M. Jones. 1982. "The Apis House Project at Mit Rahinah. First Season, 1982." *JARCE* 19:7–50.

———. 1983. "The Apis House Project at Mit Rahinah: Preliminary Report of the Second and Third Season, 1982–1983." *JARCE* 20:33–46.

———. 1985. "The Apis House Project at Mit Rahinah: Preliminary Report of the Fourth Season, 1984." *JARCE* 22:17–28.

———. 1987. "The Apis House Project at Mit Rahinah: Preliminary Report of the Fifth Season, 1984–1985." *JARCE* 24:35–46.

———. 1988. "The Apis House Project at Mit Rahinah: Preliminary Report of the Sixth Season, 1986." *JARCE* 25:105–16.

Josephus Flavius, G. 1981. *The Jewish War/Josephus*. Translated by A. Williamson. New York: Penguin.

Jurays, J. F. 1989. *Thadiyat Misr al-Firawniya*. Cairo: al-Ghad.

Kahl, J., M. el-Khadragy, U. Verhoeven, M. Abdelraheim, H. Fahid Ahmed, C. Kitagawa, J. Malur, S. Prell, and T. Rzeuska. 2011. "The Asyut project: Eighth Season of Fieldwork 2010." *Studien zur Altägyptischen Kultur* 40:181–209.

Kahl, J., M. el-Khadragy, U. Verhoeven, M. Abdelraheim, M. Van Elsbergen, H. Fahid, A. Kilian, C. Kitagawa, T. Rzeuska, and M. Zöller-Engelhardt. 2012. "The Asyut Project: Ninth Season of Fieldwork 2011." *Studien zur Altägyptischen Kultur* 41:189–235.

Kahl, J., M. el-Khadragy, U. Verhoeven, A. el-Khatib, C. Titagawa. 2009. "The Asyut Project: sixth season of fieldwork 2008." *Studien zur Altägyptischen Kultur* 38:113–30.

Kahl, J., and C. Kitagawa. 2010. "Ein wiederentdeckter Hundefriedhof in Assiut." *Sokar* 20:77–81.

Kakosy, L. 1970. "Beitrage zum Totenkult der heiligen Tiere." *ZÄS* 96:109–15.

———. 1977. "Tiergötter." *LÄ* 2:660–64.

———. 1981a. "Problems of the Thoth Cult in Roman Egypt." *Studia Aegyptiaca* 7:6–46.

———. 1981b. "Prophecies of Ram Gods." *Studia Aegyptiaca* 7:139–54.

———. 1981c. *Selected Papers 1956–1973*. Budapest: ELTE.

———. 1982. "Mnevis." *LÄ* 4:165–67.

Kamal, A. 1903. "Chapelle d'un Mnévis de Ramsès III." *RT* 25:29–47.

Kaplony, P. 1963. *Die Inschriften der aegyptischen Fruhzeit* III. Wiesbaden: Otto Harrassowitz.

Kaplony-Heckel, U. 1994. "Sowahr der stier von Medamod lebt! Ueber die orts-
    götter in den Tempel-Eiden." In C. Eyre, A. Leahy, and L. Leahy eds., *An
    Unbroken Reed*, 148–59. London: EES.

Kater-Sibbes, G.J.F., and M. J. Vermaseren. 1975–1977. *Apis*, vols. 1–3. Leiden:
    E.J. Brill.

Katalog Ausgrabungen, Auktion 19. Okt. 1995 Palais Dorotheum. 1996. Vienna:
    Dorotheum.

Kees, H. 1953. *Das Priestertum im ägyptischen Staat*. Leiden: Brill.

————. 1956. *Der Götterglaube im Alten Aegypten*. Leipzig: JC Heinrichs.

Keimer, L. 1949. "Les "Ânes Sauvages" abattus par Aménophis II pres de
    Qadesh." *BIE* 30:117–48.

Kessler, D. 1986. "Tierkult." *LÄ* 6:571–87.

————. 1989. *Die Heiligen Tiere und Der Konig, I*. Wiesbaden: Harrasssowitz.

————. 1990. "Der Serapeumsbezirk und das Serapeum von Tuna el-Gebel." In
    R. Schulz and M. Görg, eds., *Lingua Restituta Orientalis*, 183–98. Wiesbaden:
    Harrassowitz.

————. 1998: *Tuna el-Gebel II. Die Paviankultkammer G-C-C-2*. Hildesheim:
    Gerstenberg.

Kessler, D. In Press. "Spitzmaus und Ichneumon im Tierfriedhof von Tuna el-
    Gebel." In *Papers in Memory of Mohammed Moursi*. Cairo: SCA/Ministry of
    State for Antiquities.

Kessler, D., and A. Nur el-Din. 1994. "Der Tierfriedhof von Tuna el-Gebel. Stand
    der Grabungen bis 1993." *Antike Welt* 25 (3): 252–65.

————. 1999. "Ein Tierkäfig am Tierfriedhof von Tuna el-Gebel, Mittelägypten"
    in C. Becker, H. Manhart, J. Peters, and J. Schibler eds., *Historia Animalium
    ex Ossibus, Festschrift Angela von den Driesch*, 211–24. Rahden: Marie
    Leidorf.

————. 2005. "Tuna El-Gebel: Millions of Ibises And Other Animals." In S.
    Ikram ed., *Divine Creatures: Animal Mummies from Ancient Egypt*, 120–63.
    Cairo: American University in Cairo Press.

Kessler, D. Websites for Tuna el-Gebel: http://www.fak12.uni-
    muenchen.de/aegyp/tuna.html, and http://tunaelgebel.wordpress.com/bibli-
    ographie, and
    http://www.egyptologues.net/orientalia/?wicket:bookmarkablePage=:com.hypati
    e.orientalia.web.SiteDetail&site=14

Kessler, D., J. Boessneck, and A. von den Driesch. 1987. *Tuna el-Gebel I. Die
    Tiergalerien*. Hildesheim: Gerstenberg.

El-Khouly, A. and G.T. Martin. 1987. *Excavations in the Royal Necropolis at el-'Amarna 1984*. Cairo: IFAO.

Kitchen, K.A. 1969–70. "Two Donation Stelae in the Brooklyn Museum." *JARCE* 8:59–67.

———. 1981. *Ramesside Inscriptions*, vol. 4, fasc. 2. Oxford: Blackwell.

———. 1990. *Catalogue of the Egyptian Collection in the National Museum, Rio de Janeiro*. Warminster: Aris and Phillips.

Kleiss, E. 1987. "Tiermumien im Alten Agypten." *Anat. Histol. Embryol* 16:198–205.

König, W. 1896. *14 Photographien mit Roentgen-Strahlen aufgenommen im physikalischen Verein*. Leipzig: M.J.A. Barth.

Kozloff, A.P., and B.M. Bryan. 1992. *Egypt's Dazzling Sun: Amenophis III and his world*. Cleveland: Museum of Art.

Kraeling, C.H. 1953. *The Brooklyn Museum Aramaic Papyri*. New Haven: Yale University Press.

Kruchten, J.M. 1989. *Les annales des prêtres de Karnak*. Leuven: Peeters.

Kurth, D. 1983. *Die Dekoration der Saülen im Pronäos des Tempels von Edfu*. Wiesbaden: Harrasowitz.

———. 1986. "Tierkult." *LÄ* 6:572–73.

Kurushima, J. D., S. Ikram. J. Knudsen, E. Bleiberg, R. A. Grahn, and L.A. Lyons. 2012. "Cats of the Pharaohs: Genetic Comparison of Egyptian Cat Mummies to Their Feline Contemporaries." *Journal of Archaeological Science*, 39 (10): 3217–23.

Langton, N., and B. Langton. 1940. "The Cat in Ancient Egypt." *ASAE* 40:99–96.

Lansing, A, and W. Hayes. 1935–36. "The Museum's Excavations at Thebes." *Bulletin of the Metropolitan Museum of Art*, 4–39.

Leclant, J. 1980. "Fouilles et travaux en Égypte et au Soudan, 1969–1970." *Orientalia* 49:371.

———. 1986. "Fouilles et Travaux en Egypte et au Soudan." *Orientalia* 55:236–319.

Leek. F.F. 1969. "The Problem of Brain Removal During Embalming by the Ancient Egyptians." *JEA* 55:112–16.

———. 1976. "An Ancient Egyptian Mummified Fish." *JEA* 62:131 33.

Lefebvre, G., and L. Barry. 1905. "Rapport sur les fouilles executées à Tehneh en 1903–1904." *ASAE* 6:157.

Legrain, G. 1900. "Notes archéologiques prises au Gebel Abou Fodah." *ASAE* 1:5–6.

Lemaire, A. 1991. *Achaemenid History* VI. Leiden: Brill.

Lepsius, C.R. 1849–59. *Denkmäler aus Aegypten und Aethiopien*. Text 1. Berlin: Nicolaische.

———. 1853. "Ueber den Apiskreis." *Zeitschrift der deutschen Morgenländischen Gesellschaft* 7:417–36.

Letellier, B., and C. Zeigler. 1977. *Les Animaux dans l'Égypte ancienne. Catalogue du Muséum de Lyon, exposition du 6 novembre 77 au 31 janvier '78*. Lyon: Muséum de Lyon.

Lichtenberg, R., and A. Zivie. 2000. "Les momies d'animaux de l'Égypte ancienne" *Dossiers d'Archéologie* 252:48–53.

Lichtheim, M. 1973. *Ancient Egyptian Literature*, vol. 1. Berkeley: University of California Press.

Linforth, I.M. 1910. *Epaphos and Egyptian Apis*. University of California publications in classical philology 2, no. 5. Berkeley: University of California Press.

Lloyd, A. 1976. *Herodotus Book II. A Commentary* 1–2. Leiden: Brill.

Loat, W.L.S. 1914. "The Ibis Cemetery at Abydos." *JEA* 1:40.

Lortet, L.C. 1902. "Recherches sur les momies d'animaux." *ASAE* 3:15–21.

Lortet, L.C., and C. Gaillard. 1901. *Les Oiseaux momifiés de l'ancienne Égypte*. Paris: Comptes rendus des séances de l'Académie des Sciences.

———. 1902. "Sur les Oiseaux Momifiés." *ASAE* 3:18–21.

———. 1903–1909. *La faune momifiée de l'ancienne Egypte*. Lyon: Archives du Muséum Histoire Naturelle de Lyon VIII.

Lortet, L.C., and M. Hugonunenq. 1902. "Sur les Poissons Momifiés." *ASAE* 3:15–18.

Lovell, N. 1994. "The 1992 Excavations at Kom el-Adhem, Mendes." *JSSEA* 21 (22): 20–36.

Lucas, A. 1908. "Preliminary Note on some Preservative Materials Used by the Ancient Egyptians in Embalming." *Cairo Scientific Journal* 2:272–78.

———. 1911. *Preservative Materials Used by the Ancient Egyptians in Embalming*. Ministry of Finance, Survey Department Paper 12. Cairo: National Printing Department.

———. 1914a. "The Use of Natron in Mummification." *JEA* 1:119–23.

———. 1914b. "The Question of the Use of Bitumen or Pitch by the Ancient Egyptians in Mummification." *JEA* 1:241–45.

———. 1931. "'Cedar'—Tree Products Employed in Mummification." *JEA* 17:13–21.

———. 1932. The Use of Natron in Mummification." *JEA* 18:125–40.

Lucas, A., and J. Harris. 1962/1989 reprint. *Ancient Egyptian Materials and Industries*. London: Histories and Mysteries of Man.

Lucas, P. 1719. *Voyage du Sieur Paul Lucas fait en M. DCCXIV, &c. par ordre de Louis XIV dans la Turquie, l'Asie, Sourie, Palestine, Haute & Basse Egypte, &c.* II. Rouen: Chez Robert Machuel le Jeune.

Macrobius, P. 1969. *Saturnalia I*. Translated by V. Davies. New York: Columbia University Press.

Malaise, M. 1987. "La perception du monde animal dans l'Egypte ancienne." *Anthropozoologica* 7:28–48.

Malek, J. 1983. "Who Was the First to Identify the Saqqara Serapeum?." *CdÉ* 58: 65–72, 115–16.

———. 1993. *The Cat in Ancient Egypt*. London: British Museum Press.

Malinine, M., G. Posener, and J. Vercoutter. 1968. *Catalogue des stèles du Sérapéum de Memphis*, I. Paris: Imprimerie Nationale.

Mariette, A. MS a. *Papiers relatifs au Sérapéum de Memphis*. Bibliothèque nationale, Paris, MSS Fonds français, nouvelles acquisitions, nos. 22948–50.

———. MS b. *Liste complémentaire au texte publié sus le titre* "Renseignements sur les 64 Apis trouvés dans les souterrains du Sérapéum." Bibliothèque nationale, Paris, MSS Fonds français, nouvelles acquisitions, nos. 20175, fo 494ff.

———. "Liste manuscrite des objets du Sérapéum contenus dans les caisses expédiées au Musée du Louvre." Departement des Antiquités égyptiennes, Musée du Louvre, Paris.

———. 1855. "Renseignements sur les 64 Apis trouvés dans les souterrains du Sérapéum" *Bulletin Archéologique de l'Athenaeum Français*: 45ff.; repr. 1904. *Bib.Ég.* 18 [A. Mariette, *Œuvres diverses* I]: 133–255.

———. 1856a. *Choix de monuments et de dessins découverts ou exécutés pendant le déblaiement du Sérapéum de Memphis*. Paris: Gide et J. Baudry; repr. 1904. *Bib.Ég.* 18 [A. Mariette, *Œuvres diverses* I]: 311–19.

———. 1856b. *Memoire sur la mere d'Apis*. Paris: J. de Baudry.

———. 1857. *Le Sérapeum de Memphis decouvert et décrit par Auguste Mariette*. Paris: Gide et J. Baudry.

———. 1880. *Catalogue Général des Monuments d'Abydos*. Paris: L'impremerie nationale.

———. 1904a. "Mémoire sur une réprésentation gravée en tête de quelques proscynèmes du Serapeum" *Bib.Ég.* 18 [A. Mariette, *Œuvres diverses* I]: 265–310.

Mariette, A., ed. 1904b. *Mariette Pacha: lettres et souvenirs personnels*. Paris: II. Jouve.

Mariette-Pacha, A. 1882. *Le Sérapeum de Memphis*, I. Paris: F. Vieweg.

Mariette, A., and T. Deveria. 1863. *Description des fouilles du Sérapéum de Memphis*. Paris: F. Vieweg.

Martin, G.T. 1973. "Excavations in the Sacred Animal Necropolis at North Saqqara, 1971–1972." *JEA* 59:5–15.

———. 1974. "Ecavations in the The Sacred Animal Necropolis at North Saqqara, 1972–1973." *JEA* 60:15–29.

———. 1981. *The Sacred Animal Necropolis at North Saqqara*. London: EES.

Marx, M., and S. d'Auria. 1986. "CT Examination of Eleven Egyptian Mummies." *RadioGraphics* 6:321–30.

———. 1988. "Three-dimensional CT Reconstructions of an Ancient Human Egyptian Mummy." *American Journal of Radiology* 150:147–49.

Maspero, G. 1889. *Catalogue du Musée Égyptien de Marseille*. Paris: Imprimerie nationale.

———. 1902. "Un cercueil de chien." *ASAE* 3:283–85.

———. 1912. *Guide du visiteur au Musée du Caire*. Cairo: IFAO.

———. 1914. *Sarcophages persanes et ptolémäiques*. Cairo: IFAO.

Maurer, K. 2006. "Der Tierfriedhof von Tuna el-Gebel in Fruuhptolemuaischer Zeit, Zwischenergebnisse der Untersuchungen zur Ausgestaltung des Ibiotapheions' in J. Mylonopoulos and R. Hubert eds., *Archäologie und Ritual. Auf der Suche nach der rituellen Handlung in den antiken Kulturen Ägyptens und Griechenlands*, 105–18. Vienna: Phoibos.

McKnight, L.M. 2008. "Animal, Vegetable or Mineral? – Preliminary Results of the Radiological Study of Three Museum Oddities." In V. Gashe and J. Finch eds., *Current Research in Egyptology 2008—Proceedings of the Ninth Annual Symposium, University of Manchester*, 75–80. Manchester: Rutherford Press Limited.

———. 2010. *Imaging Applied to Animal Mummification in Ancient Egypt*. BAR International Series no. 2175. Oxford: Archaeopress.

———. 2012. "Studying Avian Mummies at the KNH Centre for Biomedical Egyptology: Past, Present and Future." In R. Bailleul-LeSuer ed., *Between Heaven and Earth: Birds in Ancient Egypt*, 99–106. Chicago: Oriental Institute, University of Chicago.

McKnight, L.M., S.D. Atherton, and A.R. David. 2011. "Introducing the Ancient Egyptian Animal Bio Bank at the KNH Centre for Biomedical Egyptology,

University of Manchester". *Antiquity* 85 (329), http://www.antiquity.ac.uk/proj-gall/mcknight329/

———. 2012. "Black, White and Shades of Grey—Problems and Potential of Radiography in the Study of Mummified Animals from Ancient Egypt." In G.A. Belova ed., *Achievements and Problems of Modern Egyptology: Proceedings of the International Conference Held in Moscow on September 29– October 2, 2009*, 229–33. Moscow: Russian Academy of Sciences.

McKnight, L.M., A.R. David, D.R. Brothwel, and J.E. Adams. 2008. "The Application of CT to Animal Mummies from Bolton Museum and Art Gallery, Great Britain" and "The Pseudo-Mummies from Bolton Museum and Art Gallery, Great Britain" in P. Peña, C. Martin and A. Rodriguez eds., *Mummies and Science—World Mummies Research: Proceedings of the VI World Congress on Mummy Studies*, 463–66, 687–89. Santa Cruz de Tenerife: Academia Canaria de la Historía.

Meeks, D. 1972. *Le grand texte des donations au temple d'Edfou*, Vol 59. Cairo: IFAO.

———. 1973. "Le nom du dauphin et le poisson de Mendes." *RdE* 25:209–16.

———. 1997. "Les couveuses artificielles en Egypte, Techniques et économie antiques et médievales." D. Garcia and D. Meeks eds., *Techniques et économie antiques et médiévales: le temps de l'innovation, Actes du Colloque d'Aix-en-Provence, mai 1996*, 132–34. Paris: Errance.

Meeks, D., and C. Favard-Meeks. 1996. *Daily Life of the Egyptian Gods*. London: John Murray.

Mela, Pomponius. 1827. *De Situ Orbis*. Translated by C.-P. Fradin. Paris : Drissot-Thivars.

Merceron, G. 2003. "The Diet of Captive Baboons: Results of Dental Microwear Analysis." *Nekhen News* 15:13–14.

Meyer, E. 1904. "Die Entwickelung der Kulte von Abydos und die Sogenannten Schakalsgötten." *ZÄS* 41:97–101.

Meyrat, P. 2012a. "Apis." In R.S. Bagnall, K. Brodersen, C.B. Champion, A. Erskine, and S.R. Huebner eds., *The Encyclopedia of Ancient History*. Oxford/New York: Wiley-Blackwell.

———. 2012b. "Mnevis." In R.S. Bagnall, K. Brodersen, C.B. Champion, A. Erskine, and S. R. Huebner eds., *The Encyclopedia of Ancient History*. Oxford/New York: Wiley-Blackwell.

———. 2014a. "The First Column of the Apis Embalming Ritual: Papyrus Zagreb 597-2." In J.F. Quack ed., *Ägyptische Rituale der griechisch-römischen*

Zeit, Akten der Ritualtagung Heidelberg 14.–16. Juli 2008, Orientalische Religionen in der Antike, 263–337. Tübingen: Mohr Siebeck.

———. 2014b. "Topography-related Problems in the Apis Embalming Ritual." In J.F.Quack ed., *Ägyptische Rituale der griechisch-römischen Zeit, Akten der Ritualtagung Heidelberg 14.-16. Juli 2008, Orientalische Religionen in der Antike*, 247–62. Tübingen: Mohr Siebeck.

Michailidis, G. 1968. "Elements se Sunthese religuese Greco-egyptienne." *IAFO* 66:49–88.

Milne, J. Jr. 1924. *Egypt under Roman Rule*. London: Methuen & Co.

Mokhtar, G. 1983. *Ihnasya el-Medina Herakleopolis Magna: Its Importance and its Role in Pharaonic History*. Cairo: IFAO.

Möller, G. 1913. *Die beiden Totenpapyrus Rhind des Museums zu Edinburg*. Leipzig: J.C. Hinrichs.

Mond, R., and W.B. Emery. 1929. "A Preliminary Report on the Excavations at Armant" *University of Liverpool Annals of Archaeology and Anthropology* 16:3–12.

Mond, R., and O.H. Myers. 1934. *The Bucheum*, 1–3. London: EES.

Monnent, J. 1951. "Les briques magiques du Musée du Louvre." *RdÉ* 8:151–62.

Montet, P. 1946. "Inscriptions de basse epoque trouvés à Tanis." *Kêmi* 8:29–126.

———. 1951. *La nécropole royale de Tanis II: les constructions et le tombeau de Psousennes à Tanis*. Paris: Jourde and Allard.

Moodie, R.L. 1931. *Roentgenologic Studies of Egyptian and Peruvian Mummies*. Chicago: Field Museum Press.

Morenz, S. 1973. *Egyptian Religion*. Translated by A.E. Keep. New York: Cornell University Press.

Moret, A. 1902, 1988 reprint. *Le rituel du cult divin journalier en Egypte*. Paris: E. Leroux/Geneva.

Morgan, J. de. 1897. *Carte de la Nécropole Memphite, Dahchour, Sakkarah, Abou-sir*. Cairo: IFAO.

Morrison-Scott, T.C. 1952. "The Mummified Cats of Ancient Egypt." *Proceedings of the Zoological Society* 121 (4): 861–67.

Muhammed, A-Q. 1987. "An Ibis Catacomb at Abu-Kir" *ASAE* 66:121–23.

Müller, H.W. 1964. *Ägyptische Kunstwerke, Kleinfunde und Glas in der Sammlung E. und M. Kofler-Truniger, Luzern* MÄS 5. Mainz am Rhein: Philipp von Zabern.

Mumford, G. 1997. "A Late New Kingdom Ceramic Assemblage at Mendes." In S. Redford ed., *Akhenaten Temple Project Newsletter*, March 1997, 1–3.

Munro, P. 1962. "Einige Votivstellen an *Wp w3wt*." *ZÄS* 88:48–58.

Murray, M.A. 1963. *The Splendor That Was Egypt*. London: Sidgwick and Jackson.

Muszynski, M. 1980. "Dédicace à Anubis pour Apollônios et Zénôn." In P.W. Pestman ed., *Greek and Demotic Texts from the Zenon Archive. P. L. Bat. 20*, 270–78. Leiden: Brill.

Myers, O. 1931. "The Tombs of the Sacred Bulls." *Discovery*, July, 219.

Myers, O.H., and H.W. Fairman. 1931. "Excavations at Armant, 1929–31." *JEA* 17:223–322.

Mysliewic, K. 1979. *Studien zum Gott Atum* II. Hildesheim: Gerstenberg.

Naguib, M. 1943. "'Abadat Thoth fi Hermubulis al-gharbiya." Unpublished dissertation, Cairo University.

Naville, E. 1888. *The Shrine of Saft el-Henne and the Land of Goshen*. London: Trübner.

———. 1892–93. "Professor Naville's Work of the Winter 1892." *Archaeological Report of the EEF*, 1–5.

———. 1894. *Ahnas el-Medineh Heracleopolis Magna*. London: EES.

Nerlich, A.G., F. Parsche, A.V. den Driesch, and U. Löhrs. 1993. "Osteopathological Findings in Mummified Baboons from Ancient Egypt." *International Journal of Osteoarchaeology* 3:189–98.

Nicholson, P. 1994. "Archaeology beneath Saqqara." *Egyptian Archaeology* 4:7–8.

———. 2005. "The Sacred Animal Necropolis at North Saqqara, the Cults and Their Catacombs." In S. Ikram ed., *Divine Creatures: Animal Mummies from Ancient Egypt*, 44–71. Cairo: American University in Cairo Press.

Nicholson, P., C. Jackson, and K. Frazer. 1999. "The North Ibis Catacomb at Saqqara: The Tomb of the Birds." In A. Leahy and J. Tait eds., *Studies on Ancient Egypt in Honour of H. S. Smith*, 209–14. London: EES.

Nicholson, P., and I. Shaw. 2000. *Ancient Egyptian Materials and Technologies*. Cambridge: University Press.

Nicholson, P.T. 1996. "The North Ibis Catacomb at North Saqqara." *Egyptian Archaeology* 9:16–17.

Nicholson, P.T., S. Ikram, and S. Mills. 2015. "The Catacombs of Anubis at North Saqqara." *Antiquity* 89 (345).

Nicholson, P.T., and H.S. Smith. 1996. "Fieldwork, 1995–6. The Scared Animal Necropolis at North Saqqara." *JEA* 82:8–11.

Northampton, W.G., W. Spiegelberg, and P.E. Newberry. 1908. *Report on Some Excavations in the Theban Necropolis*. London: Archibald Constable.

Notman, D.N.H. 1986. "Ancient Scannings: Computed Tomography of Egyptian Mummies." In R. David ed., *Science in Egyptology*, 252–320. Manchester: Manchester University.

Nur el-Din, A., and D. Kessler. 1996. "Das Priesterhaus am Ibiotapheion von Tuna el-Gebel." *MDAIK* 52:262–93.

Nur El-Din, M.A.A. 1992. "Report on New Demotic Texts from Tuna el-Gebel." In J.H. Johnson ed., *Life in a Multi Cultural Society*, 253–54. Chicago: Oriental Institute of the University of Chicago.

Otto, E. 1938/1964. *Beiträge zur Geschichte der Stierkulte in Aegypten*. Hilesheim: Olms/ Leipzig: J.C. Heinrichs.

Panckoucke, C.L.F. 1826. *Description de l'Egypte ou Recueil des observations et des recherches qui ont été faites en Egypte pendant l'expédition de l'armée française, vol. 10*. Paris: Pancoucke.

Pearson, J. 1805. "Some Account of Two Mummies of the Egyptian Ibis, One of Which Was in a Remarkably Perfect State." *Philosophical Transactions of the Royal Society of London* 95:264–71.

Peet, T.E. 1914. *Cemeteries of Abydos*, 2. London: EEF.

Peet, T.E., and W.L.S. Loat. 1913. *Cemeteries of Abydos*, 3. London: EEF.

Perdu, O. 1990. "Neshor a Mendes sous Apries." *BSFE* 118:38–49.

Perez Die, M. del C. 1983. "Un Nuevo vaso Egipcio de Alabastro en España." In *Homenaje al Prof. Martin Almagro Basch* II, 237–44. Marid: Ministerio de Cultura.

Perizonius, R., M. Attia, H. Smith, and J. Goudsmit. 1993. "Monkey Mummies and North Saqqara." *Egyptian Archaeology* 3:31–33.

Petrie, W.M.F. 1889. *Hawara, Biahmu and Arsinoe*. London: Field & Tuer.

———. 1900. *Denderah 1898*. London: EEF.

———. 1902. *Abydos*, 1. London: EEF.

———. 1910. *Meydum and Memphis* III. London: British School of Archaeology.

———. 1914. *Tarkhan*, 2. London: Bernard Quaritch.

———. 1912. The Labyrinth, Gerzeh and Mazghuneh London: British School of Archaeology.

Pettigrew, T.J. 1834. *A History of Egyptian Mummies and an Account of the Worship and Embalming of the Sacred Animal by Egyptians*. London: Longmans.

Piankoff, A. 1964. *The Litany of Re*. New York: Bollingen Foundation.

Pickavance, K. 1979. Robert Huntington, Bishop of Raphoe 1673–1701." In J. Ruffle, G.A. Gaballa, and K.A. Kitchen eds., *Glimpses of Ancient Egypt:*

Studies in Honour of H.W. Fairman, 196–201. Warminster: Aris & Phillips.

Pierini, G. 1991. "Acquisitions, Marseille, Musée de la Vieille Charité." *Revue du Louvre* 2:88.

Pietschmann, R. 1997. "Apis." In T. Erler, et. al. eds., *Pauly's Realencyclopädie Der Classischen Altertumswissenschaft*. Stuttgart: J. B. Metzler.

Pinkerton, J. 1814. *A General Collection of the Best and Most Interesting Voyages and Travels in All Parts of the World*. London: Longman.

Pliny the Elder. 1938. *Natural History*. Translated by H. Rackham. Cambridge: Harvard University Press.

Plutarch, J. 1970. *De Iside et Osiride*. Translated by G. Griffiths. Cardiff: University of Wales.

Porter, B., and R. Moss. 1934. *Topographical Bibliography of Ancient Egyptian Hieroglyphic Texts, Reliefs and Paintings*, vol. 4. Oxford: Clarendon Press.

———. 1974–81. *Topographical Bibliography of Ancient Egyptian Hieroglyphic Texts, Reliefs and Paintings*, vol. 3, 2nd ed. Oxford: Clarendon Press/Griffith Institute.

Posener, G. 1936. *La première domination perse en Égypte*. Cairo: IFAO.

Preisigke, F., and W. Spiegelberg. 1914. *Die Prinz-Joachim Ostraka*. Strasbourg: K.J. Trübner.

Quaegebeur, J. 1975. "Teephibis, dieu oraculaire?" *Enchoria* 5:19–24.

———. 1977. "Tithoes, dieu oraculaire?" *Enchoria* 7:103–108.

———. 1984. "La désignation 'porteurs des dieux' et le culte des dieux crocodiles dans les textes des époques tardives." In J. Bergman, J.F. Borghouts, and C. Brunon eds., *Mélanges Adolphe Gutbub*, 161–76. Montpellier: Publications de la Recherches de l'Université Paul Valéry.

———. 1991. "Les quâtres dieux Min." In U. Verhoeven and E. Graefe eds., *Religion und Philosophie: Festgabe für Philippe Derchain zu seinem 65. Geburtstag am 24 Juli 1991*, 253–68. Leuven: Peeters.

Quibell, J.E. 1908. *Catalogue Général: Tomb of Yuaa and Thuiu*. Cairo: IFAO.

Radwan, A. 1995. "A Cemetery of the 1st Dynasty." In D. Kessler and R. Schulz eds., *Gedenkschrift für Winfried Barta*, 311–14. Frankfurt: Peter Lang.

Raven, M.J., and W.K. Taconis. 2005. *Egyptian Mummies: Radiological Atlas of the Collections in the National Museum of Antiquities in Leiden*. Leiden: Brepols.

Ray, J.D. 1972. "The House of Osirapis." In P.J. Ucko, R. Tringham and G.W. Dimbleby eds., *Man, Settlement and Urbanism*, 699–703. London: Duckworth.

———. 1976. *The Archive of Hor*. London: EES.

———. 1978a. "The Archive of Hor." *Enchoria* 8 (2): 95–100.

———. 1978b. "The World of North Saqqara." *World Archaeology* 10 (2): 149–57.

———. 1978c. "Observations on the Archive of Hor." *JEA* 64:113–20.

———. 1988. "Egypt 525–404 B.C." In J. Boardman, N.G.L. Hammond, D.M. Lewis, and M. Osterwald eds., *Cambridge Ancient History* vol. 4, part 2, 254–86.

———. 2001. "Animal Cults." In D.B. Redford ed., *The Oxford Encyclopedia of Ancient Egypt*, 345–48. Oxford: Oxford University Press.

———. 2002. *Reflections of Osiris.* London: Profile Books.

———. 2011. *Texts from the Baboon and Falcon Galleries: Demotic, Hieroglyphic and Greek Inscriptions from the Sacred Animal Necropolis, North Saqqara.* London: EES.

———. 2013. *Demotic Ostraca and Other Inscriptions from the Sacred Animal Necropolis, North Saqqara.* London: EES.

Redford, D.B. 1988. "Three Seasons in Egypt. III The First Season of Excavations at Mendes 1991." *JSSEA* 18:49–79.

———. 1991–92. "Interim Report on the Second Campaign of Excavations at Mendes 1992." *JSSEA* 21/22:1–12.

——— 1994. "Some Observations on the Northern and North-eastern Delta in the Late Predynastic Period." In B.M. Bryan and D. Lorton eds., *Essays in Egyptology in Honor of Hans Goedicke*, 201–10. San Antonio: Van Siclen Books.

———. 2001. *The Excavations at Mendes: Vol. I The Royal Necropolis.* Leiden: Brill.

———. 2004. *The Excavations at Mendes: Vol 20, The Royal Necropolis.* Leiden: Brill.

Redford, S. ed. 1996. *Akhenaten Temple Project Newsletter*, Sept. 1996.

———. 1999. *Akhenaten Temple Project Newsletter*, Oct. 1999.

Redford, S., and D. Redford. 2005. "The Cult and Necropolis of the Sacred Ram at Menedes." In S. Ikram ed., *Divine Creatures: Animal Mummies from Ancient Egypt*, 164–98. Cairo: American University in CairoPress.

Reeves, N., and R. Wilkinson. 1996. *The Complete Valley of the Kings.* London/Cairo: Thames and Hudson/American University in Cairo.

Reisner, G.A. 1936. "The Dog Which Was Honored by the King of Upper and Lower Egypt." *BMFA* 34 (206): 96–99.

———. 1938. "Ancient King Gives Dog a Royal Burial." *The American Kennel*

Gazette 55 (5): 7–9, 180–82.

———. 1967. *Canopics*. Cairo: IFAO.

Revillout, E. 1885. "Comptes du Sérapéum." *Rev. Ég.* 3:140–47.

———. 1888. "Les papiers adiministratifs du Sérapéum et l'organisation sacterdotale en Égypte." *Rev. Ég.* 5:31–62.

———. 1882. "La requête d'un Taricheute d'Ibis à l'administrateur du Sérapéum" *Rev. Ég.* 2:75–78.

———. 1891. "Leçon d'ouverture prononcée à l'ecole du Louvre, le lundi, 19 Décembre 1887." *Rev. Ég.* 6:113–49.

Reymond, E.A. 1972. "Two Demotic Memoranda." *JEA* 58:254–55, 257.

Rhind, A.H. 1862. *Thebes: its Tombs and their Tenants*. London: Longman, Green, Longman, and Roberts.

Rhoné, A. 1877. *L'Égypte à petites journées, etudes et souvenirs*. Paris: Ernest Leroux.

Riefahl, E. 1949. "A Sacred Ibis." *The Brooklyn Museum Bulletin* 11 (1): 5–7.

Ritner, R.K. 1986. "Gleanings from Magical Texts." *Enchoria* 14:95–106.

———. 1994. "An Unusual Offering Table in Dallas." In *Acta Demotica: Acts of Fifth International Conference for Demotists, Pisa* 1993, 265–73. Pisa: Giardini.

Roeder, G. 1956. *Aegyptische Bronzefiguren*. Berlin: Staatliche Museum.

Rose, C.L., and E. Dietze. 1978. "Examination and Stabilization of Two Bull Mummies: Preserving Archeological Evidence of Egyptian Rituals/Technology" *Technology and Conservation* 2 (78): 32–38

Rougé, E. de. 1885. "Mémoire sur quelques inscriptions trouvées dans la sépulture des Api." *Rev. Ég.* 4:106–20.

———. 1887. "Mémoire sur quelques inscriptions trouvées dans la sépulture des Apis." *Rev. Ég.* 5:1–9.

Roveri, A-M., et al. 2000. *Aegyptiaca Animalia. Il bestiario del Nilo*. Turin: Museum of Anthropology and Ethnography of Turin University, Turin Museum of Ancient Egypt, and the Department of Human and Animal Biology of Turin, University of Turin.

Rowland, J., S. Ikram, G.J. Tassie, and L. Yeomans. 2013. "The Sacred Falcon Necropolis of Djedhor(?) at Quesna: Recent Investigations from 2006–2012." *JEA* 99:53–84.

Russell, D.A., B. Galeb, and R. Hoath. 1997. "X-raying the Gods: What Were the Mummified Horus Falcons of Egypt?" *Bulletin of the British Ornithologists' Club* 117:148–49.

Sabbahy, L. 2000. "The Mnevis Bull at 'Horizon of the Disc.'" *Amarna Letters* 4:37–43, 162.

Sadek, A.I. 1988. *Popular Religion in Egypt during the New Kingdom.* Hildesheim: Gerstenberg.

Saleh, M., and H. Sourouzian. 1986. *Die Hauptwerke aus dem Ägyptischen Museum Kairo.* Mainz Verlag Philipp von Zabern.

Sandman-Holmberg, M. 1946. *The God Ptah.* Copenhagen: G.W.K. Gleerup.

Sauneron, S. 1952. *Le Rituel de l'Embaument: P. Boulaq III.* Cairo: IFAO.

———. 1962. *Les fêtes réligieuses d'Esna.* Cairo: IFAO.

———. 1963. *Le Temple d'Esna.* Cairo: IFAO.

El Sayed, R. 1982. "Tunah el Gebel—Bilan et Projets de Travaux." *L'Egyptologie en 1979*, vol. 1, 275–78. Paris: Centre National de la Recherche Scientifique.

Schaeffer, H. 1904. "Die Auswanderung der Krieger unter Psammetich I. und der Söldneraufstand in Elephantine unter Apries." *Klio* 4:152–63.

Schlögl, H. 1978. *Geschenk des Nils. Aegyptische Kunstwerke aus Schweizer Besitz.* Basel: Schweizerischer Bankverein.

Schoske, S. 1990. *Schönheit: Abglanz der Göttlichkeit. Kosmetik in Alten Ägypten.* Munich: Staatliche Sammlung Ägyptisch Kunst.

Schoske, S., and D. Wildung. 1992. *Gott und Götterim Alten Ägypten.* Mainz: Philipp von Zabern.

Schott, S. 1990. *Bucher und Bibliotheken im alten Aegypten.* Wiesbaden: Otto Harrassowitz.

Schwartz, J. 1949. "Les conquérants perses et la littérature égyptienne." *BIFAO* 48:65–80.

Seipel, W. 1989. *Ägypten, Götter, Gräber und Kunst: 4000 Jahre Jenseitsglaube.* Linz: Landesmuseum.

Sergent, F. 1986. *Momies Bovines de l'Egypte Ancienne.* Paris: L'Ecole Pratique des Hautes Etudes.

Serpico, M. 2000. "Resins, Amber and Bitumen." In P. Nicholson and I. Shaw eds., *Ancient Egyptian Materials and Technologies*, 430–74. Cambridge: Cambridge University Press.

Sherman, E.J. 1981. "Djedhor the Savious Statue Base OI 10589." *JEA* 67:82–102.

Shin, M.H, et. al. 2008. "Mummies and Science: World Mummies Research." In P. Pena, C. Rodriquez Martin, and M. Rodriguez eds., *Mummies and Science: World Mummies Research*, 105–13. Santa Cruz de Tenerife: Academia Canaroa de la Historia.

Siegel, J. 1976. "Animal Paleopathology: Possibilities and Problems." *Journal of Archaeological Science* 3:349–84.

Siliotti, A. ed. 2001. *Belzoni's Travels*. London: British Museum.

Simpson, W.K. 1957. "A Running of the Apis in the Reign of the 'Aha and Passages in Manetho and Aelian." *Orientalia* 26:139–42.

Skeat, T.C., and E.G. Turner. 1968. "An Oracle of Hermes Trismegistos at Saqqara." *JEA* 54:199–208.

Slabbert, R., A. Du Plessis, S. Ikram, S. Cornelius, and L. Swanepoel. In Press. "Three-dimensional Model of an Ancient Egyptian Falcon Mummy Skeleton." *Rapid Prototyping Journal*.

Smelik, K.A.D. and E.A. Hemelrijk, 1984. "Who knows not what monsters demented Egypt worships? Opinions on Egyptian Animal Worship in Antiquity as Part of the Ancient Conception of Egypt", in W. Haase (ed.), *Aufstieg und Niedergang der römischen Welt* 17/4, 1984, p. 1853-2000.

Smelik, K.M.D. 1979. "The Cult of the Ibis in the Graeco-Roman Period: With Special Attention to the Data from the Papyri." In M. J. Vermaseren ed., *Studies in Hellenistic Religions Etudes Preéliminaires aux Réligions Orientales dans l'Empire Romain*, 225–43. Leiden: Brill.

Smith, H.S. 1969. "Animal Domestication and Animal Cult in Dynastic Egypt." In P.J. Ucko and G.W. Dimbleby eds., *Domestication and Exploitation of Plants and Animals*, 307–14. London: Duckworth.

———. 1972. "Dates of the Obsequies of the Mothers of Apis." *RdE* 24: 176-87.

———. 1974. *A Visit to Ancient Egypt: Life at Memphis and Saqqara c. 500–30BC*. Warminster: Aris and Phillips.

———. 1976. "Preliminary Report on Excavations in the Sacred Animal Necropolis, 1974–1975." *JEA* 62:14–17.

———. 1979. "Varia Ptolemaica." In J. Ruffle, G.A. Gaballa, and K.A. Kitchen eds., *Glimpses of Ancient Egypt: Studies in Honour of H.W. Fairman*, 161–66. Warminster: Aris & Phillips.

———. 1982. "The Excavation of the Anubieion at Saqqara: A Contribution to Memphite Topography and Stratigraphy." *L'Egyptologie en 1979*, 1. Paris: CNRS. 279-282.

———. 1992. "Foreigners in the Documents from the Sacred Animal Necropolois, Saqqara." In J.H. Johnson ed., *Life in a Multi Cultural* Society, 295–301. Chicago: Oriental Institute of the University of Chicago.

———. 1992. "The Death and Life of the Mother of Apis." In A.B. Lloyd ed., *Studies in Pharaonic Religion and Society in Honour of J. Gwyn Griffiths*, 201–

25. London: EES.

———. 2002. "The Saqqara Papyri. Oracle Questions, Pleas and Letter 's' in K. Ryhold ed., *Acts of the Seventh International Conference of Demotic Studies, Cambridge 1999*, 367–75. CNI Publications 27. Copenhagen: CNI Publications.

Smith, H.S., C.A.R. Andrews, and S. Davies. 2011. *The Sacred Animal Necropolis at North Saqqara: The Mother of Apis Inscriptions 1–2*. London: EES.

Smith, H.S., and S. Davies. 2005. *The Sacred Animal Necropolis at North Saqqara: The Falcon Complex and Catacomb, the Archaeological Report*. London: EES.

Smith, H.S., S. Davies, and K. Frazer, with a contribution by R. Bland. 2006. *The Sacred Animal necropolis at North Saqqara, the Main Temple Complex: The Archaeological Report*. London: EES.

Smith, H.S., and D.G. Jeffreys. 1977. "The Sacred Animal Necropolis, North Saqqara: 1975/6." *JEA* 63:20–28.

———. 1978. "The North Saqqara Temple-town Survey: Preliminary Report for 1976/77." *JEA* 64:10–21.

Smither, P.C. 1939. "Stelae in the Queen's College, Oxford." *JEA* 25:157–59.

Soghor, M. 1967. "Mendes 1965 and 1966. Il. Inscriptions from Tell el Ruba." *JARCE* 6:16–23.

Spiegel, J. 1975. "Versuche zur Verschmelzung von Re und Osiris." In W. Westendorf ed., *Goettinger Totenbuchstudien. Beiträge zum 17. Kapitel*. Wiesbaden: Otto Harrasowitz.

Spiegelberg, W. 1918a. "Papyrus Demotic Zen. 23." *ZÄS* 54:112, and pl. 4.

———. 1918b. "Demotische Kleinigkeiten." *ZÄS* 54:111–29.

———. 1920. "Ein Bruchsück des Bestattungsrituals der Apisstiere." *ZÄS* 56:1–33.

———. 1927. "Die Falkenbezeichnung des Verstorbenen in der Spätzeit." *ZÄS* 62:27–34.

———. 1928a. *Neue Urkunden zum ägyptischen Tierkultus*. Munich: Bayerische Akademie der Wissenschaften.

———. 1928b. "A Heart Scarab of the Mnevis Bull." *JEA* 14:12.

———. 1929. "Das Grab einen Grossen und seines Zwerges aus der Zeit des Nektanebes." *ZÄS* 64:82.

Spielmann, P.E. 1932. "To What Extent Did the Ancient Egyptians Employ Bitumen in Embalming?." *JEA* 18:177–80.

Spigelman, M., S. Ikram, J. Taylor, L. Berger, H. Donoghue, and D. Lambert. 2008. "Preliminary Genetic and Radiological Studies of Ibis Mummification in

Egypt." In P. Pena, C. Rodriquez Martin, and M. Rodriguez eds., *Mummies and Science: World Mummies Research*, 545–52. Santa Cruz de Tenerife: Academia Canaroa de la Historia.

Strabo. 1912. *The Geography of Egypt, Vol. 17*. Translated by W. Falconer. London: G. Bell & Sons.

Stricker, B.H. 1971. "Asinarii." *OMRO* 52:37.

Taylor, J. 2001. *Death and the Afterlife in Ancient Egypt*. London: British Museum Press.

Te Velde, H. 1980. "A Few Remarks upon the Religious Significance of Animals in Ancient Egypt." *Numen* 27:76–82.

Thausing, G. 1964. "Der Tierkult im alten Ägypten." *Antaios* 5:309–24.

Thissen, H.J. 1991. "Demotische Inschriften aus den Ibisgalerien in Tuna el-Gebel." *Enchoria* 18:107–13.

———. 1998. "Anmerkungen zum *Lamm des Bokchoris*." In W. Clarysse, A. Schoors, and H. Willems eds., *Egyptian Religion. The Last Thousand Years: Studies Dedicated to the Memory of Jan* Quaegebeur, 1046–47. Leuven: Peeters.

Thompson, D.J. 1988. *Memphis Under the Ptolemies*. Princeton: Princeton University Press.

Touraeff, B. 1917. "The Inscriptions upon the Lower Part of a Naophorous Statue in my Collection." *JEA* 4:119–21.

Toutain, J. 1915–1916. "La culte du taureau Apis à Memphis sous l'empire romain." *Le Muséon* 33:193–202.

Traunecker, C. 1979. "Essai sur l'histoire de la XXIXe dynastie." *BIFAO* 79:395–436.

———. 1987. "Les "temples hauts" de Basse Epoque." RdE 38:147–58.

Turner, E. 1982. *Excavating in Egypt, The Egypt Exploration Society 1882–1982*. London: EES.

Van der Horst, P.W. 1984. *Chaeremon, Egyptian Priest and Stoic Philosopher*. Leiden: Brill.

Van Neer, W., and V. Linseele. 2002. "New Analyses of Old Bones: the Faunal Remains from Hierakonpolis." *Nekhen News* 14:7–8.

Van Neer, W., M. Udrescu, V. Linseele, B.De Cupere, and R. Friedman. 2015. "Traumatism in the Wild Animals Kept and Offered at Predynastic Hierakonpolis, Upper Egypt." *International Journal of Osteoarchaeology*, 1099–1212, http://dx.doi.org/10.1002/oa.2440

———. 2003. "A Second Elephant at HK6." *Nekhen News* 15:11–12.

Van Siclen III, C. 1990. "An Illustrated Checklist for Mummies, Myths and Magic." *Varia Aegyptiaca* 6:27

———. 1997. "The Scarab on the Cat's Forehead." *Essays in Honour of Prof. Dr. Jadwiga Lipinska*, 399–408. Warsaw: Warsaw University and National Museum.

Vandier, J. 1944. *La Religion Egyptienne*. Paris: Presses Universitaires de France.

———. 1949. "A propos d'un groupe de Sérapéum de Memphis." *JEA* 35:135.

———. 1953. *Le papyrus Jumilhac*. Paris: CNRS.

———. 1961. "Memphis et le Taureau Apis dans le Papyrus Jumilhac." In J. Garnot ed., *Mélanges Mariette*, 105–32. Cairo: IFAO.

———. 1968. "La Statue d'un Grand Pretre de Mendès." *JEA* 54:89–94.

Vandorpe, K. 1992. "Les villages des Ibis dans la toponymie tardive." *Enchoria* 18:115–22.

Vansleb, F. 1678. *The Present State of Egypt*. London: John Starkey.

Vercoutter, J. 1958. "Une épitaphe royale inédite du Sérapeum." *MDAIK* 16:333–45.

———. 1960. "The Napatan Kings and Apis Worship Serapeum Burials of the Napatan Period." *Kush* 8:62–76.

———. 1984. "Serapeum." *LÄ* 5:868–70.

——— J. 1962. *Textes biographiques du Sérapéum de Memphis*. Paris: Behe.

———. 1972. "Apis." *LÄ* 1:343.

Verdel, Th., M. el Zahaby, T. Abdallah, J. P. Piguet, and A. Zivie. 1995. "Étude de la stabilité de la tombe d'Aper-El à Saqqara, 'Égypte.'" *Tunnels et ouvrages souterrains* 127:31–36.

Vernus, P. 1976. *Athribis*. Cairo: IFAO.

———. 1998. *The Gods of Ancient Egypt*. London: Tauris Parke.

Verreth, H. 1998. "A Tax List from the Mendesios of the Time of Augustus." In W. Clarysse, A. Schoors, and H. Willems eds., *Egyptian Religion. The Last Thousand Years: Studies Dedicated to the Memory of Jan Quaegebeur*, 468. Leuven: Peeters.

Vittman, G. 1995. Zwei Demotische Briefe an den Gott Thot." *Enchoria* 22:169–81.

Vogliano, A. 1942. *Un'impresa archeologica milanese ai margini orientali del deerto libico*. Milan: R. Universita, Istitu d'alta cultura.

von den Driesch, A. 1993a. "Affenhaltung und Affenverehrung in der Spätzeit des Alten Agypten." *Tierärztliche Praxis* 21:95–101.

———. 1993b. "The Keeping and Worshipping of Baboons during the Later

Phase in Ancient Egypt." *Sartoniana* 6:15–36.

von den Driesch, A., and J. Boessneck. 1985. "Krankhaft veränderte Skelettreste von Pavianen aus altägyptischer Zeit." *Tierärztliche Praxis* 13:367–72.

von den Driesch, A., and D. Kessler. 1994. "Tiermumien aus dem altägyptischen Friedhof von Tuna el-Gebel." *Einsichten, Forschung an der Ludwig-Maximilians-Universität München* 1:31–34.

Vos, R.L. 1993. *The Apis Embalming Ritual*. Leuven: Peeters.

———. 1998. "The Colors of Apis and other Sacred Animals." In W. Clarysse, A. Schoors, and H. Willems eds., *Egyptian Religion. The Last Thousand Years: Studies Dedicated to the Memory of Jan Quaegebeur*, 709–18. Leuven: Peeters.

Vyhnanek, L., and E. Strouhal. 1976. "Radiography of Egyptian Mummies." *ZÄS* 103:118–28.

Wade, A.D., S. Ikram G. Conlogue, R. Beckett, A. Nelson, R. Colten, B. Lawson, and D. Tampieri. 2012. "Foodstuff Placement in Ibis Mummies and the Role of Viscera in Embalming." *Journal of Archaeological Science* 39 (5): 1642–47.

Warman, S. 2000. "How Now, Large Cow?" *Nekhen News* 12:8.

Wasef, S., R. Wood, S. el-Merghani, S. Ikram, C. Curtis, B. Holland, E. Willerslev, C.D. Millar, and D.M. Lambert. In Preparation. "Radiocarbon dating of Sacred Ibis mummies from ancient Egypt".

Wenke, R.J. and D.J. Brewer. 1994. "The Archaic-Old Kingdom Delta: The Evidence from Mendes and Kom el-Hisn." In M. Bietak ed., *Haus und Palast im alten Aegypten*, 265–85. Vienna: Österreichischen Akademie der Wissenschaften.

Wessetsky, W. 1981. "Die Uschebti-Formel des "Sandfahrens" und die Himmelscrichtungen." *MDAIK* 37:493–96.

Weynants-Ronday, M. 1939. "Lettres inédites de Mariette." *CdÉ* 14:69–78.

Whittemore, T. 1914. "Ibis Cemetery at Abydos." *JEA* 1:246–49.

Wiedemann, A. 1889. "Le Culte des Animaux en Egypte." *Muséon* 8:211–25, 309–18

———. 1905. "Quelques remarques sur le culte des animaux en Égypte." Le *Muséon* n.s., t. 6:113–28.

———. 1912. *Der Tierkult in der alten Ägypter*. Leipzig: J.C. Heinrichs.

———. 1917. "Der Apis als Totenträger." *Orientalistische Literaturzeitung* 20:29–302.

Wild, H. 1960. "Statue d'un noble Mendesien du regne de Psametik I aux musées de Palerme et du Caire." *BIFAO* 60:43–67.

Wildung, D. 1977. *Egyptian Saints: Deification in Pharaonic Egypt*. New York:

New York University Press.

Wilson, K.L. 1982. *Cities of the Delta* II. *Mendes*. Malibu: Undena.

Woodhouse, S. 1997. "The Sun God: his Four Bas and the Four Winds in the Sacred District of Sais: the Fragments of an Obelisk BM EA 1512." In S. Quirke ed., *The Temple in Ancient Egypt*, 132–51. London: British Museum Press.

Yoshimura, S., and I. Takamiya. 1994. "A Monument of Khaemwaset at Saqqara." *Egyptian Archaeology* 5:19–23.

Yoyotte, J. 1960. "Les pèlerinage dans l'Egypte ancienne." *Sources Orientales* III: 19–74.

———. 1982–83. "L'Amon de Naukratis." *RdÉ* 34:129–36.

———. 1988–89. "Sites et cultes de Basse Egypte: Les deux Léontopolis." *Annuaire de l'Ecole Pratique des Hautes Etudes, Paris* 97:155.

Zabkar, L. 1968. *A Study of the Ba Concept in Ancient Egyptian Texts*. Chicago: University of Chicago.

Zaghloul, H.O. 1985. Frühdemotische Urkunden aus Hermopolis." *Bulletin of the Center of Papyrological Studies* 2. Cairo: El-Tobgy Press.

Zibelius, K. 1978. *Aegyptische Siedlungen nach Texten des Alten Reiches*. Wiesbaden: Ludwig Reichert.

Zimmermann, F. 1912. *Der ägyptische Tierkult nach der Darstellung der Kirchenschriftsteller und die ägyptischen Denkmäler*. Kirchhain: Druck von Schmersow..

Zivie, A. 1975. *Hermopolis et le Nome de l'Ibis*. Le Cairo: IFAO.

———. 1982. "Tombes rupestres de la falaise du Bubasteion à Saqqara. Campagne 1980–1981 Mission Archéologique Française de Saqqara." *ASAE* 68:63–68.

———. 1983a. "Les tombes de la falaise du Bebasteion a Saqqara." *Le Courrier du CNRS* 49: 37–44.

———. 1983b. "Trois saisons a Saqqarah: les tombeaux du Bubasteion." *BSFE* 98:40–56.

———. 1985. "Tombes rupestres de la Falaise du Bubasteion à Saqqara - IIe et IIIe campagnes (1982-1983) (Mission Archéologique Française de Saqqara)." *ASAE* 70:219–32.

———. 1988a. "Cat Mummy" and "Kitten Mummy." In S. D'Auria, P. Lacovara, C. H. Roehrig eds., *Mummies and Magic: The Funerary Arts of Ancient Egypt*, 232–34, n° 189–190. Boston: Museum of Fine Arts.

———. 1988b. "Un exemple d'archéologie de sauvetage à Saqqara" *Fifth*

International Congress of Egyptology: Abstracts, 299–300. Cairo: American University in Cairo Press.

————. 1990a. *Découverte à Saqqara: Le vizir oublié.* Paris: Seuil. (Arabic edition—*Maqbara 'Abriya: kashf fi Saqqara.* Translated by Emad Adly, with an introduction by the author, and a preface by Zahi Hawass. Cairo: Dar al-Fikr li-l-Dirasat wa-l-Nashr wa-l-Tawzi', 1995).

————. 1990b. "Des ministres et des chats: les deux visages de la falaise du Bubasteion." *Saqqara. Aux origines de l'Égypte pharaonique, Les Dossiers d'Archéologie* 146–147:106–109.

————. 1995 "La Falaise du Bubasteion à Saqqara: bilan des travaux et perspectives pour l'avenir" *Akten des Vierten Internationalen Ägyptologen Kongresses München 1985*, vol. 2, 291–98. Hamburg: Helmut Buske.

————. 1999. "Le vizir, les ministres et les chats. Nouvelles découvertes à Saqqara." *Boletin de la Asociacion Española de Egiptologia* 9:113–20.

Zivie, A., and L. Ginsburg. 1987. "La nécropole des chats de Saqqara en Égypte: recherches récentes." *Le Chat, Ethnozootechnie* 40:5–10.

Zivie, A., and R. Lichtenberg. 2003. "Les chats du Bubasteion de Saqqara. Etat de la question et perspectives." In Z. Hawass and L. Pinch-Brock eds., *Egyptology at the Dawn of the Twenty-First Century, Proceeding of the VIII International Congress of Egyptologists, Cairo 2000*, vol. 2, 587–93. Cairo: American University in Cairo Press.

————. 2005. "The Cats of the Goddess Bastet." In S. Ikram ed., *Divine Creatures: Animal Mummies in Ancient Egypt*, 106–19. Cairo: American University in Cairo Press.